C.R.A.P

by John Farman

Also by John Farman in Red Fox

**The Very Bloody History of Britain
(without the boring bits)**

**The Very Bloody History of Britain
(1945 to Now)**

Jesus – The Teenage Years

C.R.A.P.

COLLECTION OF ROTTEN ADULT PRINCIPLES

CRAP!

Written and illustrated by
John Farman

RED FOX

A Red Fox Book

Published by Random House Children's Books
20 Vauxhall Bridge Road
London
SW1V 2SA

A division of Random House UK Ltd
London Melbourne Sydney Auckland
Johannesburg and agencies throughout the world

Copyright © John Farman 1996

1 3 5 7 9 10 8 6 4 2

First published in Great Britain by Red Fox 1996

Set in Bembo

Printed and bound in Great Britain by Cox & Wyman Ltd,
Reading, Berkshire

Papers used by Random House UK Ltd are natural, recyclable products made from wood grown in sustainable forests. The manufacturing processes conform to the environmental regulations of the country of origin.
RANDOM HOUSE UK Limited Reg. No. 954009
ISBN 0 09 968951 0

CONTENTS

Author's Note

John Farman has never forgotten what it feels like to be young. Believe it or not, he was once young himself. The product of very straight parents (born in Luton, Bedfordshire) he was forced to suffer suburban life for many years before hitting the big city (London) at seventeen. He now lives conveniently near the prison at Wandsworth with his son Joe and his ex-wife's deaf cat. He still doesn't know what he wants to be when he grows up.

A child becomes an adult when he realises that he has the right not only to be right, but also to be wrong . . .
Thomas Szasz

I was the kind of kid my mother told me not to play with. By the time I was about ten, both parents were pleading with me to leave home. Why? I think it had something to do with my inability to believe a single word they said. If I'd found out much later that I'd been found on the doorstep with a DO-WHAT-YOU-WANT-WITH-HIM note round my neck, I think it might have made some sense. I felt as out of place in the suburbs as Prince Charles would feel at a casting for *EastEnders*, and became a trainee rebel-without-a-cause for most of my teenage years.

Teenage for most kids starts when it dawns on them that their mum isn't the most beautiful woman in the world, and that their dad can't beat everyone else's. It's at this time that you notice niggling double-standards, like when they lecture you over and over about the sin of lying, while telling the cashier at a leisure park that you are still under

that age when the price goes up. It was really embarrassing being carried in my dad's arms at seventeen. Coming from a church-going family, I could never work out why for an hour or so a week we said sorry to God for what we'd done wrong in the previous week, and then went out and did exactly the same (but with a squeaky-clean conscience). I promise you I wasn't a goody-goody, but it just   didn't seem right. Blimey, it was bad enough to notice that what was said in church wasn't what actually happened, but when you realised that your mum and dad didn't always tell the truth either, you felt really let down.

I suppose that set the tone for the rest of my life. As I got older, I realised that it wasn't necessarily my poor old parents' fault that they didn't or couldn't tell the truth. Worse than that, I realised that I couldn't always tell the truth either. Dammit, most times I couldn't even find out what the truth was!

Not being the brightest thing ever to arrive on this planet, it took me longer than most to realise that our whole society is run on an economy-size, bulk pack of porkies. The government says one thing and does another and the papers pretend to say one thing, but really mean something totally different. Even the Church, God bless it, isn't immune from selling out its integrity, just like all the other poor devils who leave childhood and fall headlong into the great grown-up (and dead scary) world.

It wouldn't be half so bad if all the powerful people and institutions that control our lives didn't set themselves up as good, honest and true; and as for pointing a highly critical finger at the kids of today, when anyone with half a brain realises what a bunch of lying wallies they can be, it all seems a real cheek!

It's not fair!
It's not on!
It's a pile of crap!

This is my personal crap-book: the stuff that gets me worked up when I should be asleep at night (or down the pub). Yours might be a completely different pile of poo. If it is, or if you disagree with what I think, let me know. I'd like to include your views in the next printing of the book (if it isn't banned by then).

THE BRITISH PRESS
LEADS THE WAY

In the old days men had the rack, now they have the press...
Oscar Wilde

You can work out more about your average Briton by the newspapers that drop through his letter box than by practically anything else. Indeed, these days it would be difficult to get many of the posher Sunday newspapers through the average sized *door*. If they get any bulkier, I wouldn't be surprised if newsagents get sued by the poor kids that have to deliver them.

Nowhere in the world is there such a diverse range (eleven dailies in all): from the Tory supporting, Queen Mother loving, status-quo protecting *Daily Telegraph*, to the Labour supporting, Queen Mother loving, us-and-them *Mirror*. Between these are all the bottom-end-of-the-middle to lower-middle tabloid format papers like the *Daily Mail* and the *Express*, or the deeply middle-class *Observer*, *Times* and *Guardian*. To the casual observer, this all seems fair enough - horses for courses in fact. After all, who would expect a captain of industry to want to read about a well-known soap star's antics in an appropriately named 'lay'-by (unless it was him in the car) or who would imagine a Dagenham hairdresser rushing out in her lunch break to find the latest developments in Maastricht?

It's so interesting to observe,
how we only get what we deserve.

So, who writes all this stuff? Very often the author of 'Gay Vicar's Maiden Aunt in Love Tryst with Blond Swineherd' comes from the very same upbringing and education as the chap who writes 'Pavarotti triumphs in Madame Butterfly' reviews in the 'serious' papers. All he is doing is writing down to the level that he thinks his audience will understand, giving them what they have grown to expect and therefore require. Any attempt at real information is smothered by salacious, sensationalising reporting, and any attempt to find the real truth is usually masked by the paper's own established opinion.

6 *Tabloids are fast reading for the slow thinking...* 9   Anon

No Such Thing as Truth

Everything you read in the papers, be they tabloid or otherwise, has been filtered, kidney-like, through the mind of a journalist. The truth about anything, therefore, whether it be Mad Cow Disease or Fergie's spending (much the same thing), is what whoever has written it decides. As any two people can witness an event and give totally different versions of what happened, the idea of unbiased news reporting is about as likely as a Prime Minister

coming clean about the state of the economy. Probably the only way to get the real truth about anything is to read every single paper every single day, then bin the lot and go see for yourself.

6 *The most truthful part of a newspaper is the advertisements...* 9
                                        Thomas Jefferson

If you consider that the tabloids (the *Sun*, the *Mirror* and the *Star*) provide the news and opinion for 19.2 of the 27

12

million who buy daily papers, and that the seriously gross *News of the Screws* - whoops - *World* sells far and away more than any other Sunday paper, a cold shiver travels down the spine. In the now-famous TV interview with the dying playwright Dennis Potter, he despairingly blamed the gutter press for the decline of standards, on every level, in Britain.

If ever you wanted to even a score, start your own tabloid and start up a war.

Rupert Murdoch, who controls many of them, seems to need no further encouragement to manipulate his fellow man. Tabloid journalists are the tarts of the industry, as they will go along with whatever opinions sell newspapers. The *Sun*, for instance, a well-known Tory newspaper, is showing all the signs of gatecrashing Labour's party because it sees the first of the guests leaving the Conservatives' party down the road. Nothing to do with policies or manifestos, just plain, playground-like swapping to the side that looks like it might win. Most papers profess to love the Royal family, but hardly bother to check the intrusive crap that comes from their lower-than-life news hounds. They enjoy the building-up of football stars into working class heroes but are the first to put their own boot in at the first whiff of scandal. They shed crocodile tears over horrible crimes, but then terrorise the innocent victims for the lurid details of their ordeals. They make loud noises about being liberal but can be homophobic, sexist and racist at the drop of a headline.

Rise and Fall

The media shape and are shaped by public opinion. A good case in point is the sudden about-turn in the treatment of our wonderful princess Diana. When she married our Charlie, any hint of a criticism would have been met with cries of treason from the readers. How times have changed. The great general public are at last showing all the signs of tiring of her, and the tabloids, conscious as always of sales, are reflecting and feeding this disenfranchisement, with candid photos of cellulite padding out those famous Royal legs, and headlines like JUST OP IT, DIANA which introduced a no-holds barred condemnation of her highly publicised ring-side viewing of four surgical operations on kids. What, only months ago, would have been seen as just another example of her wonderful hands-on caring, is now regarded as a cheap trick to strengthen her position in the publicity war over her ex-husband.

I THINK YOU'LL ENJOY THIS ONE MA'AM

Or hows about LIZ REPLACES DI AS CHARITY QUEEN OF HEARTS, which referred to the poor, neglected starlet Elizabeth Hurley, whose horrid boyfriend did those awful things in the back of a car in LA. Apparently Miss Hurley will turn up to just about every money-grabbing charity event going (in those demure little frocks), whereas Diana is starting to get a bit choosy. Because Diana, who is the Vice President of the British Red Cross, has been letting the side down, they have chosen Liz as their front runner. Mind you, it would only take Prince Charles to be caught with his Royal trousers down, in the back of his mum's limo, to get his missus back to her rightful position.

Argies Get Out

Don't go thinking that their sensationalism doesn't have any real effect. Back in 1982 the tabloids whipped up such racial hatred against the Argentineans (they're the same ones that are now searching their coastline for oil with their new chums - US!!!) during the Falklands fiasco. Yobby headlines like GOTCHA! when we sunk the Belgrano were common and designed to appeal directly to the sort of cretin that's prepared to wage war over a foul in a football match. Had it turned into a full-scale world conflagration, the poor misguided, ill-informed, tabloid-reading lads would have gone in their droves like lambs to the slaughter. Talking of football matches, the press excelled themselves during the 1996 European Cup. The semi-final match between Germany and England spawned headlines like ACHTUNG! SURRENDER, which simply fuelled the hideous nationalism that became the outstanding feature of an otherwise featureless contest. How can we possibly move forward into a future where wars are forgotten, when our tabloids are allowed to wind up the terminally mindless in such a pathetic and obvious way?

The 'Better' Papers

At the other end of the newspaper market the situation is not quite as dangerous but often just as crass. Admittedly, they do report the news in a more responsible, less sensational way, and it must be said that during the week they are, with reservations, the best bet. But when the weekend comes, oh boy, do they let rip: whole supplements devoted to *'The Style'* or *'The Culture'*. A host of self-styled sophisticates telling us which opera, ballet or art exhibition we should be seen at; hundreds of jumped-up Jane Ashers and tedious Terence Conrans, telling those that have 'made it' how they should have their homes and their children's parties and what the best people are putting in their stomachs. Ad after ad coaxing us to part with our cash in order to aspire to a style of living determined by some smarty-pants or other, or buy, in easy instalments, crap limited-editions (limited by how many they think they can flog), of hand-painted nick-nacks, sculpted by brilliant, world-famous artists (that no-one's ever heard of). Yuk! One must be tempted to ask the big question: Is the tail

REALLY! NOBODY EATS THAT ANY MORE

wagging the dog or vice versa? Do these Sunday magazines merely reflect the pretensions of its readership, or do they lead them by the nose into the wonderful world of middle-class, superficial rubbish?

Aren't we clever? Aren't we fun?
Isn't our opinion second to none?

Have you ever seen those tedious articles that compare the aesthetic merits of, say, designer garlic crushers or how Ms Sophisticate should tend her indoor herb garden. The fact that a third of the world's people don't have any food *to* flavour doesn't even enter into the frame.

Doesn't it hack you off when you see those ads for Tudor-style Wendy houses for those leafy multiple-acre Surrey gardens, when you consider that in many inner cities whole families are sharing one cold, damp room? And doesn't it make you want to throw up when, after thumbing through some glossy supplement desperately searching for something interesting to read, your hands reek of some sissy stuck-in-an-ad scent sachet. It occurs to me that the price of a weeny bottle of the stuff would cost way over what the average jobless person gets for his weekly benefit.

Something for You Lot?

But where are the advertisements specifically for young people? There just aren't any. Why? Because advertisers know that they've very little disposable income. As you've probably noticed, the only stuff that could possibly appeal to teenagers are the few patronising cartoons which look as out of place as a MacDonald's stall at Buck House. As for the amount of trees that are being pulled down to produce page after boring page of this irrelevant garbage ... my case rests, m'lud!

Sex in the Press

For as long as I can remember Britain, that very symbol of respectability, has had one of the most hypocritical and salacious popular presses in the world. For a start, every day you can buy a whole selection of 'news'papers which feature girls (and guys) in various degrees of undress, for no particular reason apart from SEX SELLS PAPERS. Fine, if that's what you want! Let's face it, lusting after naked flesh *isn't* against the law and doesn't really do any harm. But these papers want it both ways. They quite unashamedly include a whole range of lurid stories about who's doing what to whom in the world of show business and royalty (now much the same thing) and public affairs.

> 6 *The freedom of the press works in such a way that there's not much freedom from it.* 9   Princess Grace of Monaco

All this is also fine; if people are prepared to reap the rewards of publicity, they must, in turn, suffer the slippery downside, or at least be a bit more careful about being observed doing whatever they choose to do and to whom they choose to do it. But the trouble is, it doesn't stop there. This gutter press revels in pulling down those who can't defend themselves, like jackals attacking sick youngsters. And it doesn't even stop there either. After filling miles of column inches, promoting the cheapest of thrills, they then have the bare-faced gall to invest themselves with the role of our moral guardians.

> *Being two faced is bad enough,*
> *but three faced is much sterner stuff.*

While giving us stories of nude vicars in sexy romps with packs of Cubs and/or Brownies, in the sort of detail that would make Casanova cringe, or the aforementioned back-seat canoodling of a minor star, they try to make us believe they're doing us a favour. In fact, in the opportunist world of showbiz, everyone benefits – even LA hookers. It appears that no publicity is bad publicity. It's all so cynical.

Okay, it's fine to wave a finger and bray for blood if some holier-than-thou MP is caught with his vote in someone else's ballot box, but save us the moral lecture please! These protectors of our well-being hound, cajole and pay huge sums of money to people to split on their friends and lovers, and to lie and cheat into the bargain. They are prepared to print stories that even Pinocchio would have shied at, safe in the knowledge that, even if someone did have the guts to take a pop at them court-wise, the money paid out would be peanuts compared with the revenue gleaned from the increased circulation.

The reporters and newspaper owners, however, would find my anger hilarious. Their stock reply to any similar criticism is always the same: Don't blame us, we only print what you punters want. Unfortunately they've got a point. The British, more than any other race, adore watching their heroes built up to dizzy heights, but get far more of a buzz drooling over their meteoric descent to humiliation and obscurity.

True Story

I once lived in a block of flats which also housed a well-known rock star. One evening, in the bar downstairs (flash – or what?), a tabloid journalist (name available on request), working on the showbiz section (and a friend of a now *ex*-friend), asked me if I knew anything about this guy's after-dark activities (nudge-nudge). When I told her I hadn't even met the bloke, undaunted, she actually encouraged me (with the promise of folding money) to tell her something that he *might* have done; her only criteria being – as a hack – that if someone had actually told *her* this something (made up or not) it was fine to print it. Her responsibility, she claimed, was absolved. I told her to get lost (not exactly in those words), but I don't think she printed that.

If the truth you cannot find,
make it up - no one will mind.

If it sounds like I'm taking the moral high ground, I'm not. The problem really comes with all this crap running side by side with important news (isn't that the function of a *news*paper?). It's a bit like operating a central heating consultancy from a strip club; the two just don't go together. The *Sunday Sport*, on the other hand, and its weekly equivalents - all boobs and bums - though totally banal and sub-pathetic, makes very little pretence at being anything else, which, in a way, is okay (in a way). But The *Mirror*, The *Sun*, The *Star*, The *People*, The *News of the World* (or Screws, as it's better known), and The *Sunday Mirror* (have I missed any?) should carry far more responsibility for what they print. If on one page they can deal with the appalling disasters in Bosnia, using quite considerable efforts to relay the truth, then they must treat more personal matters with the same truthfulness and a little more respect.

Suffering and sex,
make wonderful text.

But Who Owns Our Papers?

Most people think that we have an independent press. Not only is that a joke, but so is the fact that most of the great press barons live far away from Britain. Rupert Murdoch (The *Sun*, The *News of the World* and The *Times*), flits between Australia and Los Angeles; Lord Rothermere (*Daily Mail*, *Mail on Sunday*) lives in Paris; Conrad Black (The *Daily* and *Sunday Telegraph*) is Canadian; Tiny Rowlands (*The Observer*) is German, spending most of his time in Africa, the Middle East or Mexico; and Robert Maxwell (who owned The *Mirror* and The *People*) was an Eastern European Jew whose present location one can only hazard a guess at (but hope its extremely hot and underground). As for David Sullivan (The *Sport* and *Sunday Sport*), I shouldn't think anyone gives a monkey's where he comes from, but I would imagine it's somewhere in Essex.

'The more national newspapers there are, the more difficult it is to tell them apart...'   Paul Foot

Big Business...

Newspaper tycoons only really need their papers to fortify, and give respectability (*News of the World* – respectable?) to, their often vast business empires. They're also a fantastic platform from which to promote their other business interests and, more to the point, trash their competitors. It's a badly kept secret that Rupert Murdoch, who owns Sky TV 'leans on' his editors to use every opportunity to praise – guess who – Sky and bad mouth the BBC, while Conrad Black breathes gently on the *Telegraph* to support the US government and the National Party in South Africa.

...but Worse

More worrying than that, because of their connections to world wheeler-dealering, most newspapers are desperately partisan politically, more than ever before and far more than – say – America. When Neil Kinnock accused the Tory press (which they mostly are) of losing him the last election, the *Sun* printed the headline 'IT'S THE SUN WOT WON IT' which was like a slap in the face with a wet kipper to the poor old boyyo.

Not only that but the stranglehold that big business has on our press means that the editors are often 'restrained' from telling the truth, the whole truth, and nothing but the truth, especially where less than strictly-straightforward big money transactions are taking place. Surely some of the journalists at the *Daily Mirror* must have known Maxwell was a right crook but for obvious reasons had to keep their typewriters well and truly off the story.

North of Watford?

Sadly it must also be noted, that it is well known that the dailies are only really interested in London (even the *Guardian* which used to be in Manchester) and the rivalry between themselves, seeming not to give a damn about the twilight zone of suburbs and small towns. They are hardly interested in real, under the skin, investigative reporting anymore, whether it be racial issues, provincial politics, the unemployed, or the fact that most of Britain is becoming more and more fed up, preferring to portray a Britain of hectic spending and travelling, which is just the way the advertisers like it.

Down Goes Rupert

Many people think that nice Mr Murdoch, not content with owning a third of our press, sees it as his God-given right to break down the class system in Britain but is going about it in a peculiar way. By attempting to drag the once fine *Sunday Times* practically down to the knee-level of the *Mail on Sunday*, with crap serialisations of the unbearably boring marital shenanigans of dimwit Di and childish Charles, he confuses quality with snobbery and real investigation with entertainment and titillation.

Unfortunately the press barons show signs of losing interest in all the different ways power is misused, but are enjoying the process of pushing themselves into the role of players in the big world power-game itself which, when you think about it, can only be a disaster for what we laughingly call democracy.

CRAP CORNER

Here's a recap of all the stuff that makes me sick about the press. Incidentally, do you bother with it at all? Do you read the newspaper your parents read, or do you add to the delivery boy's misery by ordering an extra ton of paper for your own consumption? Let me know.

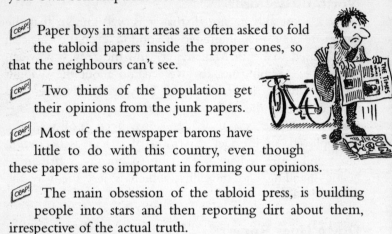

CRAP! Paper boys in smart areas are often asked to fold the tabloid papers inside the proper ones, so that the neighbours can't see.

CRAP! Two thirds of the population get their opinions from the junk papers.

CRAP! Most of the newspaper barons have little to do with this country, even though these papers are so important in forming our opinions.

CRAP! The main obsession of the tabloid press, is building people into stars and then reporting dirt about them, irrespective of the actual truth.

CRAP! Many of the big Sunday papers collude with advertisers to create the very culture which allows them to flog their gear.

CRAP! The big Sundays profess to be concerned about the state of people in the Third World, while glorifying a life of excess and dishing out an endless stream of banal style-babble.

CRAP! There's very little in the better papers for teenagers because they have very little disposable income.

CRAP! The tabloids flog indiscriminate sex in the most blatant manner, while highlighting and lampooning anyone that actually indulges in it.

CRAP! Many journalists are not really interested in the truth, and will destroy someone's life on mere rumour.

CRAP! The press barons use their papers to feather their own interests, both political and business-wise.

ALTERNATIVE MEDICINE IS THE ONLY ALTERNATIVE

Patient: *"Are you sure one bottle of this will cure my cold?"*
Quack: *"It must. Nobody ever came back for a second."*

If you were to have asked about alternative medicine twenty years ago, images of witches, hippies, alchemists and frail, bewhiskered old ladies living in woodland cottages would have sprung to mind. In the last fifteen years, however, alternative, complementary (or natural) medicine has spread like fleas on a tomcat, and has become big business. Here's a few facts and figures:

☞ 145 organisations and training centres are now flourishing, not in woodland glades, or fairy dells, but in towns and cities throughout the country.

☞ The number of alternative practitioners is growing by a ratio of 5.6 times that of 'proper' doctors.

☞ If you assume that the average fee for a chat with a non-orthodox practitioner is at least a tenner, then as much as £170 million is being handed over every year.

☞ The additional cost of all the vitamins, supplements, herbs and other gubbins, adds up to another cool £250 million.

Don't be fooled by all their patter, it's simply a case of mind over money over matter.

There's serious loot to be made out of our constantly flagging bodies, and the barons of the orthodox medical profession aren't at all wild about these new boys getting in on what for years they have seen as their act. But why should this have happened at this relatively recent period in our history?★ What's so wrong with the free(ish) medicine we've already got? Surely the bounds of medical knowledge are being pushed to limits not even imagined by our forefathers and foremothers, so why bother to start raiding the meadows and hedgerows for our lotions and potions? It seems that the whole problem has a lot to do with an instinctive British edginess over the advances in science and technology, and positive paranoia over all things synthetic and 'not natural'.

(Formerly when religion was strong and science was weak, men mistook magic for medicine; now, when science is strong and religion weak, men mistake medicine for magic...)
Thomas Szasz

Pioneering steps into the future are all right in the movies and Tomorrow's World but, as a nation, we're not that struck with newness (which could account for the fixes we're always getting into economically), especially where our personal bodies are concerned. And of course, this return to the past is coupled with the increasing bureaucracy, and the post-Thatcher government which is threatening to squeeze the life out of the National Health Service.

The NHS, as it soon became called, was the dreamchild of the late great Aneurin Bevan, who in 1948

★ Most of the therapies now fashionable are based on ideas thought up between the 1880s and the 1930s.

offered free medical service for the entire population, with free prescriptions, false teeth, glasses and even wigs for the folically challenged. But that was then and now is now. Prescriptions become more and more expensive, NHS dentists are becoming as rare as hens' teeth and the cost of glasses makes semi-blindness almost inevitable. As for doctors, their role has changed completely in the last fifty years. What used to be the family friend, who knew mum, dad and the kids by their first name, is now a harassed shadow of his or her former self. We post-modern punters, when poorly, are beginning to look round ever diverse corners in ever increasing numbers. Not only that, but it appears that even in the medical profession itself, 18 out of every 100 doctors are dabbling in alternative therapy and a further 70 are looking over their shoulders.

Whether we're suffering a chill or the pox, we are starting to question our regular docs.

The other reason for the growing interest in alternative medicine is that just about everyone seems to be getting into the health and fitness act (with notable exceptions - like me!) and are even beginning to see it as a status symbol, egged on by crafty entrepreneurs (and naff track suit manufacturers). So what? I hear you cry. If we look after ourselves, we'll be less of a burden on the state, and live longer. And surely if we cut down the number of unnatural drugs we're chucking into our bodies, and the number of radioactive gizmos which make us glow like Chernobyl on a bad day, it's got to be a good thing? If natural herbal remedies were good enough for our ancestors then, for Hippocrates' sake, they should be   all-right for us too. They didn't pump themselves full of chemicals that cost an arm and a leg, and make pharmaceutical companies amongst the richest in the world. Perhaps we should pension off our scientists, relearn all the old knowledge and skills and stop looking for 'progress' all the time.

Looking back to days of yore,
It seems quite plain that they
knew more.

     This line of thinking is not bad as far as it goes, but you must remember that those poor old yeomen of yesteryear didn't know any better. I mean, can you really believe they used to drag live cows into the bedroom of sick women in the seventeenth century because they believed their sweet breath was therapeutic? (What about the other end, I expect you'd like to know?)

     It just might be worth considering too, that the average life expectancy for men in 1840 was 41, in 1940 was 59 and in 1991 was 73. Looked at another way, in 1917, the monarch posted only 110 telegrams to people who'd reached 100 years old, compared to over 3000 last year. I don't know about you, but I know I'd prefer old age to the alternative. More than that, we don't seem to have plagues like the Black Death taking out half the population every five minutes (well, not in Britain). When did you last see a red cross daubed on a front door?

     You may have noticed the word natural cropping up now and again. Rosalind Coward, in her brilliant and brave book, *The Whole Truth: The Myth of Alternative Health* questions the whole health business, maintaining that alternative medicine pivots on the word natural, and the idea that anything to do with nature is jolly nice. You will find many more of her conclusions in chapter seven, which you might fancy taking a peek at. Natural, when related to health, is seen by some as the safe alternative to the drug-crazed, scalpel-happy approach of the orthodox medical practitioner.

Natural Therapies

The World Federation of Healing (whatever that is) describes natural therapies as those which use 'only substances, methods and modalities (whatever that means) which, in trained hands, are perfectly safe and therefore cannot give rise to harmful side effects.' Every time you blink there's a new therapy being offered. Here are just a few of the more established ones and the sort of words they use to describe themselves:

☞ **Homeopathy:** A system of medicine based on the principle that the symptoms of disease are part of the body's self-healing process, and the practice of giving extremely diluted doses of natural substances found in a healthy person to produce the symptoms of the illness being treated (*like hitting yourself repeatedly over the head if you've got a headache*).

☞ **Naturopathy:** Which is the facilitating of those natural self-healing processes. Naturopaths are the GPs of the alternative medicine world, directing their patients towards the right route to take (*and presumably taking just a little something for their trouble*).

☞ **Acupuncture:** The Chinese art of sticking needles into the bits of the patient that don't hurt to cure the bits that do.

☞ **Herbalism:** Prescription or use of herbs or plants for medication using only natural products as opposed to synthesised ones (*eye of frog or wart of toad - try telling that to someone who's just died from eating a poisonous red kidney bean or rhubarb leaf*).

☞ **Aromatherapy:** Medicinal use of smelly - or should I say fragrant - oils and essences derived from plants, flowers and wood resins (*guaranteed to make you pong like a hippy's camper van*).

And here are some more of the less well-established ones. There are millions more!

☞ **Spiritual Healing:** The alleged transmission of energy from a healer on the painful spot, through his hands or, at a distance, by telepho – *sorry* – prayer.

☞ **Crystal Therapy:** The application of different crystals or semi-precious stones to diseased or painful parts of the body *(diamonds are a quack's best friend)*.

☞ **Aura Diagnosis:** Ascertaining a person's state of health from the colour and hue of his or her aura, or energy envelope, round their bodies *(to be seen in all good porridge ads)*.

☞ **Endogenous Endocrinotherapy:** The pursuit of hormonal balance in the body by regulating the activities of the endocrine gland *(wherever that might be)* by external manipulation *(Mmm! Could be good - could be bad!)* without recourse to introduced stimulants, suppressants or supplements.

☞ **Hydropathy:** The use of water internally and externally for health and healing. The internally part involves the dreaded colonic irrigation *(or moronic irrigation in Princess Di's case)* which, when it comes right down to it, is the sluicing out of the digestive system from the only convenient orifice *(I think I'll stick to EXTERNAL if it's all the same to you)*.

☞ **Psionic Medicine:** Dowsing a small blood sample with the aid of a pendulum *(can you believe this?)* to ascertain defects and imbalances affecting a body's vitality.

To a cynic like me, and this is only MY opinion, these 'natural' (water up your bum – natural?) alternatives are a sitting duck. Just a load of jargonistic rubbish guaranteed to seduce a society where every itch has become an allergy and that has made hypochondria into an art form. But I must be fair here. Nature isn't only regarded as a something to be exploited, as admen would have us believe. 'Nature' according to many of these alternative practices, is the vital force and energy running through all things (except me, apparently) - the very thing that makes things grow and renew themselves (where's my hair going then?). Indeed in some senses, nature *is* health. So, despite all my cynical side-swipes, questioning whether all these alternative therapies actually work or are just figments of some smooth operator's imagination, is there any real harm done?

If people feel a bit cheered up by going to see someone who isn't their doctor, about their acne or athlete's foot (and don't mind parting with a lot of loot for the privilege) who am I to question it? Isn't a GP the only person who *hasn't* got a guaranteed cure for the common cold, for instance? If it really is just emperor's new clothes time again, and these mini-industries purely service an affluent society's obsession with itself - so be it. I'm all for a few people making a killing out of other people's totally unjustified insecurities and hypochondrias. Crikey, some people think the perfect doctor *IS* the one who always finds something wrong with them.

But the answer from a large proportion of the orthodox medical profession to my original question of whether there's any real harm done, is a resounding YES.

WHY?

Most people go to the doctor to talk about their ailments and to have their minds put at rest. The average GP, in a busy practice, however, has to turn his or her patients round every five to ten minutes (they say the best way to guarantee a doctor making a housecall these days is to marry one). Most alternative practitioners, on the other hand, charge by the hour, and - surprise surprise - seem to have all the time in the world (are you getting my drift?).

Keep 'em talking, that's the scam, even if you're just a sham.

29

Therefore, it doesn't take Sigmund Freud to work out that, as our favourite occupation is talking about ourselves – by spending time with us – these people make us feel special, even cosseted, and not just a number on some overworked, and thoroughly shagged-out doctor's register. It's common knowledge that because our population is becoming increasingly older (and therefore more medically dependent), progressive governments find it more and more difficult to hang on to even a semblance of Bevan's dream of good, comprehensive (and free) medicine for all. No government can possibly own up to losing this particular plot, because, of course, it's a potential vote loser. So what does the average not-very-well-man-in-the-street do if he can't get the attention he feels he deserves? Simple. He goes to someone who appears to really care and believes *anything* he is told.

BUT, despite falling hook, line and sinker, into the idea of alternative medicine, most people like to leave at least one foot in the proper doctor's camp, just in case. *BUT,* and this is the even bigger *BUT,* like having a flirtation outside a marriage, they feel embarrassed about telling him or her that they're seeing someone else for fear of being thought of as disloyal or sneaky. Most of the time this is okay, but more and more cases are turning up of patients, with quite serious conditions, forgoing the advice of their GP in favour of the comforting words of the alternative practitioner. In other words they are choosing to believe the one who advises them on the more optimistic and least painful option.

If visiting the doc's means its going to get hurty,
go elsewhere and hope he's not shirty.

How's Your Head?

This, of course, opens up a new bag of worms. How much of our health is due to the actual nuts and bolts mechanics of how our bodies work, and how much is due to our mental well-being? What's happening in the old brain department?

"How long can I live without a brain Doctor?"

"I don't know. How old are you?"

The pursuit of health, this current craze of the eighties and nineties, is thought by some to be as much to do with how we think as what we do. We can actually *choose* to be ill or not. Because of a whole new set of rules that for one reason or another we can't seem to keep up with, a brand new term has entered the language:

!!! STRESS !!!

Stress is a word that my mother and father or their parents would hardly have used, but these days it's passed around as freely as a joint at a rock festival. Like everything that starts to get mentioned a lot, whole new industries have started up to try to find ways of cashing in on them. *Transforming Consciousness* has become the new *IN* term. So what's new? Hippies were trying to get their heads round all that stuff decades ago *(and look what happened to them).* Even quite respectable people were *turning on* and *tuning in* with the help of acid, speed, grass, uppers, downers and John and Yoko *(Memo: I really must write the The Farman Book of Jolly Silly People).* This time round it's all a bit different. Most of the new boys in the 'good-health-through-getting-your-head-together' business turn up their noses at 'artificially introduced' stimulants, tending to regard the body as a temple (mine's more like a tram-shed). One of the conditions to the alternative health movement's promise of fitness, is that we change our mental outlook and chuck the drugs, though you'd never guess that if you'd met some of the practitioners I've known.

> *Just because we've the gift of speech, must we practise what we preach?*

Here are a few of the new outfits set up with the sole intention of unscrambling our minds:

☞ **Pre-Creation or Soul Therapy:** Through this 'system' *(notice how many times that word's used)* a person is able to make contact with his Soul or Divine energies, literally rejuvenating his whole being. In this expanded state of awareness he is easily able to release deep seated blockages *(sounds like a laxative)*. Not only from life, early childhood traumas etc., but also from other incarnations. This therapy also helps most physical-emotional-mental-psychic, and sexual conditions' *(like not having someone to do it with?)*.

☞ **Neuro-Linguistic Processing:** Teaches the actual processes of human communication, which allows us to understand how we can make significant changes to our processes of communication. 'It is possible to describe any human activity in a detailed way that allows you to make deep and lasting changes quickly and easily' *(haven't we heard that somewhere before?)*. Also available is *Re-Beliefing,* which offers freedom from all mental stress *(that's nice)* and freedom from all psychological problems *(that's fantastic!)*. Applicants move through the various stages towards becoming a TOTAL ACHIEVER *(me, me)*. They will be confident, optimistic people, able to talk to anyone, command attention and be winners *(me, me, me)*. They will often look years younger than they really are *(My! that's truly fantastic)* as *Re-Beliefing* slows down the ageing process as one erases old beliefs *(like the belief that you're being conned stupid)*.

Or best of all:

☞ **Reiki Therapy:** 'Reduce tension and stress, expand creativity and productivity, renew and revitalise your energy, support personal growth and transformation *(into what?)*, enhance the quality of your life.'

So are we really all stressed-out crazies? Blimey, the way they carry on makes us sound like a bunch of deprived, angry, frustrated nutters. Surely, never in the whole history of the human race, have we been represented as so damaged or such prisoners to our past. The *Networking Movement,* for example, also tells us that 'we suffer from blockages from the past (send for Dynorod), and that, just like packing up junk food, we should do the same for our minds . . . we have to feed ourselves and others spiritually. The past is a whole load of rubbish and junk, simply effluent from an affluent society.'

In my humble opinion there never has been such a marvellous opening for someone with the gift of the gab, a spare room (and a photocopier) to cut into this rich vein of insecurity. There are literally thousands of these outfits, all punting similar messages.

Feeling sad and a little confused?
No one with cash is ever refused.

The one uniting feature that links most of these gurus, therapeutic societies and indeed just about every common or garden high street counsellor, is that they need absolutely no training or qualifications to set up shop. In fact you or I could, this very day, shove a brass plate on our front door saying something like.. ➡

> **John L. Farman**
> *(Freelance Guru and Cosmic Therapist)*
> _____
> Improvement of stress-related conditions,
> physical conditions, apathy, depression,
> tiredness, bad breath and boring friends

then shove a card in the local newsagent or a small ad in the local paper, and sit back and wait for the punters to pour in. Thousands, if not millions, of people go to these operators, many of which have little more than a course at the local adult education centre behind them, and many a lot less, parting with hodloads of cash on the basis that a problem shared is a problem halved (and that nobody else can be bothered with their continual bleating).

Genuine or Not?

To retract slightly, quite a lot of counsellors *have* had an intensive course of training, and have indeed been through

therapy themselves (all shrinks are barking) which must make them a little more qualified to listen in on other people's misery (and ease their hard-earned loot off them). And many of the multitude of alternative practitioners, healers or call them what you will, have also studied their 'craft' before working with the general public.

BUT – and let this be a warning

Andy, a barman in my local pub (a 'resting' actor) recently earned £500 for two hours' work by posing as a faith healer when one of a group of ten fell ill just before a *Festival of Faith*. Nobody spotted the imposter. This could prove either of two things. Either all the other 'healers' were charlatans, or it really is the *belief* in the healer that does the trick. This, of course, makes spotting the difference between the quack and the serious, trained practitioner virtually impossible.

Therapy at the Bookstore

If you don't want to be a therapist or counsellor yourself, but you feel a burning need to help people and make a pot of gold in the process, might I suggest you write a book about it. First, however, you must find an angle that hasn't been tried that many times before. Here are a few existing titles to ponder:

☞ *Getting What You Want* by J.H.Brennan

☞ *Choose Happiness* by Elizabeth Smith

☞ *Success Through a Positive Mental Attitude* by Napoleon Hill (how could you fail with a name like that) and Clement W. Stone.

or even:

☞ *How to Make a Man Fall in Love With You* by Tracy Cabot (presumably for women).

There are literally hundreds of small publishers producing thousands of different titles, all offering us fantastic, fail-safe solutions to our various problems. Every single one encourages the individual's dream that their character, and therefore their life, can be changed by simply reading – and that there *are* real solutions to everything. We, of course, *know* this to be perfectly reasonable. That's why we find that by simply spending a few quid in Dillons, we can transform ourselves into happy, well adjusted, fulfilled, good-looking, great in bed, kind and incredibly popular individuals (depending how many we buy). Isn't it wonderful that there are so many people willing to sacrifice their time massaging our insecurities and weaknesses.

Far be it from me to suggest that if every one of these self-help books was put on a huge fire, it would not make a scrap of difference to mankind (unless you're the publisher), bar keeping a few people warm for a couple of hours.

CRAP CORNER

What do you think about alternative medicine? Do you think I've uncovered a whole series of half-truths, or am I barking up the wrong tree? Why not let let me know? Here again are the main points.

The more fantastic developments in medical science become, the more sceptical the public gets.

The government have no problem with alternative medicine. It simply takes the spotlight off the lamentable state of the health service.

If natural medicines were so damn good in the past, how come people's lives were so much shorter before medical science was developed.

The word 'natural' is all but meaningless in the nineties as it has come to mean anything and everything that advertisers want.

The word *chemical* sends most 'alternatives' into spasm, even though many chemicals occur naturally anyway.

It's mostly people who live in cities who go on and on about all things natural.

'Natural homeopathic treatments' pander to a society that has made hypochondria into an art form.

The perfect doctor is the one who finds something wrong with you.

CRAP! Alternative medicine can be dangerous if allowed to fly in the face of modern medical knowledge.

CRAP! Many people would have it that much physical sickness is caused from things cerebral. In other words, it's what's going on in our heads that makes our bodies hurt.

CITY FRAUD'S NOT
PROPER CRIME CRAP!

> ❛ *A stockbroker is a man who can take a bankroll and run it into a shoestring...* ❜
>   *Alexander Woolcott*

Hands up all those who didn't have a behind-the-hand giggle when the slightly slimy Nick Leeson (that not-very-bright-Watford-boy-made-good who gambled on the Tokyo and Singapore money markets) brought down one of London's oldest and most prestigious commercial banks. The naughty lad had been using 830 million of Baring's very best millions to prop up his own dodgy dealings, which began to go wrong when an earthquake struck in Kobe, Japan.

> ❛ *I have always found that a gambler's word is better than a banker's...* ❜
>   *Al Farr*

It seemed poetic justice for all of us who don't earn our daily bread, or should I say the jam on our daily bread, by simply shifting a decimal point a couple of places.

Basically, if you live by the VDU screen you should certainly not expect sympathy if you die by it. Unfortunately, when these big players hit the skids, the shock wave usually engulfs a legion of small investors, the recipients of charities and the thousands of dear old ladies whose meagre pensions are all that's left of a lifetime's *proper* work by their sadly departed husbands. The only people who rub their hands together with glee are the lawyers.

*❛ My definition of an utter waste, is a coach-load of lawyers
going over a cliff, with three spare seats... ❜*   Lamar Hunt

Mighty Maxwell

Take a good, hard peek at the sadly seedy Robert Maxwell
affair for instance. Most of those transactions mentioned
earlier didn't actually break any laws. Some did, however, and
most of the bigger frauds were carried out by ruthless men
whose inner circle of lackies turned a blind eye. Far from
being regarded as the fat, evil cheat that we now know he
was, he was revered by all around him. And it wasn't as if they
didn't *know* what a cruel ruthless so-and-so he really was. The
truth was that they actually admired him. It was those very
characteristics that symbolised the get-rich-at-all-costs greed
of the eighties. Sure, many of his former colleagues and
partners turned round when it was proved that he was a cheap
crook, and said that they'd been bullied and terrorised, but
that was for fear of being sucked into the ever-deepening poo
themselves. It didn't take Nacker of the Yard to work that out.

*❛ Business is like oil, it won't mix with anything but
business... ❜*   J. Graham

The Boss is Always Right

Companies, it was generally thought, had no responsibilities
beyond making as much dosh as possible for their
shareholders. A boss should be able to hire and fire at will if
he so desires, and even stick his filthy mitt into his employees'
pension funds should he need some extra loot to bale out
other operations. That's exactly what Robert Maxwell did.

We all snigger at other countries who have, in the
past, been dominated by bad dictators like Ferdinand Marcos

or Idi Amin, but fail to realise that in a slightly lesser way the Maxwells of this world were cast in the same mould. Okay, he didn't actually murder or torture people, but he certainly had the power to hire and fire on a whim and so ruin the lives of the good and honest people who got in his way. He also spent the hard-earned pensions of 32,000 loyal employees to the tune of £44 million (mind you, he did get a jolly nice boat out of it).

Unfortunately, the slob actually got away with his crimes by dying, so there's no one to humiliate or string up at the nearest lynching tree. If the nasty old toad was murdered, then it certainly wasn't worth a penny of tax payers' money trying to work out who did it. Good riddance we say! It's just a pity that someone didn't listen to a report from the highly-respected Board of Trade who, as long ago as twenty years before his death, branded him a cheat and a liar, totally unfit to run as much as a station sandwich bar.

Old Maxwell quite cunningly
decided to drown,
So missing conviction
and being sent down.

But his crime is only the most obvious example of a whole load of frauds and manipulations of company laws which work against a section of the community that naively trust others to look after their money, or the company they work for. At last, Labour leader Tony Blair, through his gimmicky sounding 'stakeholder' plan, has suggested that employees just might be given the right to know how the company they work for is being run and even have some say in it.

REAL Crime?

But still British society doesn't think that financial fraud is as bad as robbing a bank, mugging a pensioner, or even fiddling the dole office. This is proved by the badly kept secret that prisoners convicted on fraud charges go to nice open prisons, and are often allowed to keep their PCs and mobile phones so that they can continue their dodgy businesses.

Most people, in fact, believe that if you defraud a huge company or national institution it's almost fair game. If, for instance, an individual neatly skims off a few grand from – say – a bank or an insurance company, many of us secretly think 'good for him'. We hate those faceless organisations, full of soulless pen-pushers, especially the way they treat us if we ever get into money troubles or need to make a legitimate claim when something gets lost or stolen.

Insider Dealing

Just like the old David *v* Goliath story, beating the system appeals to most of us and there are some city crimes that not only make fortunes for the perpetrator but also, it could be argued, seem to damage no one directly. The Stock Market, which is linked to trading centres worldwide, is the place where shares in all public companies are traded. A public company is one that you or I, if we've got the loot, can buy a bit of. Buying and selling shares is really a form of legitimate gambling just like poker or the gee-gees, and shares are bought in the hope that their value will go up fairly quickly, yielding a quick, profitable buck for the buyer. 'Insider Dealing' is the trendy new term used when an individual uses information that only he or she has, when buying or selling shares. For example:

Your rich Uncle Ted owns a company that manufactures the famous *Acme Egg Whisk*. One Sunday when you're round at Acme Towers (his palatial home), he tells you that he knows of a way that you and he could make a small fortune real quick. He's just about to clinch the biggest deal in egg-whisk history – the whole of China is about to go mechanised in the whisking department. When the deal goes through, he claims, the value of his company, and therefore the shares, will explode. He suggests that on Monday you (as he's not allowed to do it) ring up your stock broker (which we all, of course, have) and buy as many shares as possible. He'll even lend you the money. In return, you split the vast profit with him. Simple, and no harm really done; the shares would have gone up anyway so all it means is that you and Uncle cash in big time as well as any one else who has shares in Acme. The fact is, however, that what you both did is actually breaking the law. Using information that only you could possibly know – to make profit – means you are cheating against the fair working of the system. Illegal it may be, but surprise, surprise, hundreds of transactions are made on this basis every day.

Just before we climb aboard the moral band wagon and condemn these people to bread and water for the rest of their days, let's examine what you or your nearest and dearest would do in either of these following situations:

1. You are walking past the staff room at college and you see some papers on the floor. Just before you knock on the door to hand them in, you glance down and see that they're the questions for the exam you haven't revised for. Do you hand them in immediately and get the college goody-goody prize, or do you have a quick shifty through them to see what you're going to be asked (and then hand them in and get the college goody-goody prize)?

2. You are about to park your car and you remember a friend telling you that the meter at the end of the street registers the money that you've put in but rejects the coin after doing so. Do you keep putting the same coin in until you've got the maximum time, and then pocket it, or do you go and find a meter maid to report the faulty machine?

You see the connection? They might not seem to be that closely related to big financial fraud, but if you were held down and tortured, you might be forced to admit that they are just weeny versions of the same thing: that is, using a particular piece of information to your own advantage. Both of these examples have happened to me, and I know jolly well what I did - the right and honest thing. And my name's Mother Theresa.

...and Accountants

Most people in ordinary jobs don't have accountants. They are taxed at source and receive their pay packets with the dreaded income tax removed. Other, more cunning people, have accountants who admit to using every method possible to reduce their client's bill. This might involve them putting your money offshore to countries that don't charge the same rate of tax (or any at all); building up vast semi-artificial expenses so as to make your amount of profit look smaller; allowing members of your family to be included on the payroll for non-existent jobs even though they might not even know what the business involves, simply to reduce your liability; and so on and so forth. There are literally millions of legitimate ways that a clever accountant can reduce the amount of tax his paymaster pays to far below what Joe Public has to suffer, just by juggling figures. Why isn't something done about this glaring inequality and carefully dressed fraud? I'll tell you. Because all the people that make the decisions that influence our tax laws, are in on the act! To change the way the system works would be like crafting a big, heavy stick to beat themselves with.

43

The Moral Maze

So, do you think it's right that the better the accountant you employ the less tax you pay? Or do you think that we poor workers pay too much tax anyway? Come to that, do you think that making money out of pure speculation without actually making anything, as they do in the Stocks and Futures Markets, should be encouraged – or do you think it morally indefensible?

The Black Economy

But don't go thinking that it's only the rich who get away with murder. There's a form of fraud that's even more common than all the aforementioned scams put together. The amounts might not be so great, but the effects on the economy are just as damaging. How many times have you heard a builder, plumber, window cleaner, telephone engineer or washing machine repair man tell you that he or she can do the job required FOR CASH at a much cheaper rate? How many times have you noticed in your corner shop, that the money doesn't go straight into the till but a drawer under the counter, or how many times does a minicab driver simply put the fair in his pocket without making any record of the transaction. Why are they all doing it? To avoid showing an income that might be taxed.

And another thing. How many times have you heard people say that they would prefer not to have a cheque, because it makes their paperwork a bit complicated? Rubbish! A cheque has to go through a bank, and the Inland Revenue have a nasty habit of requiring to see bank statements when assessing your tax.

If, after all this, you think England's bad, go to Spain or Italy or some of those hectic third world countries. The Black Economy, as it's called, is so rife, that it's surprising they have any public services at all: whole economies floating on a sea of back handers and dodgy cash.

Postscript

Nick Leeson, who opened this chapter, will get the last laugh on everyone. While serving his six and a half year prison sentence, he'll write a book of his dirty dealings. Well to be precise, someone will write it for him (I've already explained that he's not the brightest thing since Einstein). He has already been paid a £450,000 advance for the work (called predictably *Rogue Trader*). But that's only part of it. On top of that there will be shed-loads of loot for the film and TV rights and all the various telly spin-offs. Eventually he'll have his own chat show no doubt. Who says crime doesn't pay?

CRAP CORNER

Lets look at the double standards thrown up in this chapter.

CRAP! Baring's Bank were perfectly happy to support Leeson when he was making them loads of money, but seemed strangely reticent when he wasn't.

CRAP! Hundreds of people can be put out of work by one solitary phone call, from one person who doesn't give a damn, to another.

CRAP! Nobody minds a crook and a bully when he's on their side or when he makes them money, but watch their allegiance when he's found out.

CRAP! When a Third World country's involved, mass swindling is called tyranny: in the sophisticated western world it's called business.

CRAP! One of the very best ways of making a fortune is to do something really dreadful and then write about it.

❛ The difference between a dead skunk and a dead banker in the road is that there are skidmarks by the skunk... ❜ Anon

EATING ANIMALS IS BAD FOR THEM

As far as the Vegetarian Society is concerned, a vegetarian is someone who doesn't eat any meat or meat products, poultry or fish and who only eats free range eggs. A vegan refuses to eat anything that has even looked at an animal, refusing to consume milk, butter, cheese, cream or honey (bees – animals?). Here are just a few of the arguments wielded forth by vegetarians:

☞ God put all the creatures on this earth to share its resources. Eating our fellow occupants is barbaric and obscene.

☞ Farms are turning into little more than animal factories with profit being the only consideration.

☞ Animals hate being kept indoors, preferring the wide open spaces.

☞ All animals have deep feelings and share the same ability to feel pain and fear as us. Our methods of slaughtering them are disgusting and cruel.

☞ Britain alone could support a population of 250 million on a vegetarian diet.

☞ Four fifths of all agricultural land in the world is now used to feed animals for us to eat.

☞ Fish are sensitive too.

☞ Margarine, biscuits, ice cream, cakes, tinned soups and noodles all contain fat from dead animals.

☞ Sweets, jelly, wine gums, thick yoghurts as well as jelly

babies and lipstick contain gelatin or glycerol which is made from the boiled up bones of farm animals, including horses (shock horror).

☞ Even Polos contain hooves, horns and bones.

☞ Real vegetarians don't wear leather. It's cruel.

Writer Bill Bryson's favourite animal is the cow. (One of my favourite animals is Bill Bryson.) If you stand by a gate, he mused, they will most often walk over and look at you with beautiful, trustful, baleful eyes. You can then talk to them, feed them grass and feel real close for as long as you please. Best of all, he says, when you get bored, you can eat them! Chickens, on the other hand, really get the short straw. They're the only animals I know that get eaten before they're born or after they're dead.

WANNA BITE OF MY BIG MAC?

Many of you will call this tasteless talk heresy, claiming, as stated before, that filling our stomachs with those creatures we are fortunate enough to share Mother Earth with is barbaric and unnecessary, and that those that do it should be rated lower than dogs in the ecological chain. Woof woof!

❛ *Vegetarianism is harmless enough, but it tends to fill a man with wind and self-righteousness...* ❜ *Sir Robert Hutchinson*

Big Eaters

The average person who lives say 70 years will probably chomp through 550 chickens, 36 pigs, the same number of sheep and eight cows or horses (if French) and God knows how many Mars Bars. He will wash that down with over 18 tons of milk and have 10,000 eggs for his breakfast.

If he didn't, it doesn't necessarily follow that all those uneaten beasts would be contentedly mooing, baaing, oinking and clucking in idyllic picture book meadows and farmyards. The saddest thing, whether you like it or not, is that many of them have precious little use other than to provide us with food, so the poor dears would probably join the dinosaur, dodo and sincere politicians in extinction in a blink of the eye (evolution-wise), and anyway – what about the mustard industry?

Okay, you could say, so we might not have those animals any more, but we'll still have the indigenous wildlife to enjoy and they'd have all the fields to themselves. Sorry, wrong again. It's a well known fact that the mass cultivation since the war, the trashing of the hedgerows and the use of murderous sprays, has decimated our wildlife faster than an army of big game hunters with flame throwers. In Britain alone 24 songbirds are currently in danger and throughout the world so much natural habitat has been lost, that extinction is overtaking some species 50 – 100 times faster than the expected natural rate. Just to cheer you up more , the species that still exist today, are the product of 3.5 billion years of evolution, which in terms of time-scale puts everyone (including us) in danger★. Anyway, getting rid of animal pasture land would not create vast areas of parkland and forest: just more room for high yield crop production, ghastly new towns, car parks, motorways, shopping malls and Vegetarian Centres.

' *Vegetarians have wicked, shifty eyes and laugh in a cold calculating manner. They pinch little children, steal stamps, drink water and favour beards...* '

J.B. Morton - 'Daily Express'

★Why not try my Endangered Species Cookbook, including tried and tested recipes such as Osprey egg omelette and Panda with stir fried bamboo shoots. Tasteless? Moi?

But wait, I hear all you veggies (4% of population) cry, the devouring of our fellow mammals is declining anyway – so put that in your gravy. Well, again that's sort of true, but as the consumption of red-blooded cows and sheep dips ever so slightly (on account of turning us mad), we are gobbling up more pigs and chickens than ever before. In fact, overall, we are consuming 50% more meat now than we were 40 years ago – so put that in your soya soup!

> *The only place for fowl or pork*
> *Is on our knife, or on our fork.*

The Choice

The main problem seems to be that the poor beasts that we actually eat don't have much say in the matter. We humans, because we're clever and organised, pull whichever species we choose from the freezer as the fancy takes us. It's not really fair. At least big, cross animals like lions and crocodiles can occasionally get us back, but who's ever been savaged by a sheep or a cow (or a Welsh rarebit for that matter)?

But is this really the point? Isn't there a great danger of dropping into the way of thinking that animals are really the same as us – but in fur coats? From birth, our mummies, daddies, and teachers regale us with stories in which all the beasts we know and love, talk to each other in much the same way as we do. Take the *Tales of Beatrix Potter*, *Wind in the Willows*, *Bambi*, or even *Deputy Dawg*. A small kid could well grow up thinking that when they're not actually in our company animals chatter away about their masters, or who they're currently going out with, or what they're going to do when they grow up and so forth.

Nice 'n' Nasty

The point I'm trying to make is that because of our upbringing, we give every animal qualities and personalities that we've assimilated through kids' books. Sheep are always kind and quiet, snakes are sneaky and vicious, rabbits are jolly and industrious, and wolves are vicious thugs that kill for the fun of it. The fact that rabbits spend practically all their time screwing and eating, and wolves are generally no more aggressive than our own pet gerbils, doesn't get considered.

Spot the Beast

We even contrive to make the animals that we eat look as anonymous as possible. Old-fashioned butcher's shops used to look like horror film sets (Silence of the Lambs?) with dead pigs, rabbits and chickens hanging by the feet and dripping blood for all to see. These days, meat in supermarkets is as neatly packaged as pasta or Polos, and often we can't tell what animal each bit actually comes from. Come to that, we don't even call meat by the actual animal's name. Cows become beef, pigs become pork, and it's only relatively recently that we've started calling sheep lamb instead of mutton. Along this line, many people find eating fish almost impossible if the head is still in place. Those baleful, sightless eyes – urggh!

All's Well in Never Never Land

We actually want to believe that cows and sheep long for sunny pastures full of lush grass and buttercups, and hate being shut up in a dingy sheds, because that's what WE'D prefer. Have you considered that what might look to us a jolly nice open landscape to stand around eating our lunch in, might cause an animal unbelievable discomfort due to lack of shelter from the blistering sun or the freezing rain? Just a thought.

We reckon that if a pig looks a bit pissed off, it could be because it's more than likely just been separated from its piglets and is shut up in a gloomy pen all day, or that cows look so fed up because all they seem to do is walk backwards and forwards eating grass and having milk squeezed out of them (why isn't milk green?). I don't know if you've noticed, but despite the pictures in Farmyard Friends, all animals have only one expression, and that's usually pretty fed up or, dare I venture to suggest, stupid. It's all very nice to put human emotions into your own Tiddles or Rover, but if you've ever seen a pussycat literally torturing a bird to death, or a dog sniffing another's bum (or, heaven forbid, worse!), you'll begin to see what I'm on about.

If only our animals could stand up and speak, I wonder if they'd be so docile and meek.

While I'm about it, everybody gets their knickers in a twist about the consumption of calves, lambs or deer, because they're rather dear and pretty, but you don't get that many losing sleep over slimy fish, crusty lobsters, snotty oysters or squidgy snails. As for frogs, who gives a fig about them?

❛ *Three million frogs' legs are sold in Paris – daily. Nobody knows what becomes of the rest of the frogs…* ❜

Fred Allen

A Job for Life (or Death)

It might be said that animals know their place. A pig doesn't sometimes feel that he'd like to break out and work in a bank, or a cow doesn't get delusions of starring in a pantomime (Oh yes she does!). Like it or not the animals that we eat have been bred for the job, not just from their parents and grandparents, but from countless generations over thousands of years. They've got nothing else to do but be eaten. Hens, for instance, don't fly because there's no point, and anyway, they've got nowhere to go. They are now brought up in the

only place that they expect to be
brought up in – a battery cage, not
clucking around in a farmyard being
fed by jolly, rosy-faced farmers'
wives, as purists would no doubt prefer.

But what about all those
chickens you can buy in our
supermarkets with *Free Range* printed
on their plastic macs? Surely they must have had a much
better life, mustn't they? Sorry, not always true. Five times
more hens die from aggression, fear and stress in large 'free
range' enclosures and often, in those that have an inside or
outside alternative, half the birds choose to huddle together
inside in the smelly darkness.

But Where Will It End?

If it sounds as if I believe that anything goes in the great
pursuit of profit through food production, I don't. This
unnatural selection can get out of hand, as supermarkets (the
main culprits) demand more and more for less and less.
Broiler chickens that grow so fast their legs can't hold them,
turkeys too fat to bonk (mind you, I know humans like that),
beef cows too muscled to give birth unaided and soon,
believe it or not, featherless chickens, hibernating sheep (to
save winter grub) and, would you believe, attempts are now
being made to breed out all ability to feel stress or pain in pigs
– Suffering Sausages! In other words totally brainless animals
that are closer related to a brussel sprout or turnip than to
yours truly.

Let us hereby make a pledge,
not to turn animals into veg.

The Choice Is Ours

Animals do suffer, and anyone who's ever
seen (or smelt) the inside of a battery
chicken farm will never be the same
again. Here are a few horror stories:

☞ 30% of all chickens reach the slaughterhouse with at least one broken bone.

I FEEL WELL AND TRULY PLUCKED

☞ Turkeys are often painfully de-beaked to prevent damage to others.

☞ A milking cow often lives in a state of total exhaustion due to the 30 or 40 litres of milk that must be poured out of it every day.

☞ Pigs suffer real stress from cold, damp concrete inside and heat exhaustion outside (pigs, unlike the popular expression, can't sweat) and intense stress when transported.

☞ Sheep suffer from anything from foot rot to heat exhaustion also when transported.

Whether or not you believe in vegetarianism, certain things must be done. We must either clean up our act, making intense farming conditions as humane as possible (which IS possible), or spend more money when at the supermarket by choosing only the animals that have not been so intensely farmed, or develop the poor dumb critters so far scientifically that they become something else entirely. The very last alternative is that we stop eating them altogether and put the few remaining examples into zoos. "Ooh mummy, can we go and see the hamburgers?"

Meat or Veg?

For me the issue isn't really whether we eat meat or not – that must be down to personal choice. How far do you go anyway? Vegans, as mentioned earlier, are the most far left of the vegetarians, refusing to eat anything that's even been sniffed by a living creature. But what if you took it even further? What about Vegetable Rights? In one of G K Chesterton's books he put it like this:

Mr Mick not only became a vegetarian, but at length declared vegetarianism doomed ('shedding' as he called it finely 'the green blood of the silent animals') and predicted that men in a better age would live on nothing but salt.

Seriously (for once)

I have a deep respect for vegetarians who refuse to eat meat for non-sentimental reasons, and there are many of them. What seems to be the debate of the nineties, however, is whether animals, who can't speak up for themselves, should have the same rights as us? When you get a situation where a top company like Fisons produces a cattle feed that actually contains dead cows, you realise that ethically you are getting into some very hot water. If cows wanted to eat each other, they'd be at it all the time. No wonder it sends them loopy (and us loopy when we eat *them*). It says in the Bible that you should never cook a kid (small goat, that is) in its mother's milk - it's not respectful. I don't always agree with everything in the Good Book but it certainly has a point here.

CRAP CORNER

For me, eating meat or not, is simply a matter of personal choice. Meat eaters, however, must be aware of what they are actually doing. There are hypocrisies and delusions on both sides. These are the main points:

CRAP! Vegetarians would have it that meat-eaters are destroying the balance of nature. On the contrary, as omnivores (people who eat meat and veg) we help perpetuate it.

CRAP! We are constantly told that the grazing of cattle is ruining our Brazilian rainforests and consequently the ecological structure of the world. What about the endless, treeless tracts of wheat fields that, if left alone, turn into near desert?

Vegetarians would have it that if we didn't farm animals the fields would return to their natural state - a haven for wildlife. They wouldn't.

The reduction of natural habitat throughout the world for wild animals is as much to do with intensive crop cultivation as the rearing of animals.

"Meat eating is decreasing" is a popular vegetarian cry. If you were a pig or chicken you might disagree. The flesh of these animals is being consumed in ever greater quantities.

Meat eaters pretend to their children that farm animals are extremely nice and our true friends. They then put them on their plates.

Vegetarians have a habit of assuming that animals think and feel like they do, and try to make meat eaters feel guilty. There is no evidence for this!

There is a general assumption that animals are happier to be out in the open. There is no evidence for this either.

Intensive farmers imagine that the animal is a simple machine-like organism with which he can do anything he pleases. An animal should have rights like we have. These should be internationally drawn up - and then stuck to.

Most meat eaters (like me) prefer to buy their dead animals looking like nothing in particular. This helps them avoid realising what they are actually consuming.

FOREIGN AID ACTUALLY HELPS PEOPLE (CRAP!)

6 If only it were as easy to banish hunger by rubbing the belly as it is to masturbate... 9 *Diogenes (412 -322 BC)*

How do you fancy a highly paid job, requiring no particular skills, offering loads of foreign travel and practically limitless expenses? Mmm - yes please? Not only that, but you'll never be required to show results, and everyone will think you're a truly fab person for doing it. If this sounds like a job as presenter for one of those naff TV travel shows, you're wrong. Tell us more, I hear you cry. Surely no such wonderful opportunity exists?

Oh yes it does. Read *The Economist* correspondent Graham Hancock's almost unbelievable *Lords of Poverty* - he'll put you right. In the highly-lucrative world of charity and aid-for-the-less-fortunate-than-ourselves business, armies of 'helpers' surf on a wave of almost limitless cash and self-congratulation. Make no mistake, charity is a big, buxom, beautiful business (if you're on the 'doing' end), and the sums involved are like international telephone numbers. Allow me to let you into a secret. You don't have to make an actual, countable (or even accountable) profit to keep the people involved in its running extremely comfortable. And who supplies the dosh? Three guesses. We, the richer countries of the world, do! As one African refugee quipped, "Why is it that every US dollar comes with twenty Americans attached to it?"

To be fair, most of Britain's top twenty-one voluntary agencies, like Band Aid, War on Want and Save the Children, manage to keep their administration costs down to below 10%. But some of the big boys could (if held down and tortured) tell a very different story.

'Administration', by the way, is the key term and is used to cover anything from first-class air travel to five star hotels, fab lunches to sumptuously catered 'conferences', to luxury cars, to servants, to 'room service' (and 'service' covers a multitude of sins), to... you get the picture?

So what's so wrong with raising money,
It gives them bread and gives
us honey?

Here's just a fraction of Mr Hancock's evidence, so judge for yourself.

☞ The International Hunger Project, which received $6,981,005 in 1985, sent no more than you or I did (probably less) to the world's starving, apart from a mere $210, 775 that went out as grants to other relief agencies (who were all trying to get in on the same scam). The rest was used for the aforementioned 'administration' (like a phone bill of $500,000).

☞ The British branch of the Hunger Project collected a cool £192,658 of which only £7,048 carelessly slipped through their fingers and actually got to the needy.

☞ In 1985, International Christian Aid was investigated by the US State Department, who found that only 41% of their vast income converted into hard cash to help the Third World.

☞ In 1986 War on Want's director George Galloway spent £20,000 in 18 months on luxury hotels while discussing the needy. (And blow me! They're one of the good charities.)

☞ UN officials working to relieve the suffering in

Phnom Penh received more in two days' allowances than the relief programme would provide for your bulk standard hungry Cambodian over twenty-seven months.

☞ The Khartoum Hilton did surprisingly brisk business during the catastrophic Sudanese drought of 1985. The $150 a night (without brecky) rooms were filled to capacity with delegates who'd pitched up to 'assess' the situation. Despite four months of hard assessing, not one single extra well-drilling rig was erected or one extra tumbler of water extracted.

Hancock gives several examples of the sort of delegates, aid agency officials, relief workers, priests, authorised sightseers, peeping Toms and disaster groupies, call them what you will, who simply pitch up at the nearest luxury hotel to a current misery centre, pop out to have a sympathetic peek at the starving (in their bought-or-rented-for-them air conditioned four-wheel-drives), before dashing back to down the last cocktail before the sun dips behind the palm trees round the hotel pool, heralding time to go in to a four-course slap-up dinner. What a relief.

CARING TAKES SO MUCH OUT OF ONE.

It's an ill wind that blows nobody any good. Most of the stuff listed above was, however, simply due to inefficiency, gross overstaffing and those wonderful caring folks' astounding ability to milk the system. Unfortunately there are almost as many incidents of downright corruption, bare-faced stealing and almost laughable inefficiency. Over to Mr. Hancock again.

☞ One voluntary organisation working with UNHCR (the bit of the United Nations concerned with refugees) in Beirut used UN funds to buy tents, blankets, bed sheets through four made-up companies at 300% mark up. Not only that, but the amounts purchased were far more than there were refugees to actually sleep in them, even allowing for the far smaller amount that actually turned up. The loss was somewhere in the region of $500,000 dollars.

☞ During the emergency in Somalia, a number of prefabricated health centres were built, costing $2 million each. They would have cost $1 million but someone decided to put two, instead of one, flush toilets in each (a million dollars for a bog?). The fact that there was not one metre of plumbing to attach them to where they were going seemed not to have been thought relevant. When they arrived in Mogadishu it turned out that the prefabs were miles too wide for the trucks that had to carry them, and it was even suggested that they cut them in half (not the trucks - the centres). Only one health centre was ever put up, and it turned out to be too hot inside to be of any use. The air conditioner seemed not to work. Why? - no electricity - of course!!!

☞ Among the totally useless drugs (mostly salesmen's samples) off-loaded on war-torn, famine-ridden Somalia (one of the hottest countries in the world) was a consignment of frostbite treatment. Better still were electric blankets, Go-Slim soup and a fab new chocolate drink for dieters. Unfortunately, on arrival they found that you tend not to get a lot of hot people trying to get warmer or emaciated ones trying to lose weight.

☞ Following the fall-out from the Chernobyl power plant blowout in 1986, a load of contaminated food, illegal in Europe, started turning up in aid shipments. In 1988 a bunch of extremely peckish African countries had given the thumbs down to a whole cargo of EEC food because it practically glowed in the dark.

☞ The Germans really are a caring race. They sent 1000 polystyrene igloos for the homeless - any old homeless.

Unfortunately, these particular homeless lived very near the equator and, after finding that the igloos were too stifling to enter, discovered they couldn't dismantle the flipping things. They ended up burning them which, I should imagine, made them even hotter.

☞ In Bangladesh, a tricky little gang of surprisingly rich local 'commission agents' pocketed an estimated $136 million from aid transactions. All in only eight years.

☞ Best of all was one British charity's recent response to an African cry for edible help. Who ever packed up the crates must have had their mind on other things (or a wicked sense of humour) as, when they were opened, they were found to contain packs of tea (so nice for those impromptu afternoon tea parties in one's cardboard shack), tissues (for dabbing the corners of one's mouth after said tea) and Tampax (guaranteed to swell in one's stomach, so relieving the hunger pangs).

YOU SIMPLY MUST COME ROUND TO ME NEXT WEEK.

Farmer's Friends?

Another great cock-up can be observed when relief agencies send too much aid, so wrecking what remains of an indigenous economy. Consider this. There you are, a Third World farmer, minding your own business, struggling away against all odds to raise a crop in a hot, dusty, water-deprived area. The word gets out in the west that you and your fellow countrymen are going a little short in the old grub department. Suddenly lorry loads of wheat turn up on your doorstep, and Mrs Abukubulawa and all her neighbours, quite understandably, go for the new stuff rather than paying you for yours. Brilliant! Thanks to the kindness of thousands of people in a country you never even heard of, your neighbours get their shopping buckshee, and you go out of business.

Third world poor from North to South
Look their gift-horses in the mouth.

Give 'em More

Here's a fab scam; if you want to make
money out of other people's misfortune – simply exaggerate
the scale of the problem. The American charity World
Vision, which has a very successful branch in this country, put
an ad in the *National Catholic Reporter* in 1981 claiming that
12,000,000 people were on their last legs somewhere in
Africa. It was a pure, no-other-interpretation-possible,
money-grabbing fib. The pictures of the admittedly starving
people were at least three years old and, although the natives
weren't exactly enjoying champagne lunches with canapés
and lobster, in five-star restaurants, the crisis was well past.

❜ What fun it would be to be poor, as long as one was
excessively poor! Anything in excess is most exhilarating… ❜
Jean Anouilh

International Christian Aid have been known to go
bigger and better in the money-for-sympathy stakes. In one
of their tear-jerking, wallet-loosening documentaries they
claimed that there were 1.5 million refugees in Somalia.
Wrong! There were only a third of that number. They also
said that the fighting was getting worse when the very reverse
was true, and that the children were not receiving enough
calories to survive when, in truth, the poor little mites were
getting too much damn food. All a bunch of
porkies just to keep their huge organisation
topped up.

❜ Too many people have decided to
do without generosity in order to
practise charity… ❜ *Albert Camus*

Help for the Hapless

The principle, I'm afraid, behind the whole aid business, is that the poor impoverished people in the third world should be regarded as fundamentally helpless and, more to the point, fundamentally stupid. They are, according to those that dish aid out, the victims of countless disasters, shortages, wars and climatic catastrophes. They have too many children because they don't have anything else to do in the evenings and, because they are incapable of helping themselves, they must line up patiently to wait for we, big white Father Christmases from distant lands, to sort out their lives for them.

Let Them Grow Cake

This, of course, is total crap and about as patronising as that caring Margaret Thatcher's classic comment about the Ethiopian farmers. You can almost hear her slimy, mock-soothing, mock-Tudor, so-so patronising voice when you read the words. "We have to try to teach them the basics of long term husbandry." Yes, Margaret, I'm sure those brave ingenious farmers, who've fed their families for centuries off their tiny, unyielding, often parched, deeply eroded, handkerchief-sized hillside plots, were lining up for any advice they could get from a two-bit grocer's daughter from Grantham, whose suburban constituency members would be hard put to maintain a window box, let alone an allotment.

❮ Resolve not to be poor: whatever you have spend less. Poverty is a great enemy to human happiness; it certainly destroys liberty, and it makes some virtues impracticable, and others extremely difficult... ❯   Samuel Johnson

❮ ...and it means that you have to suffer insufferable prats like Maggie Thatcher... ❯   John Farman

Whoops!

One small peak at all the gobsmacking failures and total cock-ups of the major aid agencies will more than convince anyone that most of them haven't a clue what they're doing (and care even less). For instance:

The United States Agency for International Development had this brilliant idea to create a fish farm in Mali, West Africa, a country so hot that it makes hell sound like a cool-box. They assumed that the lake they got the natives to dig could be filled from a nearby canal. In theory, very true – but nobody thought to check whether the canal contained water all the year round. It didn't. As fish have a tendency to like being in water most of the time, a highly expensive diesel pump had to be brought in to suck water from several kilometres away. Next they discovered that fish like to eat while they're growing up, but drat it, on investigation, they discovered there were no pet shops locally. Therefore, the fish food had to be imported, again at great expense. The net result was that each kilo of fish, when all the expenses were put against it, cost a mere $4000. It would have been cheaper for each Malian, every time he fancied a fish supper, to fly over and buy the said swimmers at Harrods.

If this was just one isolated incident it wouldn't be so bad, but Graham Hancock lists a liturgy of stupid, expensive mistakes; like new roads that are split by wide rivers with no bridges to join them up; highly technical, state of the art equipment installed in such remote places that no one has the foggiest how to use it; huge dams (that were never asked for) that take away the homes of thousands and then kill them with fatal water-borne diseases; and wonderful resettlement projects for migrants which leave the poor blighters poorer than they were before, and break up their very tribal existence. The list goes on and on.

Helping others to help themselves
If you're shocked by what you've read so far about aid to stricken countries, you ain't heard nothing yet. Wait till you

realise what's going on in the business of mobilising and disbursing money to poor countries. Every year, 10,000 men and women attend the meeting of the World Monetary Fund and the Governors of the World Bank (see corrupt, inefficient organisations). Admittedly, now and again, some good work gets done, but over and above that, it is a lavish bunfight for all those remotely involved in the aid business (and a lot more hangers on). Here are a few interesting observations:

☞ When not nodding off or fast asleep at the compulsory meetings the delegates can be found at a host of cocktail parties, lunches, afternoon teas and dinners, the opulence of which would make our greedy Royal family's eyes water.

☞ The total cost of the 700 events cost a mere $10 million dollars.

☞ The average cost of a dinner per person was around $200 dollars (enough to feed some poor starving kid for months).

☞ One of the conferences, held at one of America's most plush hotels – the Sheraton, Washington, had 550 guest rooms converted into offices, miles of telephone lines installed and 54,000 watts of floodlights (though no one seemed to know what they were for).

☞ Every three years the Bank/Fund meeting takes place in a developing country. In 1985 it was held at the Hilton International in Seoul, the capital of South Korea (whose turn it was). Most considerately, the Korean government destroyed 128 buildings in the poverty struck red light district, just so's they could build a bigger hotel car park. It probably wasn't that much of a problem, however, as most of the prostitutes were like as not tucked up in the hotel rooms servicing the delegates.

Let's all meet to discuss the poor,
That's what half the money's for.

How Much?

The money raised is called Overseas Development Assistance (ODA) and tends to run between $45 billion and $60 billion a year. This might sound quite a lot of dosh but not when you consider that the last time anyone counted:-

☞ America spent more than $22 billion a year on fags.

☞ British women spent more on make-up and scent than the extremely rich Swiss spent on aid.

☞ The USA and Russia spent more than $1.5 billion A DAY on 'defence'.

☞ The boss of Lazard Frères, a huge American company, earned more than the combined yearly ODA budgets of Ireland and New Zealand.

☞ The highest percentage of Gross National Product (the amount of money a country earns) devoted to overseas aid came from - would you believe - Norway (at only 1.2%) while America, the richest country in the world, was near the bottom with a magnificently measly O.23%.

☞ Good news, in 1979 Britain was the most generous of the top seven industrialised nations. Bad news, we are now near the bottom. Purely co-incidentally, the Tories have been in power throughout most of this period.

What About the Workers

Yes, what about the aid workers that actually work abroad? It's generally recognised that if you manage to get in on the action, you're likely to earn far and away more than your qualifications would allow anywhere else. For instance you can expect a free furnished house (bills paid), and free freighting of all your goods and chattels (car, kids, budgie, wife etc.). Okay, some of the places you are expected to live might not be exactly Hampstead Garden Suburb but, as there's seldom anything to spend money on, the capacity for saving a large percentage of your highly inflated salary, is enormous.

But these perks are nothing compared to what you can expect if you work for the UN charity UNICEF (United Nations Children's Emergency Fund). Compared to someone like a poor OXFAM fieldworker, they live in the lap of luxury, with villas, cars and servants, and the use of first class air travel to simply go sign a letter. As Hancock put it:

Whatever noble mission the United Nations may once have had has, I am now convinced, long since been forgotten in the rapid proliferation of its self-perpetuating bureaucracies. Rather than encouraging humility and dedication, the world body's structure seems actively to reward self-seeking behaviour and to provide staff with many opportunities to abuse the grave responsibilities with which they have been entrusted.

In other words jammy jobs for all the boys!

A Clearer View

America coughs up a mighty 25% of the UN's running costs, but they are often not happy with what they get for their cash. One incident that pissed them off was when there was a decision to build a $73 million conference centre in Ethiopia (when famine was big). Cynical Senator Kassebaum piped up and confirmed that it would cost the US $18.5 million simply to enable their UN delegates to stand on the 29th floor, so gaining a better view of the country starving to death.

❝ *Charity separates the rich from the poor...* **❞**   *Eva Peron*

Here are a few more examples of the UN's or UNICEF's uses and abuses of the money given to them:

☞ The annual flagship publication *State of the World's Children Report* is produced by an external consultant. It would appear that the huge gang of highly paid professional journalists and other communicators, who waft around UNICEF's information office, aren't quite up to the job.

☞ Over in their Belgian office, Joe Verbeck, the director of UNICEF's Belgian committee, was accused of abusing his position (amongst other things) by organising a child sex ring which operated for many years. He got off due to 'lack of evidence', but another member of his staff got ten years. Police had discovered a photographic studio in the basement of UNICEF's offices, set up to take dirty pics of kids – mostly from the Third World (at least there was *some* connection). On UNICEF's main computer was a list of 400 wealthy 'Euro-pervs' and a much longer listing of all the youngsters available for sex.

☞ Some time ago the President and Executive Board of the United Nations Educational, Scientific and Cultural Organisation(UNESCO) claimed reimbursements for $1,759,548 for travel and hotel bills for a single year. At the Food and Agriculture Organisation they get through $17 million for travel alone.

☞ The rector of the UN University is paid three times as much as the Norwegian Prime Minister.

☞ Personnel and administrative costs take 80% of the UN's expenditures. Not bad for an organisation dedicated to struggling tirelessly for world development.

Let's Talk

One brilliant way of spending huge tranches of money and giving everyone concerned a jolly no-expenses-spared time, is to invent subjects for conferences and hold them in exotic places. How's about these for starters:

The United Nations Seminar on the Existing Unjust International Economic Order, on the Economics of Developing Countries, and the Obstacle That This Represents for the Implementation of Human Rights and Fundamental Freedoms – which sounds a right barrel of laughs. Or the relatively concise:

United Nations Conference to Review All Aspects of the Set of Mutually Agreed Equitable Principles and the Rules for the Control of Restrictive Business Practices.

Or how's about my idea for a conference:

United Nations Conference to discover more and more ways of extracting money from governments and private organisations, in order that we can buy ourselves an even better standard of living and make it look like were doing some good.

Don't make the title short and snappy,
Obscure and long will keep 'em happy.

It goes without saying that the poor Third World people, whom these conferences are designed to help, know nothing about their existence, wouldn't understand a word if they did, and are similarly totally unaffected by their conclusions.

But Seriously

I suppose it's somewhat churlish to lampoon all these organisations for wasting millions of the tax payers' money, while pretending to help the poor and develop Third World countries. After all, it keeps them in jobs and it seldom does any actual harm. Or does it? It might help at this stage to examine how the terrible situations that lead to the heartrending pictures on our tellies come about. Let's take a peek at famine.

6 *The war against hunger is truly mankind's war of liberation...* 9
                                                            J F Kennedy

Famine or Why Some People Starve to Death Unnecessarily

If you want to know more about famine read the great P J O'Rourke's *All the Trouble in the World*. He comes out with some amazing stuff. Believe it or not, he tells us, there is enough food in the world – and there has been since the late sixties. Since the mid-eighties, moreover, there has also been sufficient for everyone world-wide to have a correct and healthy diet. Okay there wouldn't be an awful lot of Big Macs or Chicken McNuggets involved, but a more vegetarian diet, though a bit boring, is a much more practical and healthy way to feed the masses anyway. And, if at any time there wasn't enough grub, there's absolutely tons of extra unused agricultural capacity standing waiting. (America, for instance, only has 2.4% of its labour force making food.)

It isn't a question of land either. The largely inefficient French produce more wheat than Australia and Argentina put together. The problem is, as you must have guessed, the grub's often nowhere near the right places at the right time, which is why we have the phenomena of the food mountain.

Just because we see starving people on the news every five minutes doesn't mean the problem's getting worse either. In 1950 almost a quarter of the world was constantly peckish, as opposed to only ten percent now. It's just that these days there's a full news crew on the spot before you can even say "What time's supper?"

What Causes Famine?

Famines, contrary to popular belief, are seldom caused by what we think they're caused by – drought, flood, greedy insects or disease – but more often than not some kind of political jiggery-pokery. The Chinese famine of 1958-61, which broke the world record, involved none of those things. It was simply the result of those horrid Marxists sticking their noses into the way the peasants had been farming quite successfully for years.

❜ World poverty is primarily a problem of two million villages, and thus a problem of two thousand million villagers... ❜   *E.F. Schumacher (not the racing driver)*

Famines are not always accidental either. The Nigerian government used starvation as a neat weapon against its arch foe Biafra. So did the Ethiopians to the Eritreans, the Muslim Sudanese against the Christians, and Spurs against West Bromwich Albion. Moreover, can you believe this? Famines aren't always caused because there's not enough food! The most recent dreadful famine in Bangladesh needn't have happened at all – they'd just had one of their best rice harvests ever. Someone (probably with a lot of spare rice to flog) put it about that there was a shortage, so that rice prices doubled overnight. As day follows night, hoarding started to occur, causing prices to go through their mud huts' thatched roofs and a nice new black market to open for business shortly after. This played right into the hands of their already corrupt leader Mujibur Rahman, who never missed a chance to make a few quid out of his poor fellow countrymen. So people starved for no good reason. The United States put the tin lid on their fate and sealed it tight, by refusing to send aid because the naughty Bangladeshis (unknown to the starving peasants) were selling jute to the naughty Cubans, their enemies (petty or what?). So you see what we're up against.

‘ Charity is the power of defending that which we know to be indefensible… ’
                                                                    G. K. Chesterton

Making Things Worse

‘ Money is better than poverty, if only for financial reasons… ’
                                                                    Woody Allen

It's all very well the UN and the World Bank having all their grandiose and expensive schemes to ease the load of the Third World peasant, but what if a) they don't want help and b) the situation is made a thousand times worse by their intervention. Here's a few examples, supplied by Graham Hancock, where world aid has severely trashed the way of life of the very people it set out to help.

☞ In Ethiopia's Awash Valley, the nomads had been happy for centuries using their dry season pasture lands. Nowadays these lands have been sown with crops and barbed-wired off, reducing the poor natives to total poverty having had their whole way of life and culture destroyed. Consequently they have to queue for grub which is handed out by the holier-than-thou aid agencies.

☞ Huge hydro electric dams, and the vast lakes that tend to go with them, have sprung up in Africa, Asia and in Latin America pushing out thousands - no - millions of the indigenous population, and committing them to a nomadic lifestyle.

☞ The rain forests of Brazil were initially removed to provide pasture for cattle and to progress the lifestyle of the inhabitants. These days it's almost too late to make good the damage that's been done to the Indian population as they face mass genocide from greedy developers.

☞ If you have the misfortune to live in the Cordillera mountains in the Philippines you'll be well hacked off with progress and foreign aid. The mining, logging and hydro-electric dams have practically destroyed the very existence of the 500,000 inhabitants.

☞ Nestlé, those master chocolatiers, also control nearly half of the £180 million baby food and milk business in India. According to a report in *The New Generation* (the magazine of the National Childbirth Trust) they recently failed to turn up following a summons to answer criminal charges concerning the labelling of infant formula milk and cereal foods. Apparently they had refused to print a crucial warning in Hindi on the milk tins. Their defence was that the majority of the good folk of India's 900 million that use baby milk, are rich and educated and can therefore read English (actually, only 4% of Indians read English and over half of them don't read at all).

It turned out that in one Bombay hospital alone, seven out of ten premature babies were dying when fed by bottle alone, and that as soon as they returned to the dreaded breast (which, I'm told, was almost certainly designed for the job), nine out of ten survived. Nestlé alleged that throughout India many babies needed 'topping up' with their formula and the labelling was a mere technicality. All heart! I hear you cry.

If God, in his wisdom, had thought
powdered milk best,
He wouldn't have given a woman
a breast (or two).

And Cost?

So what about all these 150,000 experts, external advisors, consultants and official aid personnel, that are at any one time scouring the world looking for good to do?

72

Well one good UN expert can cost a cool $100,000 minimum which, if my abacus serves me right, adds up to around $150 billion (35% of the total official aid pot). World Bank experts, however, come a little bit dearer at around $150,000 which adds up to $22 billion, which is over half of all the money they'd had to play with in the first place.

Conclusion

‘ We need inequality in order to eliminate poverty... ’
Keith Joseph

Due to the kindness of the 'world with money', the 'world without money' receives loads of loot every year. As this amount is over thirty times more than in 1950 we should all be able to pat ourselves on the back and conclude that we're thirty times kinder. Or are we? Surely if the targets set in the North to help those in the South are reached, it will be 'a good thing'. Here again Graham Hancock puts us right.

Aid (or money to help folk) is just one way that currency moves from North to South. But the best kept secret of all is that money also moves from South to North, or poor to rich. There are loads of other transactions apart from global Overseas Development Assistance. Please remember that Aid is money LENT to poor countries to help them out of a fix. There's no such thing as a free subsistence lunch! Owing to a severe decline in bank lending and the rising interest on the loans being paid back, the water's started flowing the other way against all the rules of nature. In other words the rich countries are now getting back more than they're giving ($39 billion's worth in fact). And you won't see many governments shouting about that. So who's helping who here? Here's some examples:

73

☞ During the years 1986–88 the World Monetary Fund received almost $8 billion from the Third World.

☞ Between 1982 and 1987 British banks (the ones that repossessed our houses) pulled back more than $80 billion in loan repayments from Latin America alone, (that's £40 from every man woman and child). We were actually giving them a phenomenally generous 8p each, per year, in aid.

☞ We give India 15p per person and Kampuchea 0.0026p to spend at their leisure. By comparison, the good folk of Gibraltar (largely populated by monkeys and retired colonels) and the few in-bred Falkland Islanders (scene of the finest victory in modern warfare) receive £748 and £5 each per year respectively.

On top of all that, the money these countries do receive, as was suggested before, often does more harm than good, ruining the environments and the lives of the people they were intended to help. This cash often keeps horrid dictators in power, corrupt agents loaded and provides fantastic livings for a vast bunch of hangers-on that would be hard put to get jobs buttering bread in sandwich bars in their own countries.

Life Before Aid?

The world got on perfectly well before aid was even a twinkle in the rich countries' eyes, and practically fifty years after the first money started being pumped in, those countries are in less of a position to cope than they were before. From being proud and tenacious, they are reduced to sitting, cap in hand, to see what we'll give 'em next. If this is untrue, then it stands to reason that the countries would be much better off than they were before, which they most certainly are not. That's supposing the money actually gets to them in the first place. By the time all the aid agencies, experts, commission agents, corrupt politicians and wheeler-deelers have had their sticky hands in the till, there's often not enough to buy as much as a new begging bowl.

Aid, according to Hancock, is therefore a complete waste of money, and should be stopped before it does any more harm. And so say all of us!

CRAP CORNER

Not very inspiring reading eh? Not exactly the sort of stuff to make you rush to send your money to some high profile charity. Here are the main points thrown up in this chapter:

CRAP! The charity business is one of the only pursuits that deals in large amounts of money that seldom have to be accounted for.

CRAP! Chasing the needy is a very lucrative and comfortable profession needing very few qualifications.

CRAP! Charities are an excellent way for manufacturers to offload surplus, often useless and sometimes dangerous equipment.

CRAP! Relief aid is a wonderful cover for fraud.

CRAP! Relief aid can often muck up a poor country's agricultural infrastructure.

CRAP! It's quite a good wheeze, if you're in the do-gooding biz, to exaggerate a problem so that you can collect more money and pocket the difference.

CRAP! Governments of sophisticated industrial countries are excellent at telling impoverished third world agricultural countries how to run their business, even though they may know nothing about it.

CRAP! Millions of pounds are spent on lavish conferences to discuss the sad plight of the poor.

CRAP! Famine is so often caused, not by lack of food, but political corruption and game playing.

CRAP! The problem of starvation is not necessarily getting worse, its just that we hear about it quicker.

CRAP! Vast amounts of money are wasted by putting in imaginative schemes without researching their practicality.

CRAP! Major companies cynically flog their products to simple people who don't really need them.

CRAP! These days some rich countries receive more back in interest on old loans, than they actually give away.

CRAP! Aid can often have the reverse effect on a proud culture and people, reducing them to non-productive beggars.

EVERYONE GETS A GOOD EDUCATION IN MODERN BRITAIN

> **6** *The schools ain't what they used to be and never was...* **9**
> Will Rogers

A few facts for your perusal:

☞ The pound in 1971 would be worth over £7 today.

☞ The amount of personal wealth has risen since 1971 by 600%.

☞ The sum spent on state schools has risen by only 53% in the same period.

☞ The total spent per student on further education in the UK, is less than in any other large industrialised country.

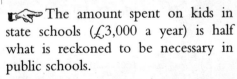

☞ The amount spent on kids in state schools (£3,000 a year) is half what is reckoned to be necessary in public schools.

☞ Teachers' pay is lower in relation to average earnings than it has been for twenty years. (If you pay peanuts, you get monkeys.)

☞ Kids from the professional classes get sixty times more university degrees than those from the working, manual or semi-skilled classes.

Beware!

Before I stick my foot neatly into my own mouth, it has to be said that statistics about education can be made to support whatever you want to say, and our government and 'leaned-on' press trade on this fact more than anyone else. For instance, if you go to a private school, you are less than likely to be put into an exam you might fail. (They're not daft, it would look bad in the performance charts!) In a state school, everyone is entered for everything as this increases funding. Therefore, contrasting results would be slightly ludicrous as you are not comparing like with like. Having said that, it's my book, so I'll use any means possible to illustrate my point. All's fair in love and pursuasion!!

In a country where jobs and opportunities for the young are as rare as a supermodel's A Levels, class (or who your parents know) is one of the strongest determining factors as to what becomes of you when you leave or get kicked out of school. Anyone who denies that if daddy heads a major company, and their school chums have similarly well-heeled old folk, their opportunities aren't just that little bit better than the average kid in the street, needs to be manacled to the average down-town employment office for a couple of days, and made to swallow their words.

No need to join the employment queue (let Daddy pull some strings for you).

It's no exaggeration to say that one of the great scandals is the run down of most state schools to which 92% of all British kids go, and the concessions and tax loops that have been available to parents who already have the money (or credit rating) to pay for the alternative. It is no exaggeration to view it as a sophisticated method of social engineering: a smart way of making sure that those with money have easy access to educational achievement, social networking and a method of making sure their kids only mix with 'the right kind'.

Even the canny assisted place scheme is a load of CRAP. By offering a financial leg-up to some lucky offspring (whose humble parents are a touch short of the odd six grand plus) to go to a public school, the government is simply underlining the fact that it must regard them as much better. If your parents are middle class (see page 127) they could also be to blame. After all it was them (or a majority of them) who put in a government that won't spend the right amount of money on state education. Why? Because that cash will come out of their pockets in the form of taxation.

The bulging classrooms (thirty plus), non-replacement or repair of necessary equipment (chairs!) or buildings, shared books, shitty pay for teachers etc. etc. that result from all this, have made our state schools the laughing stock of Europe. And it must be said, most wealthy people don't give a stuff.

❛ *In large states public education will always be mediocre, for the same reason that in large kitchens the cooking is bad...* ❜
Friedrich Nietzsche

Brief Historical Note

To go through the history of how we've got the schools we have today, would require another book (not ANOTHER bloody book!), but let me start by saying that children first *had* to go to school in Britain in 1870. For years we seemed as a country to be happy with the old grammar and secondary modern school system, which forced all children to take an exam that would affect their whole future at the tender age of eleven (the dreaded eleven plus). The brighter children would then troll off to the grammar schools and the not-so-brights would go to the others. This might on the surface seem desperately unfair, but you must take into consideration that in those days there were far more jobs opportunities and it was perfectly possible for a bright secondary mod kid to do better than extremely well on leaving school – my brother for instance. The comprehensive school, which largely replaced these grammar and secondary moderns (which still exist in a few places), was the brainchild of the 1975 Labour government, which believed that by sweeping away the eleven plus and educating kids, from the almost Neanderthal through to super-brainiacs, within the same walls, the overall standard would rise. Children from less fortunate backgrounds, in theory, could move more easily through the ranks and consequently fulfil the socialist dream of an equal chance for all. The idea was that after primary school the little dears would be divided into three bands and each of the local secondary schools would be given a quota from each. The top 25% would go into the higher band, the middle 50% would

CLEVER AVERAGE SLOW

be next, and the slower kids would represent the last 25%. Sadly, for them, it didn't work as (a) the more popular secondary schools tended to take the cream of the three bands and (b) it could be said that the system spawned a new elitism within the individual schools which was just as questionable, if not worse, than the system it replaced. The 'bad' students who never worked having the greater influence on the ones that did, just like the old saying – bad apples always affect the rest of the barrel.

New Terms for Old

Since the Education Act of 1988 a number of new terms have been passed around like Royal princesses. We hear them every day, but do we know what they mean? Here are a few.

National Curriculum

This document actually defines exactly what children should be learning at various stages throughout their school career. It was worked out by a panel of educationists appointed by the government. Dangerous for starters.

Opting-Out

The Tories saw a lot of education authorities as hives of loony lefties, so they decided to give schools the freedom to go outside the local authorities and take their grants direct from central government. It turned out to be an ill-conceived bribe as, though in the short term it meant that some schools got a bit more money (because they didn't have to pay for their own administration costs) they soon found that they had to buy in a lot of the things that would have been given to them by right of passage.

> **The Tories simply waved their magic wand, and lo and behold we'd all been conned.**

The whole business of opting-out was advertised, by the ever-cunning Tories, as giving more choice to frustrated parents but, when it came down to it, it simply meant that the best schools could grab the best kids, as everyone in any given area naturally wanted their littl'uns to have the best chance. So how did they (and do they) make the selection? By looking at the parents' occupations, listening to their accents and finding out if they live in nice roads - silly! Mind you, if you happen to live way out in the sticks you'd have no choice anyway as your 'selection' would be made by nearness more than anything else. The government, poor dears, were not a little surprised by the relatively low number of schools that took up the opt-out option.

Grant Maintained Schools
This is the term for the actual schools that did opt-out and chose to be funded centrally.

Local Management of Schools (LMS)
The others.

Sink Schools Stink

Not many people know that kids today, like gunslingers in westerns, have prices on their heads. If a child goes to a certain school, he brings with him about £2,500 per year in funding – a neat little package. Not surprisingly, there is quite a lot of competition for young bums on seats, as schools operate best with maximum money. I know a headteacher who calls his pupils 'bags of gold' and refers to the whole set-up as a franchise – Kentucky Fried Education?

If you have a densely populated area with a lot of schools, they soon work themselves into some sort of pecking order. As most parents from most social groupings want the best for their offspring they try to get their nearest and dearest into the ones with good reputations, leaving the rest... to the rest. Added to all these floating kids, over the last few years, there has been a meteoric rise in expulsions and exclusions owing to disruptive behaviour (and usually terrible academic results that show badly on the highly-rated league tables). These kids usually work their way down the slippery slide to the only establishments that will have them. The schools at the bottom of the pile soon became labelled 'The Sink Schools'. This is what happens if you bring market forces to bear on something that should be free of such things.

Us and Them

The net result is that through this selection process and the assessment of children through the National Curriculum, we should very soon have the us and them situation back in place – just like the old grammar and secondary modern school days. The bright kids from the nice homes (with books, computers and front gardens) will go to the best schools and get educated proper-like, and sod the others.

Strangely enough, however, it doesn't always work like that. Expensive schools aren't always the best, which should give us all satisfaction. Public (or fee paying) establishments have no requirement to follow the National Curriculum, meaning that they can teach what they like and to whatever standard they choose. Also, teachers in state schools currently either have to have the Post Graduate Certificate of Education or a Bachelor of Education degree. Public school teachers have no stated academic requirement, though it must be said that the governors usually go for graduates from either Oxford or Cambridge – not because they'll be better teachers (which they're usually not) but because it looks flashier on the glossy prospectus (which is the bait to lure the parental dosh).

In order to avoid coming a cropper,
We make sure our staff all speak proper.

HEAD TEACHER

And Now?
John Major, June 1992:

I was brought up among people who had little. Yet we were no different from the next man or woman. We had our own hopes, our own ideas, and our own ambitions. Just because you have little money, it does not follow that you need little choice, that you are only fit to follow where others lead. People in those circumstances long to have choices...

Ah, choices! That's exactly what the government seems to have been determined to surgically remove. The joke is that the way things are going, poor little Major minor, whose daddy worked in a circus, and who managed to come good after only making the 'C' stream at the local grammar, would probably have been condemned to stacking shelves in Kwik-Save for the rest of his life had he been made to suffer his own poxy regime. At least the old system, which was abandoned for being elitist, was based on some kind of educational merit rather than class. Practise what you preach Mr Major. What about these fabulous results after fifteen years of Tory rule? Half of all eleven year olds are found to be substandard in English and arithmetic according to the National Curriculum, and the standard of spelling amongst teenagers is the wurst ever ricordid. Makes yu prowd eh?

...and Labour?

The opposition are, of course, diametrically opposed to grant-maintained schools. According to them, they represent the sort of elitism, through money and position, that they are determined to destroy. Well, they say they are. Just to show that this whole chapter isn't a party political broadcast on behalf of the Labour party - catch this.

Harriet Harman, the rather Sloaney Shadow Transport Secretary and bright light of 'New Labour' (who went to the £6000 a year St Paul's School) sends her eldest son to the exclusive London Oratory and her younger one to the famous, public school style, St Olave's Grammar School for boys. Well who can blame her? The Labour controlled borough of Southwark (where she lives) has some of the worst exam records in the country. If you think that's hypocritical, her butter-wouldn't-melt-in-his-mouth leader, Tony Blair (who went to a fully-fledged public school) also sends his kid to the London Oratory, or should that be Ora-TORY. By the way, although Harriet is the MP for the gruesome borough of Peckham in South London, she actually lives in a large elegant Victorian maison in rather posh Dulwich. Surely she must be aware that most of her constituents wouldn't have that choice of school, as they just might not have a spare car and driver (non-working mum or nanny). To be fair it's probably much easier telling everyone how the poor and underprivileged should live, if you don't have to do it yourself. To be even fairer, Ms Harman - when trying to wriggle out of it - asked her tormenters why her kid should suffer for a crap and well-knackered (my words) education system that wasn't of Labour's making. Not a bad try, girl, but many people think she missed a golden chance to put her money fair and square where her mouth WAS.

'Socialism is only workable in heaven where it isn't needed, and in hell where they've got it...'   *Cecil Palmer*

That great socialist dream of a brave new world where the poorest and most underprivileged of kids who show promise, could go on to university, and have a fair slice of the economic cake (let alone a view of the cherry on the top) is now as realistic as Jeffrey Archer being asked or asking to join the Cat and Fiddle darts team, despite the reforms that each progressive parliament promises on the approach to each general election. It's the stuff revolutions are made of.

Pull up the drawbridge, stand and wait - don't let the bastards through the gate.

This, dear reader, is the main area where the hypocrisy that underlies the education system is obvious to all who don't have a vested interest in shoving their heads under the sand, and it is for this reason that all the riots, lootings and joy ridings in poor, no hope, inner city slum areas, are not only par for the course but, in some respects, understandable. Forget all those chinless toffs at their poncey hunt balls, or the Fulham bread-chucking, Fergie-clones who act like spoilt wan...self-abusers - they're totally irrelevant. If you're one of those kids who have been brought up in a home where the only person to greet you when you get back from school is the budgie, the only access to what's going on is tabloid crap, talking properly's reserved for snobs, a cultural outing means a trip to Legoland, the most educational thing ever watched on the telly is *Pets Win Prizes*, or where there's not a single book in the house (unless you count the bloody Argos catalogue) then God help you.

But then, so what? You wouldn't be reading this book anyway.

*It beats me why they should
want to improve,
They'd be so out of place if
they ever did move.*

The Great Political Football

Educational policies come and go like music trends and are created by the almost whimsical current political mood of the day. Unfortunately, they are almost always rather short-term and never seem to take into account the education prospects of our youngsters. It could be said that in one way things are not much better than when I was a kid in the fifties (when education was unbelievably dull and rigidly structured). But because kids are being used more and more as laboratory rats for some new education minister's pet fancy, I think they could actually be worse. Any free-thinking individual must agree that education should and must be dragged out of the political arena and allowed to swim in the clear water away from the ludicrous and selfish cut-and-thrust of the two major political parties. After all, what is education for? Do we want it simply to give us exam results? Or do we want it to push our students towards a vocational training so that they are more fitted for some kind of job at the end of it all? Or do we simply want it to prepare us to use our time more constructively if the future becomes one where only a few people actually have jobs? Perhaps this is something that you could write to me about.

CRAP CORNER

Political parties and the papers that support them manipulate statistics to reinforce their policies.

CRAP! In Britain you can still get the best education in the world, provided you can pay for it.

CRAP! In Britain you can get one of the worst educations in the world, and it serves you right for having poor parents.

CRAP! If you're rich or upper class, don't fret about the poor getting above themselves, or the class system breaking down. Poor education for the masses will take care of all that.

CRAP! Middle class people want a good education for all, as long as it doesn't cost them anything.

CRAP! The opting-out scheme was a neat trick of the Tories to give us the illusion that we had more choice.

CRAP! Children are selected for grant maintained schools as much for their social background as their ability.

CRAP! John Major makes a lot of noise about an education system where everyone can flourish, while cutting back the money to the very schools that need it most.

CRAP! Labour politicians really care how the country's kids are educated, and can't wait until they all go to schools that are as good as the ones their kids go to.

CRAP! The British have long lost the plot as to what education is for. In a world that is changing faster than you can blink, we seem unable to make a connection between education and the needs of the country – either present or future.

CRAP! Education policies seldom are in place long enough to see whether they work. Children are being used as guinea pigs by educationists and politicians alike.

IT'S ONLY NATURAL TO BE NATURAL

CRAP!

> ❛ *What a troublesome affliction to have to preserve one's health by too strict a regime...* ❜
>
> *François, Duc de La Rochefoucauld*

In the chapter about alternative medicine, I mentioned Rosalind Coward's controversial book on alternative health which pushed and pulled at the definition of the *natural*, a term which seems to be creeping into every aspect of our lives.

Advertisers are anything but stupid and realise that by simply tacking on this sadly misused word, magical attributes are given to their products, which the gullible punters will fall for every time (which they do in droves). Food, vitamins and mineral supplements, not to mention all the junk we slap on our bodies, are nearly all promoted as *natural* with no artificial ingredients. 'Be gentle on your skin as nature intended – naturally' says the ad for *Fleur* aromatherapy.

Everyone seems to have been sucked into the virtues of eating *naturally*, of living as *naturally* as possible, and following *natural* principles. *Natural* and goodness go hand in hand. Whizz round your supermarket and read off the names: *Harvest Crunch, Common Sense Natural Breakfast, Natrel*, etc. etc. Not a hint of that nasty modern technology, just fields, mountain streams, meadow herbs, bunny rabbits, baa lambs and all things pure and good (yuk!).

The public are suckers,
it's so easy to cheat.
Just use the word NATURAL,
in what they wear, drink or eat.

Actually, *Natrel* deserves a special mention, for its TV commercial. You know, that one where the minute this naked couple rub the miracle deodoriser under their arms they turn into trees. Blimey, if I turned into a tree I'd be more worried about becoming an instant target to any passing pooch who fancies a pee or, much more to the point, some hungry squirrel searching for nuts!

Good and Evil

Anything natural comes from God; anything chemical comes from the devil, or those horrid, greedy, pale-eyed, white-coated lab-dwelling boffins with steel-rimmed specs, which is why we don't get products like Techno-Brek cereals, Syntho-Sham shampoo, or Chemi-Karsy lav bowl freshener. I suppose it would be churlish at this juncture to note that many chemicals do actually occur naturally or are derived from natural substances, but we won't pour cold water (Perrier, of course) on the 'naturalists' ill-conceived manifesto, will we? But where do we get this soppy view of nature? Sure, it's fab for the odd country walk or sunny picnic, but nature can be awful too - stingy, bitey, chilly, smelly and most often downright brutal. We might like images of dear little fox cubs gambolling in sunlit meadows, but tend not to linger too long on concepts of their mummy ripping the guts out of an equally dear, if somewhat absent-minded, little bunny to feed them. We gaily watch sweet little Robin Redbreasts tearing worms out of the ground, but seldom wonder whether the worms have got their own wives and kids waiting at home.

Sure, nature's mostly claw and tooth,
But what have ads to do with truth?

The point I'm lurching towards is that we select from nature what we want to see and what we want to believe. We can afford to be drippy about it, because, as a rule, we don't have anything to do with it. I bet an Aborigine who lives out in the bush doesn't wax lyrical about the joys of nature, or insist on naturally-enriched herbal shampoo when he trails into the Wallabaloo Cash and Carry.

Health Foods

❛ *Some breakfast food manufacturer hit upon the simple notion of emptying out the leavings of carthorse nosebags, adding a few other things like the unconsumed portions of chicken layer's mash, and the sweepings of racing stables, packing the mixture in little bags and selling them in health food shops...* ❜
Frank Muir

To qualify as a proper health store, the stock should follow these rules:

1. Vegetables should be as close as possible, timewise, to their death, and look as if they've just come from the ground. Plenty of good honest earth.

2. Food should be WHOLE and not fractions of foods produced from refinement.

3. Food should be non-toxic, containing no colour, preservatives or additives (bang go my Hoola Hoops!).

4. The store should facilitate a diet offering a wide range of nutrition.

Health food stores are a little like sex shops; I can never quite work out what most of the things are for. Nothing they sell in them looks remotely edible, and generally the proprietors appear to be such weedy specimens that you feel slightly loath to follow their example. Like them or not, however, the health food movement has traversed our land, and despite my snidey quips, has become part of the modern high street. Brown bread eaters are no longer seen as faddy or cranky, obsessed with their and everyone else's bowel movements and in the smarter suburbs, for instance, it's regarded as rather refined to buy unrefined food. We're even beginning to witness little corners with confidence inspiring names like *Country Corner* or *Nature's Way* in our mammoth, prefabricated, edge-of-town supermarkets.

❛ Nutrition makes me puke... ❜　　　*Jimmy Piersall*

Worthy Foods
Fibre rich, refined grains (no *white* bread, flour or rice) and everything whole (whole grain, wholemeal etc) and everything raw; anything that looks dull and inedible; and anything that comes from animals that are not pretty or furry – like chickens or fishes.

Many of the products sold in health food stores, like soya proteins, tofu, seaweed, bean sprouts and lentils, have been attributed with almost magical qualities, carrying all the wonderful vital energies of nature.

One way that you can tell organically grown fruit or vegetables is that they don't look nearly as nice as the stuff doused in chemical pesticides and fertilizers, and are considerably more expensive.

❛ The first time I tried organic wheat bread I thought I was chewing on roofing material... ❜　　*Robin Williams*

Wicked Foods

Animal fats, refined grains, all processed foods. This just about removes everything that we really fancy to eat, from hamburgers to hot dogs to doughnuts. Anything sweet, anything gooey; anything with red blood in it; anything frozen; anything that's been near a machine. Here are a few little devils that might surprise you.

> NOBODY MESSES WITH BIG MAC

☞ Vitamins. Everyone thinks that vitamins make you well and exceedingly frisky. Unfortunately most of those used as additives come from animals. Vitamin D3, for instance, which is in most breakfast cereals, is a slaughter house by-product.

☞ Most cakes and Christmas puddings contain suet, which is minced up animal fat.

☞ Most cheese, unless otherwise specified, contains rennet which is made from calves' stomachs.

☞ Anything red is either to do with blood or mashed up Cochineal – a kind of bug.

☞ Worcester sauce is made from anchovies, and most bottled or tinned tomato juice contains a little. If you have a soft spot for this smelly little fish or his relatives, then avoid these products.

We Are What We Eat

Food freaks will tell you that what you eat affects every aspect of your life. At various times it has been suggested that diet alone can effect the onset of AIDS, wrinkles, hair loss, loss of … er … memory, and even ageing itself. A bad diet has been held responsible for juvenile delinquency, violence and suicide (I've heard about what can happen if you don't eat your greens, but this is ridiculous). Vegetarianism is on the increase, especially among the young, which is not surprising when you consider the lengths the government went to to stop us finding out about Mad Cow Disease.

The *British Medical Association* have also told us that veggies show a lower incidence of obesity, coronary heart disease, high blood pressure, blood disorders, cancer and gall stones.

❛ I went on a diet, swore off drinking and heavy eating, and in fourteen days I lost two weeks… ❜   *Joe. E. Lewis*

BUT if there is so much evidence for eating a wholesome, natural, uncooked, right on, animal free, no leather-shoed diet, why don't we all do it? I'll tell you why (or rather Rosalind Coward will tell you why). A lot of the stuff we are led to believe about food is (to borrow the title of my book) pure unadulterated C.R.A.P.

The British are on the verge of becoming food obsessed. We've reached a stage where it is implied that if we don't pay attention to our diet, the consequences will be terrifying. For a rich society like ours, food is about choice, and that choice is now coming under social pressures. By eating health foods, many individuals feel they are making a stand for the wonders of nature and delivering a kick in the balls for consumerism and the power and influence of the masses. They therefore feel they are making the choice between illness and health, life or death.

Could it just be that they're deluding themselves? Couldn't the reason that so many people have got their knickers in a twist over food processing and food poisoning be because they get in the way of the old food-to-good-health route? In a society like ours, where food production is so incredibly mechanised, and where turning out as big a profit as possible is what it's all about, even food which we think of as raw has been submitted to processes that we have absolutely no control over. For instance:

☞ Did you know that people who live on so-called junk food show the lowest pesticide levels?

☞ Did you know that tomatoes (unless tinned) carry the highest pesticide levels of all?

☞ Did you know that some natural foods and uncooked foods can be poisonous and stand far more chance of decomposition?

☞ Did you know that the common or garden frozen pea loses less of his vitamins than his raw relatives who have to be cooked longer?

☞ Did you know that the advantages of canning and freezing, which halts the possibilities of microbiotic decay, far outweighs the risk of sickness from these processes?

Taking these things into consideration, the dream of mutating into a fit, healthy race by eating a natural diet, is as realistic as me opening a health food shop. If we really want to improve the quality of our grub it would take a complete political re-look at how we produce it, and the environment we produce it in.

> *My wife went on a diet. Coconuts and bananas. She hasn't lost any weight, but she can sure climb a tree...*
> *Henny Youngman*

CRAP CORNER

Here are the main points in this chapter. Let us know what you think.

CRAP! The word natural is all but meaningless in the nineties as it has come to mean anything and everything that people who have something to sell want.

CRAP! It's mostly people who live in cities who bang on and on about all things natural.

CRAP! Health food freaks see diet as the be-all-and-end-all of practically everything that's evil in the world.

CRAP! The need to satisfy the ever-opening mouth of the consumer society and to make a swift profit often means that the food you get in the supermarket is fresher than that from the farm shop.

CRAP! By eating health foods many people believe they are kicking the system and making the ultimate choice between life and death. This isn't necessarily true.

THERE WAS NO TIME LIKE THE SIXTIES

CRAP!

When its three o'clock in New York, it's still 1938 in London...

Bette Middler

YOU REALLY SHOULD HAVE BEEN THERE

Every generation, from the beginning of time, must have suffered from their parents boring them silly, with endless stories of how much better or how much tougher life was when they were young. Here are a few examples from history.

1. *God, to his best boy Jesus*: "You're lucky sonny. When I was a lad, I didn't have all the things that you've got these days - trees, flowers, mountains or girls. I had to make them all myself."

2. *Noah to his grandchildren*: "Just think of this, before you were born, your father and I had to build a bloody great boat to save all those animals that you take so much for granted."

3. *Henry VIII to his daughter*: "Times were much better in my day. When I became fed up with your mum, I simply had her topped."

4. *Prince Philip to his boy Charles*: "You don't know you're born these days. Years ago we'd have been hung, drawn and quartered for screwing another man's wife while still married."

5. *Mr Jackson to his son Michael*: "You're lucky son. When I was young, I was black."

Why is it that ever since parents were invented, they have felt the need to describe the period that they were young in as somehow better, or harder, more exciting or more dangerous than the one they're currently in? My theory, for what it's worth, is that we poor middle-agers always have so little going for us compared to the young, that we feel the need to impress them. Tragic or what?

(*Nostalgia isn't what it used to be...*)   *Graffiti*

In a world that changes faster than the Lib Dems' policies, it could be argued that parents find it easier to tell their kids even more bullshit than ever they'd had to put up with themselves. The reputation of some periods has grown and mutated like Chinese whispers. Here's a classic example:

The Fabulous Sixties

Almost no decade in the history of England seems to have had so much said about it than the nineteen-sixties. Kids today sit open mouthed at the tales their parents tell of peace and love, flower power, rebellion, the beginnings of rock, AIDS-free-free-love, Mary Quant and oodles of drugs guaranteed to have you floating just below the ceiling from Friday night to Monday morning. The poor old dears' eyes roll back in their heads as they describe 'Swinging London', the conquering of space, the birth of the Beatles and the invention of a jolly fast plane called Concorde. Okay, strap me down, shine the bright light in my eyes, and I'll tell all. This is what the sixties were really like...

It's time to tell the honest truth,
About my sad (and distant) youth.

The Truth

I, like all my mates, had suffered some of Britain's drabbest years, recovering from a war that had brought it to its knees. We were the classic children of the sixties. When they began, I was in my early teens, the Cold War with Russia was at its chilliest and the Communist world was facing up to us capitalists and pulling extremely ugly faces. John F Kennedy, a young, chubby-faced, honest-looking senator from California, became the President of the most powerful country in the world and seemed such a brilliant contrast to our pompous little Harold Wilson. Having watched the horrendous Vietnam war from a safe distance, we British kids were somewhat relieved to view someone that at least looked like we could vaguely relate to keeping us all out of the Third World War (even though it did turn out that he was bonking practically everything that moved).

America the Brave

America seemed great to us. Its own youngsters always seemed to be having a great time and were being entertained by the likes of Elvis, Little Richard, Buddy Holly and Eddie Cochran while we, as always, had to make do with cheap imitations like Cliff Richard, Billy Fury and a silly, bearded, antipodean import called Rolf Harris. The only stuff worth listening to was from the other side of the big pond, and even when the Beatles came along in 1963, anyone who was vaguely 'with it' (a quaint sixties term) thought they were a bit sissy compared to the emerging rhythm and blues of hardly known groups like the Rolling Stones, the Yardbirds or would you believe, Rod Stewart (who wasn't awful then). We male teenagers giggled at the likes of Cilla Black (who was awful then), Dusty Springfield and Lulu, preferring to lust after the sexy black American girl groups like the Ronettes or Supremes, who were just beginning to turn up for the first proper rock concerts.

Home Grown

Our British sixties only really kicked off well after half time. In 1967, those sinful Stones got well and truly busted at Keith Richard's house in Lewes and elevated to superstardom amongst the young. Keith and Mick were done for possession of dope, and an ever so pretty young convent girl (but ever so bad pop singer) called Marianne Faithful became a role model to all those young middle class innocents who were dying to fall prey, and lose all, to those larger than life pop stars, and poncey photographers (like David Bailey). They were rich and trendy. Most of us weren't, however. They, according to our parents, symbolised the way that British youth was sliding down the karsy, and in a million households the topic of conversation rarely veered from "When are you going to get that hair cut?" "Surely you don't think you're going out looking like that?" or "What were those funny pills that fell out of those silly flared trousers last night?"

You could almost hear our parents' groans, at any mention of the Stones.

Fashion Alert

Carnaby Street and the Kings Road became full of daft, sissie-looking kids parading around in pink satin flares and hideous floral-pattern blouses (and that was just the boys) bought from boutiques (the new 'in' word for shops) like Grannie Takes a Trip and Lord John. The press went on and on about *Swingin' London* being the fashion and music centre of the world, and for a very short while we actually believed it. Our desperately straight mummies and daddies went on and on about the moral breakdown of society and how much they respected *their* parents when they were our age.

❛ *Nobody is healthy in London, nobody can be...* ❜
Jane Austen

Most of us youngsters, however, were too busy scurrying hither and thither, trying to live up to our dreadful reputation, looking desperately for the bit of London that was actually swinging. Images of all-night drug-crazed orgies to the strains of Hendrix and Cream flooded through our heads, but where the hell were they? If you went hunting in Carnaby Street it always seemed to be happening in the more upmarket Kings Road. When you rushed back to Chelsea it had just moved on to somewhere else. I can remember driving up and down the Kings Road on a Saturday afternoon (I was at art school during the week), in a mauve Mini Moke, looking a total prat, trying to push all the other non-Mokers out of the sight line of one of the rash of foreign film crews. These were mostly Belgian (where nothing has ever happened) or German (who wouldn't recognise trendy if they tripped over it) and were desperately trying, like us, to find something remotely *swingin'* to capture, like an exotic butterfly, and send home.

Rebels Without a Cause

Oh yes, we were rebels all right. We must have been; we had long hair and took loads of mind-expanding drugs (well, some of us knew someone, who knew someone else who once did). The trouble always seemed to be that we were never quite sure what we were rebelling against. Sure we listened to the endless moaning and droning of Bob Dylan, but if truth be told, few of us could understand a word of what he was going on about. The problem was solved in the same year as the great Stones' bust. Someone drew a funny little upside-down Y, with an extra line splitting the V, made the symbol into badges, and we all pinned them on our new politically correct duffle coats and took them on long dreary protest marches. What were we protesting about? Search me!

Someone said something about nuclear bombs, but most of us went because out parents didn't want us to, and anyway, it was a chance to get out of those soppy flowery clothes, and meet a different sort of bird.

You should thank your dad and mom,
  for all they did to ban that bomb.

Hippiedom – No Thank You

To be honest, I was never a hippie. When everyone else was allegedly turning on and tuning in, I and a couple of art school mates got caught up in the latest fashion from America's west coast. We were 'Beach Boys' (the surfing sound was at its zenith). I know it sounds a touch weird to be prancing around, surf board on roof-rack, searching for the ultimate wave in the centre of a huge city, but we students, for a couple of rather warm summers, preferred the clean-cut American style clothes and the short bleach-blond crew-cuts to the rather dweeby, droopy hippie look of everyone else, and so did the sort of girls we were after. To be honest, I only got on a surf board a couple of times, as it was so bloody cold (Cornwall certainly ain't California), and so bloody difficult. We, therefore, mostly hung around the beaches and cafes of Newquay chatting up, and almost impressing, young girls who were down on holiday from places like Wigan or Bootle with their mums and dads.

Later, when at the Royal College of Art, some of us drew pictures for the famous underground magazine *Oz*. A few druggy Australian hippies had set up home (overground) in a beautiful house in trendy Kensington and, from a position of great comfort, took the piss out of the British way of life. Well I think they did. The paper was so badly produced, with type running over those ghastly hippie, psychedelic, hallucinogenic drawings, that most times it was impossible to read anyway. In the end it got busted by the obscene publication squad because of the infamous 'schoolgirl' issue which, if my memory serves me right, had featured a drawing of someone like Rupert Bear doing something very strange to someone like Mickey Mouse. *Despite* the fabulously pompous John Mortimer QC defending it, the case was actually dismissed.

'Is marijuana addictive? Yes in the sense that most of the really pleasant things in life are worth endlessly repeating...'

Richard Neville (Editor, OZ)

Total Crap

Despite all the ill-remembered junk that has been trotted out almost parrot fashion, there was no real protest in the sixties! Wearing silly clothes never made the world a better place; joss sticks and perfumed candles never really led us into deeper consciousness; drag guru Timothy Leary never said anything that remotely applied to us; the *I'm Backing Britain* campaign was only a daft media con and not an inspiring unifying celebration; *Hair* was actually yet one more dreadful musical; *Concorde* became the fastest white elephant since Dumbo; and the moon – after all that fuss and expense getting there – turned out to be as interesting as a car park in Milton Keynes and not the least bit worth landing on.

PAY AND DISPLAY

You'd have to be a total goon, to want to spend time on the moon.

Sorry, the sixties was just a huge, commercially-driven, media–inspired fashion statement. London never really swung – it just told everyone it did. Actually the term 'swinging' turned out to be a proof-reader's boob. The typesetter was meant to put 'singing' after Harold Wilson's annoying habit of humming every time he lit his pipe. The extra 'w' stuck.

And love was never actually free – it just pretended it was. Okay the contraceptive pill meant you could, in theory, do 'it' without fear of spawning a kid called Moonbeam or Saffron, but we lads still had to find the girls to do 'it' with, and that wasn't nearly as easy as history has led us to believe. Despite tireless efforts, and appalling Jack Kerouac chat-up lines ("Hi babe, what's going down here?"), we found we couldn't actually change sexual attitudes overnight. In fact, the ideal woman was so pale and skinny in those days that I'm now surprised we wanted to pull them anyway. And as for all the art and music that poured out of the sixties, where is it now? For every good bit there was a gigantic pile of pretentious crap served to a totally pretentious clientele. The only good things to come out of the decade, as far as I'm concerned, were a healthy questioning of everything our parents stood for... and mini skirts.

CRAP CORNER
So what after all this, will the sixties be remembered for?

CRAP! The sixties was a decade that all those who were around, will review nostalgically, remember what it was really like, and then lie about.

CRAP! The only person that swung in 'Swinging London' was James Hanratty who was hanged in 1962 for a murder he might well not have done.

CRAP! The only reason my parents respected their parents, was because they got it in the neck if they didn't.

CRAP! Love was only free if you were as rich as the Rolling Stones and could afford to spend a fortune on a girl.

CRAP! Most of the clothes of the sixties were so badly made that they fell apart instantly. Even if they had lasted, however, we'd all be far too embarrassed to get them out.

BRITAIN CAN'T SURVIVE WITHOUT A ROYAL FAMILY

CRAP!

‛ A king is an ordinary kind of man who has to live in a very extra-ordinary kind of way that sometimes seems to have little sense to it... ’
                                                    King George V

My attitude to the Royal family usually falls somewhere between the 'heads on pikes at the palace gates' or the 'why are we so cruel to the poor dumb critters?' schools of thought. It's ages since I thought they were really necessary and I can't be pinned down on the old 'they're wonderful for tourism' angle as I can't stand tourists either. But when push comes to shove, I suppose there's something rather quaint about them, so - like red double decker buses or policeman's helmets - I'd probably miss them if they weren't there. Or would I?

There's no doubt that the poor loves have had a pretty tricky decade and now that our dashing (or dashed) heir to the throne is divorced (heaven forfend), more and more erstwhile loyal subjects are beginning to ask that big question that in days gone by has only been whispered (for fear of severe head removal): "Could we get along just as well without them?"

I DON'T SUPPOSE I COULD CHANGE MY MI.....

If we're going to be nationalistic or even racist about it, they haven't got a leg to stand on. Her side of the family's German (renamed mysteriously after a brown soup), and old Phil, when all's said and done, is plain and simply Greek.

Margaret Thatcher, who Queen Lizzie couldn't bear, would have been far more suitable from a 'who's really British' perspective and before she was found out (and then kicked out) must have thought this herself, as she even started talking like them. "We are a grandmother" she exclaimed using the royal we when one of her awful sprogs reproduced (mind you, I think it might have been her version of a joke).

Where Did We Get Them From?

I suppose the question we must ask is how far do you want to go back? Once upon a time back in 520, for instance, England was divided into seven parts and each one had a Royal family. Now I don't know about you, but the one we've got's quite enough for me. Then we became open season for anyone with a bent towards conquering and for the next thousand years everyone from Danes to Swedes to Norwegians to Italians to French to Dutch all had various goes at ruling us. When did the Germans get in on the act? It all came about in 1714 when *their* King George was sent for to be *our* George I. Tell you what, if you want the full story, buy *The Complete Bloody History of Britain* by me.

Media Groupies

One of the reasons that I, like many others, have become somewhat disenchanted with the Royals relates to their relatively new and relatively seedy affair with the media. In olden days, all they showed us was all that sparkly guff; - royal weddings or the odd imperial visit from someone from somewhere we'd never heard of. Even now those events are perfect for the media, specially the telly. You know the sort of thing. Some bottom-licking, hush-voiced commentator, heart-set on a knighthood, eulogising over the fab family in those grovelling, obsequious tones (that we've all grown to know and loathe) as they waltz up the Mall in their top-of-the-range horse-drawn carts, or stand like rather overdressed glove puppets on their Buck House balcony giving us those sincere-as-a-car-salesmen, royal waves.

That sort of publicity's fine, however, and just what's required to keep us loyal, servile and flag waving. But, sadly, the other sort ain't, and could be exactly what, if they're not careful, will cause the very crowns from their very heads to topple.

❦ The life of one Welsh miner is of greater commercial and moral value to the British people than the whole Royal crowd put together, from the Royal great-grandmama down to the puling Royal great-grandchildren... ❥   Keir Hardie (1894)

Apathy Rules OK

While many of us flounder around at the bottom of the 'US' pile, they still manage to stand firm on the top of the 'THEM' pile. The reasons are not that complicated. Our monarchy remains unchanged largely because we as a nation can't really be bothered to do anything about it and newspapers of all denominations have cottoned on to swelling their circulations with any picture they can beg, borrow or steal. Even a snap of Prince Charles picking his nose (or Fergie picking someone else's) will pip Pamela Anderson's boobs, or Eric Cantona's temper, to the front pages.

Over the last decade or so, our Royals have practically fallen over in their race to out-do each other in the self-publicity stakes. But now, just like being hooked on a rather fancy drug, they can't seem to shake the news leeches off. Not only that, but having willingly supplied the tabloids with enough crap to keep the presses rolling for years, they now try to enforce their us-and-them veto by, tortoise-like, pulling back when this attention doesn't suit (publicitus interruptus), and play the old 'we-are-the-premier-family-in-Britain-and-should-be-allowed-to-live-our-lives-in-privacy' card. They want to do exactly as they like, but be treated with the sort of awe that even God himself wouldn't turn his nose up at (if he's got one). It's like a huge joke that everyone from politicians to paupers is in on. And this joke is that all the members of our Royal family are in some way superhuman, a protected species like swans or VAT inspectors. That's why we listen quite calmly to silly Prince Charles' half-baked opinions on everything from architecture to agriculture, or his ex-missus who reckons she's cornered the market on child care (this is the same princess who doesn't even spend Christmas with *her* kids). One minute the professionally-coy Diana is saying that she wants to end all her public engagements because she can't take the strain, and the next she's seen at every glitzy showbiz event possible and making ghastly '*True Confessions*' on telly, claiming to want to be the 'Ambassador for Caring'. Pleeeeease! I reckon I could be the 'Ambassador for Absolutely Everything' if I could get access to the £751,005 that she blows every year.

We want our royal cake that's true,
but please don't ask us to share with you.

And another thing. How come the House of Windsor is above criticism and even the law? In the aforementioned aren't-I-a-sincere-and-truly-wonderful-person interview her Royal Highness mentioned that not only had her phone calls been intercepted by the palace, but her letters had been opened by the prince's henchmen. As Roy Hattersley pointed out in the *Guardian* recently, phone tapping and diverting the mail are actually illegal, so why was nothing done about it if it were true?

Value for Money

I'm afraid this double standardisation from on high doesn't work with me. If the truth be told, I've always preferred my kings, queens, princes and princesses to be really special - sliding around in snazzy motors and coaches, wearing their crowns and fondling their orbs. George V used to wear his personal crown every day while signing the State papers so, if it was good enough for him, why not them? Isn't that why we pay them shedloads of cash? Like:

☞ A Civil List that gives the Queen (the richest women in the world) £7.9 million a year to pay her expenses.

☞ Another £3.6 million a year in rent from the Duchy of Lancaster.

☞ She also receives the Grant in Aid, a vast tract of loot not only designed to keep up her Royal Palaces but to pay for all the homes for the hangers-on, and family (like the five million quid spent on that vulgar ranch-style shack on the edge of Windsor Great Park for that delightful young, but sadly divorced, couple Andy and Fergie).

The Royals believe we should give them this money with no questions asked. I mean, why should we need to know what 'By Appointment' marmalade the Queen Mother (isn't she wonderful?) has on her toast, or how many times her stupid corgis go for a wee? It should be none of our business. And why should *we* be concerned with how much the whole caboodle costs, and who does what to whom, as their wonderfulnesses tip-toe around the corridors of Buck House or Windsor Castle? Attempting to gain information about their personal lives should be punishable by death or at least a very long, all expenses paid stay in the Bloody Tower. The Royal family *should* be better than us and because of that should be permitted to do as they like – albeit quietly! It is not for us to seek to examine their ways under a microscope. They know what is best for their subjects and it is our duty to look up to them for moral guidance in all things. Do I sound convincing?

A Fine Example

Their attitude to sex and marriage, as Britain's premier family should be an example to us all. Prince Philip, bless him, is very much of the old school, keeping whatever everybody suspects he gets up to well out of the frame. Tiny rumours come and go, but unlike the donkey at the kiddies party, no one can pin anything on him (probably 'cos no-one can be bothered).

6 *I'm prepared to take advice on leisure from Prince Philip. He's a world expert on leisure. He's been practising it for most of his adult life...* 9
Neil Kinnock

The others are a different story, however. The press's most recent fascination with the sex life of the Royals started several years ago with the aforementioned Prince (randy) Andrew, who broke all the rules by consorting with the sort of girls that the rest of us red-blooded male Brits fancied. None of your Camillas, Lucindas or Lavinias, with pointy chins, turned up collars and horsey voices; he went out with gorgeous soft-porn stars and fab fashion models. Though many say he probably *didn't* bestow his royal favours on them, we all thought he might, and that was enough. Why should we give him the dosh to take out the sort of classy babes we couldn't get our own hands on? The funniest thing was that, having had all that five star action, he went and married the kind of Hooray Henrietta we all thought he should be mixing with in the first place; the sort we wouldn't have been seen dead with (and now he won't either). Then, joke of all jokes, she turned out to be more of a slapper than the rest of them put together.

Here are a few of the latest royal indiscretions to illustrate my point.

☞ In 1992, Andrew's wife Sarah, Duchess of York (née Fergie), was photographed TOPLESS, and having her toes sucked (there's a lot of it about) by her personal 'financial advisor' in the South of France. Not only was the freckly but feckless femme-fatale still married, but also on the royal payroll. Despite the 'just good friends' line that we were all asked to swallow, her mother-in-law, good Queen Bess, 'was not amused'. But Fergie turned out to be the sucker, for whether or not she followed his financial advice, she still ended up three million in the red (but with spotless feet).

Just reveal one royal boob, and see your cred go down the tube.

Prince Charles caused a right royal rumpus when he admitted, after endless press pressure, that he'd been hoisting his aristocratic leg over a rather long-in-the-tooth, albeit far more suitable, (but married) Camilla Parker Bowles. Poor Charles had thought he'd kept his slightly more than common adultery so quiet but our defenders of all things decent, the press, did their duty as always. Her that Must be Obeyed, the Queen Mother said that she wouldn't have Mrs Bowles in the house (or any of the Royal Households).

The poor, shy, hard done by, butter-wouldn't-melt-in-her-mouth, Lady Diana Spencer (ex-missus of our future king - in case you've forgotten) has for a long time seemed rather confused as to whether royalty was in some way connected with show business, fashion, sport or art, as she seems to have been linked with everyone from the likes of Eddie the Eagle to Zig and Zag. In 1995 there was a scandalous rumour that she'd been consoling herself with 'scrummy' rugby union star Will Carling. If true, I doubt whether she was after the £40,000 a year that he could now earn from his sport. Blimey, she must spend that on knickers (at least £4000 at Donna Karan alone!). Joking apart, delightful Di remains to the rest of the world, the quintessential image of an English Princess. Vive la Republique!

If you've blown your chance at Queen, why not try another scene?

☞ The palace, in true hypocritical style, still saw fit in 1990 to trash Thomas Hardy's *Tess of the D'Urbervilles'* chance to star on a postage stamp, as they didn't relish the idea of an unmarried mother appearing next to our gracious Queen.

Double standards we have mastered, We won't have Her beside a bastard.

Love and Hate

Seriously, the silly billies have put themselves in a bit of a no-win situation. From loving them unreservedly, as we did just after the war, the British public have now learned to adore and disapprove of them in equal dollops – and at the same time (actually, not *quite* equal. It is now reckoned that 40% of the public would actively prefer them to go).

We adore titles and heredities in our hearts, and ridicule them with our mouths. This is our democratic privilege...
Mark Twain

The daftest aspect is that their exploits are no better or worse than any others in the whole of royal history but, by letting their petticoats show, they've gone and shot themselves in the foot and given us yet another soap opera. As a well known royal observer once so perceptively pointed out, 'they've let in daylight upon magic'. We can see the whole shebang for what it really is. Whenever you do such a thing, mystery disappears and the subject becomes as fascinating as last week's lottery tickets. This was never more obvious than when the Queen did that hilarious 'week-in-the-life-of 'documentary in which she appeared to be living in such a sheltered, twilight world of palatial privilege, that she probably wouldn't have realised that kids were sleeping rough on the streets not half a mile from her own silk-lined bedroom.

I SAY! WOULD YOU HOMELESS MAKE LESS NOISE. SOME OF US ARE TRYING TO SLEEP

6 *Queen Elizabeth is a woman who acts her age, which is 50. She has, in fact, acted that age since she was little more than twenty...* **9**   *Fern Marje Eckman (1976)*

Vive la Republique?

Many people believe that all this fuss about the actual star players in *Buck House* - the soap opera, is totally irrelevant. Whether Britain continues with a Royal family should not be down to one single incompetent generation. The issue is much more important than that. Few could deny that having a Royal family (or *this* Royal family) encourages the British to look to bygone days rather than the present (let alone peer into the future). In that respect I've probably been far too hard on our present crop. Is it really their fault that they often seem as inappropriate as a modern dress version of Shakespeare? Unlike burning at the stake, steam engines or typewriters, we, the British, have hung onto them just like we have the House of Lords, and made them the joke that they are, simply because we can't bear the idea of the alternative.

And what *is* the alternative to this increasingly boring and magic-free royal family? A republic with an elected president as top man or woman? This often seems rather attractive and a hell of a lot cheaper (the majority of British believe this will happen in the next 50 years). But what scares us is that having a president could mean giving one person all the power *and* all the pomp, which would be as dangerous as handing a disturbed four-year-old a sub-machine gun (see Adolf Hitler, Mussolini or President Nixon). Let's face it, our present Mr and Mrs Windsor aren't even allowed to make a decision about what colour phone boxes should be, let alone who we should go to war with (which I think's pretty healthy). One could go further and say, thank God we *did* have a proper queen when Her Supreme Mightiness Maggie was in charge of the government. Her mania for power, coupled with her hideously superior and condescending manner would have made her akin to the wicked queen in Snow White. "Mirror mirror on the wall, who's the most powerful of us all?"

As usual, Labour MP Mr Hattersley put our minds at rest, claiming that our presidents would almost certainly be political neutrals - people that everyone quite liked - who would perform their official functions with charm and efficiency but would know to keep their traps shut about the big issues (like Michael Aspel or Gabby Rosslyn?). The danger with this, of course, would be that you might end up with the kind of jokers they elect in the United States of America. When you consider that a proven crook, a dippy peanut farmer, an ex-western film star (with Mad Cowboy Disease) and a bad saxophone player have been the best they could come up with in recent years, it doesn't say much for republicanism. But at least it would get rid of this highly expensive absurdity and wipe away the worst aspects of an elitism based purely on class.

The Happy Medium?

But, whether we like it or not, the answer to the problem probably won't be the transference from one crappy regime to another - we British are far too reserved. It will no doubt be a shaky compromise. But - and this is the big BUT - if the Royal family, now fifty in all, is to go forward into the twenty first century, it must shed all that gross fat that has accumulated and solidified through history. Get rid of all the

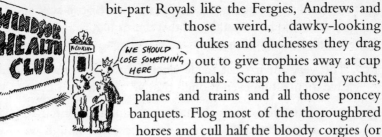

bit-part Royals like the Fergies, Andrews and those weird, dawky-looking dukes and duchesses they drag out to give trophies away at cup finals. Scrap the royal yachts, planes and trains and all those poncey banquets. Flog most of the thoroughbred horses and cull half the bloody corgies (or send 'em to Battersea), chuck all those hangers-on off the civil list, and turn half their estates into theme parks (Merrie Olde Windsor, Balmoral World of Adventure etc.). Keep the Queen, her hubby and mum indoors much, much more, and for heaven's sake don't let any of them make prats of themselves on the telly again. . . .Pause for removal of tongue from cheek.

Seriously though, unless they can detach themselves again from the arrogance of the aristocracy, stop being the very promoters of the class system, separate themselves from wealth and privilege and move naturally again between the likes of you or me, they will be responsible for their own fate.

CRAP CORNER

<u>STOP PRESS</u> *AT THE TIME OF GOING TO THE PRINTERS, OUR QUEEN, REALISING THAT THE WRITING IS UPON THE WALL, PROPOSED SEVERE REVISIONS TO THE WHOLE ROYAL CIRCUS.*

As you've probably guessed I really don't care whether we have a Royal family or not. As far as I'm concerned they're a vaguely amusing irrelevance that costs the country rather too much money. What do you think?

CRAP! Many people believe that Royalty are good for tourism. Sorry! A recent poll showed that these days they're way down the list of attractions, somewhere between policemen's helmets and half-timbered houses.

CRAP! The Royal family as an institution is seldom questioned because the British public cannot imagine it not being there.

[CRAP!] While they epitomise the British and the British way of life, it should be remembered that there's hardly a drop of British blood in any of them.

[CRAP!] The very media that made them into stars, refuses to leave them alone even though they've had enough.

[CRAP!] Like footballers or rock stars, we constantly listen to their opinion on just about everything even though we know it is seldom more educated than yours or mine.

[CRAP!] Princess Di claims tearfully one minute to hate media attention, but the next, just like a kid whose neglected toy is taken away, is seen trying to attract it at every opportunity (that suits).

[CRAP!] If the Royals say they need all the money they receive to keep the whole shebang going, how come that from the time of Queen Victoria (who was at one stage nigh-on broke), the Queen has become one of the richest women in the world.

[CRAP!] The Queen is the head of the Church of England which regards 'away-matches' within marriage as a heinous sin. Shame she didn't pass that on to the others.

[CRAP!] Just as our Royalty aren't allowed to make a decision about anything remotely important, a president would be similar: a symbolic leader, manipulated by the House of Commons (without the help of The Lords).

[CRAP!] The whole idea of a privileged Royal family prolongs the worst aspects of the class system and prevents Britain from becoming a fully-fledged modern democracy.

Democracy means government by the uneducated, while aristocracy means government by the badly educated...

G. K. Chesterton

BRITAIN IS BECOMING
A CLASSLESS
SOCIETY

CRAP!

6 *Without class differences, England would cease to be the living theatre it is…* 9
Anthony Burgess

This is the longest chapter in the book and my editor has pinned me to the floor and won't let me free before I make it perfectly clear that everything you are about to read is only MY OPINION. Feel free to disagree (at your peril).

A Classless Society?

Labour leaders have always made a classless society their aim, but the Tories have always seemed quite happy with the way things are until it became diplomatic to claim otherwise. John Major, that one-dimensional stool pigeon of the upper class Tories, went one step further and once claimed that Britain was becoming a classless society, based on the supposition that it must be if he, a middle class lad, could make it to PM. He soon had to modify this as can be witnessed in this speech.

6 *When I have talked of a classless society or an opportunist society, I mean that it just does not matter whether you come from a tiny, scruffy back-to-back in a pretty poor housing area or from one of the best mansions in one of the best parts of the town.* 9

This, of course, was and is either a load of hypocritical rubbish or gross naivety. One thing you can be sure of, in a Britain that changes as fast as a trainee lion-tamer's trousers, is that, despite 2000 years of what we call civilisation, the class system is still with us. But surely, I hear you groan, we don't have serfs and villeins anymore, and knights and barons aren't nearly as thick on the ground, so how can you make such a claim? Also, we're aeons away from that grumpy old Karl Marx's 'large proletariat and small bourgeoisie' malarkey. Isn't Britain, therefore, becoming one huge, ever so fair and ever so happy, classless family?

Fraid not! Sure, we don't have to tug our forelocks to our betters these days, or wait for them to toss us the odd coin at Chrissy so that we can have a lump of gristle in our gruel, but those that rule and own most of the wealth in our country have far more subtle methods of keeping us in position. The famous Gallup polls (those opinion people that stick their nose into every aspect of our lives), regularly monitor how this class struggle is going and have reported that the problem (if it is such) has almost doubled in the minds of the British people in just under thirty years.

But class is not just state of mind,
To think that means you must be blind.

Also, whereas in days of yore it was very much an us-and-them scenario, with everyone knowing their place, the class structure has become far more complex and layered. We now have the upper class, the upper middle class, the middle class, the lower middle class, the working class and below them those poor sods who have no bloody class at all (and somewhere in the middle we have the nouveau riche). Many would say that it's this very class system that's ruining, or has ruined, our country. Where most other nations have become almost egalitarian, we hang on like grim death to the status quo. If you live abroad, you will probably notice that respect is usually achieved by money and not much else. In America, for instance, you are what you earn. The poor aren't nearly so envious, as they still believe the system is open for them to achieve money and status (the same thing) themselves. Anybody can hit the jackpot, become president, or marry Elizabeth Taylor (and most have). In France, it's not unusual to see the bank manager drinking in the local bar with the road sweeper, while in Germany the road sweeper probably earns so much money that he probably owns shares in the bank.

Onward and Upward

The national sport in this fair land, isn't soccer, as we are led to believe, but the corporate move towards, and sometimes even into, the class above. For all except those at the bottom, that is, who have no options, or those at the top, who are kept well busy trying to keep the rest of us commoners out!

It's important to try and up one's class; so let me pass, then kiss my arse .

But what has it got to do with a book like this? you might ask.

The class system in this country is as great a source of hypocrisy and double standards as any other we might mention. From the very top to the very bottom of the social pile, the adult of each species (for that's almost what they are) pass down to their offspring all the values and opinions they will require to either hang on to their perceived social position or climb up into the one above.

Whether you like it or not, you and yours will fall into one of these social classes, with maybe a couple of characteristics borrowed (or nicked) from one of the others. Everything we do, say, watch or wear identifies us (even you) so let's have a look at them in more detail starting, naturally, with our (or at least my) much betters.

The Aristocracy

Just like whales, tigers and kindly, co-operative traffic wardens, the aristocracy are an endangered species. None of the rules of society apply to them, and you can only see them en masse at Royal weddings or funerals. Those that live in Britain are as diverse racially as the staff in the average Pizza

Hut, and the only thing they have in common is they've long forgotten what real work means. Money-wise, you'll all be pleased to know that our dear Royal Family own the biggest slice of the financial cake in Britain, weighing in (in 1990) at a cool £6,700 million, which let's face it, most families could scrape quite happily by on (with a modest lottery win thrown in). Until recently they used to set the whole standard of English behaviour – a sort of bench-mark for the gentry – but recently, due to circumstances beyond – correction – *within* their control, have fallen slightly from grace (see page 105).

> ❛ *An aristocracy is like cheese, the older it is, the higher it becomes...* ❜
> *Lloyd George*

The Upper Class

Like all things to do with class, the real brainteaser is finding where to draw the line. You could of course do it purely by money. For instance, in 1985, 1% of the population owned 33% of the booty. This figure had been steadily falling over the years, until that friend of the people (provided they're loaded), the fab Mrs Thatcher, put a stop to the rot. But you and I know it just isn't as simple as how much cash you've got. After all, you can be dead ordinary and own a palace (albeit tacky) and frightfully well-connected living in a caravan. So don't go thinking for one milli-second, that if you win 20 extremely big ones on the lottery, that it will push you straightaway into the upper class. Sorry! You can't buy posh! Anyway, the upper class won't allow

you in as they're a close-knit bunch of super-rich families (or close-knit nits). Another very important factor is that it's very, very difficult to build up the level of stash that they've got, without some sort of grand inheritance. It's probably this factor alone that has become the major constituent of the slippery-sided, caviar-topped wall that keeps the rest of us out.

> *The stately homes of England*
> *How beautiful they stand*
> *To prove the upper classes*
> *Have still the upper hand...* Noel Coward

This wall is cemented together by all the networks that are in place to keep their bloodline pure – namely marriage, family friendships, the 'old boy routine', business and financial handshakes and, most important of all – school (Eton, Harrow etc.) and university (Oxbridge). All this stuff gives them their enormous undeniable, unknockable power which means that, when push comes to shove, the upper classes still occupy most of the high ground in the business world, politics, the civil service, the military (you don't ever see those boys getting shot) the Church and the judiciary. Okay, you might get a handful of geriatric working class heroes struggling into the House of Lords (a neat way of showing them the back door of the Commons), but you can bet your pension the poor old blighters don't often get asked home for tea with the others.

Just because you're now a Lord,
don't mix with whom you can't afford.

So if you just happen to be one of those bushy-tailed, if somewhat misguided, social-climbers who thinks they can ease (or sleaze) their way into the toff's world, the odds are not good. They might go out with you; they might even take you to their beds; but, if only for fear of being severed from the family stack, they'll never marry you. To sum up, if you went to Biggleswade Comprehensive, then Salford University, smoothed out your northern accent and then made a humungous packet on the stock exchange enabling you to buy all the bits and pieces that you think make you one of them (see nouveau riche) – wise up! You might as well try dating Princess Di (actually, the way things are going, you'd probably have a better chance). Be content to be the high roller of the class below (or several even). Here are a few ways to help you identify if you're upper class.

Ten Principles of the Upper Class

1. Always address the lower echelons by their Christian names (they will never do the same).

2. Always claim to prefer horses to people.

3. Always vote Tory and read the *Telegraph* (The *Times* has gone so far downhill since that terrible Aussie bought it).

4. Always holiday at least once a year in Scotland with relatives.

5. If you *are* Scottish, never have even a remote Scottish accent.

6. Always make a total prat of yourself when drunk.

7. Always claim to have no expendable cash, insisting it's all 'tied up'.

8. Invite Mick Jagger to dinner at least once.

9. Do everything you can to avoid death duties.

10. Sadly, regard the Royal Family as rather common.

❛ The Queen's a very pleasant middle to upper-class type of lady, with a talkative retired Navy husband... ❜

Malcolm Muggeridge

Ten Things You Must Never Do If You're Upper Class

1. Never learn any form of dress sense or style.

2. Never learn to dance with any sense of rhythm (except the Highland Reel).

GOSH CAMILLA, YOU'RE A SUPER ROCK AND ROLLER

3. Never carry actual cash. (Actually they never have any - it's all tied up).

4. Never appear in *Hello!* magazine.

5. Never have black people in the house (especially not servants - that's not done).

6. Never drive flash cars or aeroplanes.

7. Never speak to your children before they've left prep school.

8. Never follow any convention (like eating nicely, walking upright or having chins).

9. Never go into shops. (Have everything brought round the back.)

10. Never give anything to charities (just your name).

The Upper-Middle Class

These are the people that also have been used to having lots of money, but unlike the aristocracy, have either made it themselves or are not too far down the food chain from the people that did. These are the company bosses, lawyers, newspaper editors, barristers, publishers etc. that can be regularly seen driving or being driven in flash motors like Rolls -Royces, 5 Series BMWs, big Mercedes or Daimler/Jaguars, or standing about, gin and tonic in hand, on large yachts and cruisers in and around the sunspots of Europe wearing silly caps and navy blue blazers.

Be it limo, plane or yacht,
be sure to show off what you've got.

Their wives spend most of their time alone, or with the woman that 'does', in the home counties, or the more luxurious surrounds of major cities, doing good works, organising fetes for the local church or passing holier-than-thou judgements on the poor sods from the lower classes who are unfortunate enough to come up in front of them at the local magistrates courts. Their children have names like Rupert or Lucinda and go to good public schools - maybe not always the Harrows, Etons or Roedeans, but certainly the Stowes, and Rugbys and Benendens. These kids, post-school, mostly end up in West London where they have made Fulham and Clapham such 'super' places to live (if you don't mind the words *bonking*, *dosh* or *yah* ringing in your ears in every pub, wine bar or bistro, or being prevented from parking by more GTI convertibles than you can shake a shooting stick at).

We can't think why they think it rude,
to shout so loud and throw our food.

How to Spot Them

The family, though not often seen together (kids away at school and husbands - simply away) can always be guaranteed to congregate at local agricultural shows or point-to-points where they strive to look identical in those toad-coloured Barbours, brown trilbies and green wellies. If you're becoming confused, they can be differentiated from the aristocracy by their cars and dogs. The upper classes tend to drive rather beaten up Land Rovers and

Suburus (as they have nothing to prove) crammed with scruffy lurchers and whippets, while our upper-middles arrive in immaculate Range Rover Vogues (doesn't the name say it all) or any of the other ponced up four-wheel-drives that wouldn't know a muddy country estate if they sunk into one. In the canine department they tend to go for Labradors (only black) or Springer Spaniels (only stupid).

Otherwise try the five-a-side rugger at Twickers, the racing at Ascot, the polo at Windsor or that ludicrous floating Pimms-fight called Henley (pronounced *Henleh*) where they all contest to look more ostentatious than each other, while completely ignoring some rather sad athletes who float by, as fast as they can, in long thin boats.

I say, who cares who's really won,
it's cost simply loads to have such fun.

It's a well-known fact that few of them understand culture, still believing that Andrew Lloyd Webber is our greatest composer and tending to congregate at the most expensive venues like Covent Garden, Glyndebourne or the filming of Gladiators (only joking) where they can be seen in DJs and shapeless, strapless, shiny frocks, talking about who was at what, with who - and when.

Unlike the aristocracy, Mr and Mrs Upper-Middle have taken a bit of a caning through the recession. Even their hero Maggie couldn't save them from tumbling property values, sinking shares and punitive exchange rates. As for the poor nippers, Rupert and Lucinda, who, with their respective partners Emma and Guy, bought charming cowboy-converted ex-Battersea workman's cottages for a quarter of a million quid each, the poor dears have both slid into a negative equity trap (see also page 130) which mummy and daddy find almost as unmentionable as their offspring bringing home ethnic minorities. Hardest hit of all were the poor Lloyd's Names, that illustrious bunch of wealthy (but not quite enough!) near-toffs who, having quite happily been coining it for years (for no input whatsoever) got caught well and truly with their hands in the international cookie jar, by having to pay up unlimited amounts of this unearned loot due to vast American environmental claims.

You just can't know how much it hurt,
to get so rich – then lose your shirt.

If you read any of those unbelievable society mags, like *Tatler* and *Harpers* you will see that the greatest aim of any upper-middle class parent is to get one of their offspring mated to someone from the shelf above. Just as race horse owners take their fillies to be serviced by the purest stud, these folk will spend fortunes just to give their children, and therefore the family, a leg up (or over) into the aristocracy (almost as much as the aristocracy spend trying to stop 'em).

Shout hooray, and raise your glass,
we've finally made the upper class.

Ten Principles of the Upper Middle Class

1. Despite believing in nothing, always turn up regularly at the local church.

2. Always bank with Coutts or Williams and Glyn's (never anything common like the Midland or National Westminster).

3. When asked about Rock and Roll always say you like the Beatles (as they're the only pop group you've ever heard of).

4. Always have a flat in 'town', or if in town, somewhere to get away to at the weekend.

5. Always shout at foreigners and waiters (it's the only way they understand).

6. If not formal, always call dinner 'supper'.

7. Always vote Tory and read – sorry – 'take' the *Telegraph* (the *Guardian*'s just for lefties and lesbians).

8. Every home must have an Aga, but as they're so bloody impractical, always have your cook or wife (same thing) use a proper oven or microwave.

9. Try to own racehorses (or parts of such).

10. Only stay with friends when abroad (hotels are *so* vulgar).

Ten Things You Must Never Do If Upper-Middle Class

1. Never buy anything foreign unless it's a property abroad.

2. Never let anyone else chair committees in your local village.

I SAID I WANTED BRITISH ORANGES IN MY MARMALADE

3. Never wear man-made fibres (especially not in bright colours).

4. Never question a bill in a restaurant (too vulgar).

5. Never allow black people into your house, unless to play in the steel band at your daughter's wedding bash (and make sure that's outside in a marquee).

6. Never let your car get more than two years old (unless you have a private number plate).

7. Never admit anything bad about the Royal Family.

8. Never allow sex before marriage (but have plenty during - if possible with other people).

9. Never admit to knowing (or being) a homosexual.

10. Never wear anything gold (it's slightly common).

The Middle Classes

I know a lot about the middle classes, because I'm now one of them (though not particularly my fault). My family didn't always used to be, as my mother's mum and dad came from Leeds and my father's came from the East End of London and were all united by an extreme shortage of funds. Our bit of the family (my mum and dad), like the largest percentage of the middle class, had clawed our way up from the blue-collar working class, through lower middle class and out into the sunny, fresh air of the white-collared, non-manual-labouring middle class. My poor cockney mother (Lord love 'er) was stranded like a beached whale in the smartish London suburbs, owing to my dad's rather meteoric success in the city (where he'd started as a messenger boy) and rather inconsiderate early demise (from exhaustion). It was, therefore, only my brothers and myself who were truly middle class, as we went to goodish state schools, had always known a telly and a family car, and had even known people to come round to eat at our table (if only twice). I became an illustrator (rather middle class), my elder brother became a successful broker like my father (extremely middle class), and my younger, would you believe, a vicar (which is about as middle class as you can get).

How to Spot Us

We middle classes (in case you're not one of us) are all the people that fill up the roads with nice clean cars, live in houses with neat front gardens, have sensible amounts of kids, bring these kids up as well as possible, vote Conservative, Liberal or sometimes - in nostalgic deference to our mis-spent roots - Labour, join clubs and societies, have occasional beards (if men) and occasional coffee mornings (if women). We respect the police, believe in capital punishment (but say we don't), love pets and nature programmes on telly and, although seldom vegetarian, prefer our meat not to look like anything in particular. We believe in owning not renting, buying not hire purchase and prefer Sainsbury's to SuperSave. We are now by far the most powerful group in the country.

But we poor old middle classes have had it really tough over the last few years. There we all were, bustling along in the mid-eighties, having woefully suffered that wobbly plot-lost Labour government of the seventies, fully believing our saviour Maggie Thatcher's promise that she'd put the *Great* back into Britain. And why shouldn't we? Our houses were going up in value by 26.8% a year and, therefore, for a while, we could earn almost as much on paper as we would from working. Okay, it was a shame that all those who didn't own anything were missing out but that was life and it wasn't our fault.

If everything's okay for you,
sod your friends and neighbours too.

Building societies, bless their silver-lined cotton socks, were falling over each other to lend us as much money as we could possibly squander, and if we were flush enough to buy shares in all those privatised companies that we stupid British once owned anyway, we could scrape the fat off the top within weeks. At last we had a strong leader, prepared to fight our corner in international affairs, support a free economy and stand up for the sort of person who believed in working hard for a decent standard of living. Sounds good eh? Unfortunately it was all a load of pure, unadulterated bollocks!

We should listen to what we're told,
all that glisters is not gold.

Foundations of Straw

All the money that appeared to be being made was being made by simply shifting around – you've got it – money. At a time when smart Essex kids in the city were pulling in unbelievable fortunes, our manufacturing base was plummeting (as we weren't making nuffink) and unemployment was soaring. Suddenly the extremely fertile shit hit the all-devouring fan, and Britain was plunged into the deepest recession that most of us could remember. Redundancy became the big word and suddenly chaps who thought their futures (and membership to the golf club) were secure, were chucked on the 'sad bastards' scrap heap, mortgaged up to their eyeballs, with expensive company motors and even more expensive wives at home. All those who'd taken their kids outside the now declining state school system found it difficult to meet the fees for Rippemoff Hall or Chinless Manor. On top of all that was the family membership to the local sports centre, the wife's second car (a Clio naturellement) and the payments to BUPA which they'd joined because the Tory government, who didn't give a stuff about the health of ordinary people, had practically strangled the life out of the NHS. Some of their grown up sons and daughters who, thinking they'd bought themselves into the upper-middle class, and having delighted in the label Yuppie (Young Upwardly Mobile Professional Person), were caught like their 'betters' with their 501s down; they found themselves owing the HP on expensive cars like BMWs and Porsches and, as a result of building society mis-management, with negative equity in their properties (the value having dropped below the amount they'd borrowed to buy them). Those dear old building societies, that had been so kindly and co-operative only a couple of years before, simply nicked *their* houses back and sold them for whatever would clear what they'd lent. As for the banks, as soon as there was even a cloud on the horizon, their lovely friendly, we're-only-here-to-help managers called in their loans to small businesses and happily watched them go to the wall.

❝ *We of the sinking middle class …may sink without further struggles into the working classes where we belong, and probably when we get there it will not be so dreadful as we feared, for, after all, we have nothing to lose but our aitches…* ❞
George Orwell

It doesn't take us very long,
to pull the rug when things go wrong.

And have we learned our lesson? Do moths ever avoid naked flames? Of course not. Here are a few of the things that go to make us middle class.

Ten Things one must do to be Middle Class

1. Never admit to reading the tabloids. If you have them delivered, make sure they're wrapped in the 'big' papers.

2. Never admit to your kids what you did when you were their age.

3. Install a bidet in the bathroom, but don't bother to use it (even if you do know what it's for.)

4. Always make loud sympathetic noises when you hear of the financial trouble your friends are in (but giggle inwardly).

5. Always pretend that you hardly ever watch television, and if you do - only documentaries.

6. Let everyone know you know homosexuals and 'coloured' people (it's so trendy and politically correct).

7. Pay lip service to all the conservation groups (but carry on polluting as usual).

8. Change your mind about state schools being crappy and run down (especially if you can no longer afford the alternative).

9. If your wife has to work 'cos you're short of cash, make sure she says that she's doing it to be fulfilled.

10. Tell everyone that if you won the lottery you wouldn't change a thing in your life.

YES THANK YOU GEORGE WE'RE MUDDLING ALONG FINE

Ten Things You Must Never Do If Middle Class

1. Never watch anything with Noel Edmunds or Bob Monkhouse in.

2. Never admit to going to fairgrounds or leisure parks (go – of course – but never admit it).

3. Never call the lavatory the lavatory ('Loo' please!).

4. Never envy people in *Hello!* magazine, and never admit buying it.

5. Never discuss politics or religion at dinner parties (just house prices and the ozone hole).

6. Never live in a street with a caravan in a front garden or a satellite dish stuck to a house.

7. Avoid French products (until the bastards start behaving themselves) but by all means have a little place in Provence.

8. Never go on package holidays (or at least never admit it).

9. Never give the homeless people on the streets money. It only encourages them.

10. Never admit that there could be any other reason for Third World poverty, other than having too many children through carelessness.

The Lower Middle Class

The lower middle classes have also had a bit of a struggle over the last few years. They're the ones with the most egg on their faces, having denied their background completely to vote for the 'you'll-never-have-it-so-good' Thatcher. They watched her trash the unions that their working class fathers and grandfathers had struggled so hard to build and then, just when they'd had their corporate balls surgically and expertly removed, wondered why their bosses ran all over them. But like gamblers that never know when to go home, they continued voting for her until well after her own sell-by date, hoping against hope that the gravy would start flowing again. But, just like gravy, the economy congealed and as near as dammit dried up.

Don't give up on Mrs Thatcher,
there's never been a man to match 'er.

But as you've probably realised, the class system only moves upwards not downwards, and the new lower middle class would never slide to being working class again. They found their views and aspirations far more accurately expressed in the 'better' tabloids like the *Mail*, *Express* and *Today* and, having achieved what they perceived as middle class accoutrements like matching avocado bath suites, fully fitted MFI kitchens, wine when people come round, plastic garden furniture and a garage with an up-and-over door, were not going to give up without a fight. But what a fight it's turning out to be, especially for the men folk.

A lot of these families consisted of a manual working husband and that reasonably new concept, a non-manual (is that womanual?) working wife; the joint income allowing them luxuries and a spending capacity that their parents only dreamed of. This had come about because bosses had cottoned on to the fact that out there on the estates of identical toy-town houses that surround the dormitory towns was a huge workforce that could not only do most of what had been hitherto men's work but would do it much better, for far less money and, much more to the point, not make so much fuss about it. The trouble came when the demand for manual work fell away. Hardly anybody was building houses, cars, ships or anything else big anymore, so when dad lost his job, mum had to be the breadwinner (and baby-maker, cook, cleaner and clothes-washer) while the old man tried in vain to think of other things to do that didn't involve going to the pub or the betting shop.

Most women just have all the luck – eat, sleep, work and fend for the children.

How to Spot Them

The lower middle class are everywhere. They provide all our services like telephones, post and car repairs; they police us, own our smaller shops and bury us when we're dead. They usually drive small, underpowered cars so as to save on the fuel consumption and often put soft toys on the back shelf. They love things like Comic Relief Day, not because they're into giving to charity, but they like having a red nose on their car (and sometimes never take them off!). We can see them at ice rinks, bowling alleys and all those large half-timbered suburban pubs that have sold franchises to catering chains flogging substandard food at inflated prices; "Hello, I'm Tracy, your waitress of the day. Would you wait here to be seated?"

> ❛ *The one class you do not want to belong to and are not proud of at all is the lower middle class. No one ever describes himself as belonging to the lower-middle class...* ❜ *George Mikes*

They go on package tours to foreign places like Torremolinos and Ibiza where the natives have cottoned on to only selling English beer and food, but strangely patronise all the fast-foreign food outlets in Britain like those selling Italian pizzas, Turkish kebabs, and the sort of Indian and Chinese cuisine the Indians in India and the Chinese in China wouldn't be seen dead eating. Their older children are the lager-louts and loose-living slappers that have ruined all the countries that can be got to within a couple of hours from Luton Airport. The lower middle class can be seen en masse at theme parks like Alton Towers, Waterworld or, if not too 'recessed', Disneyland in Paris or Florida. But perhaps the best way to see them in their purest and most unadulterated form (apart from a few middle class meanies) is at car boot sales. Car boot sales always amaze the other social classes, who wonder why anyone should want to buy someone else's almost worn out lavatory brush or twenty year old, totally unreliable Teasmade. My theory is that it's the social event that brings them together, and that the very same lavatory brush and the very same Teasmade return week after week. The money just circulates in such a way that a trainee statistician could spend hours of harmless fun constructing a graph to illustrate its final demise.

Boot sales serve a worthwhile function,
to shed crap gear without
compunction.

Ten Principles of the Lower Middle Class

1. Always do all your shopping at those huge prefabricated superstores on the edge of your town or pedestrianised shopping malls.

2. Only have proper coffee or non-sliced bread if you have 'company'.

3. Always spend days comparing the prices of something you want to buy.

4. Always believe that it's just a matter of time before you win the lottery and further believe that money can solve all problems (which, of course, it can!).

5. Admire the people featured in *Hello!* magazine.

6. Aspire to owning one of those 'hairdresser's jeeps' smothered with naff slogans and decals.

7. Love caravanning.

8. Only buy your children the plastic extruded, *My Little Pony*-type junk advertised on TV.

9. Always eat picnics as close as is humanly possible to your car and preferably the main road.

10. Always believe that people with upper class accents know best.

Ten Things You Must Never Do If Lower Middle Class

1. Never miss *Gladiators*, *Blind Date* or *Celebrity Squares*.

2. Never buy anything fresh, or without a telly advertised brand name, at the supermarket.

3. Never miss a refreshment stop on the motorway.

4. Never read books, apart from thick ones with gold lettering, on holiday.

5. Never tip waiters.

6. Never buy clothes without patterns on.

7. Never give children names that they don't share with TV, film or pop stars.

8. Never lose a minute's sleep over anything that doesn't directly concern you (foreign wars, famines, earthquakes etc.).

9. Don't be unfriendly with ethnic minorities at work but by all means slag them off at all other times.

10. Don't think about spending a penny on your children's education until it's far too late.

The Working Class...

Up to only a hundred years ago the working class consisted of all the people that actually worked, as opposed to all those who didn't. These days practically everyone, right up to the upper middle classes, needs to work to survive (at least to the level that they have become accustomed to). Indeed, because of this, many middle class people will fling up their soft, smooth hands and claim to be working class (which is a bit like the *Sun* suddenly including an education supplement). Clearly the term must be redefined.

It's much easier to think of them as all the people that actually earn their daily bread by the sweat of their own brow – the ones that actually produce something or physically cause something to be physically different. Practically everything that we eat, own, drive, live in or work in has been produced by the working class, having been told how, when and where to do it by everyone above them. The real working class are in some respects similar to the upper class, in that they know who they are and have no real desire to be anything else, to the point that even if they do start making enough money to move on, they show little or no interest. Unlike the upper class, however, they are becoming less and less involved with politics, which is not surprising when you think of the bunch of seemingly self-obsessed wallies – the Labour Party – that were supposed to represent them over the last 89 years. Like the lower middle class, at least half the working class chose other parties in the 1987 elections (which just goes to show how confused some people can get).

But it must be said that the working class are substantially better off than they were 50 years ago. They don't have to go to the end of the garden to relieve themselves, and most, these days, have most of the symbols of modern life: fridges, cars (albeit old), washing machines, life-size tellies and can now talk to each other on the phone (without shagging out their pigeons), and some have even cottoned on to how to restrict the size of their families.

Life for us is much much better,
thanks to God (and the French letter).

...and Where We Can See Them

Like the lower middle classes, the working class are everywhere.
They drive our buses (when not in their own Reliant Robins,
Ladas or Allegros), dig our roads, build our houses, grow our
food and clean our public lavs. They live in inner city high-rises,
on council estates and caravan parks. Many of them are ethnic
minorities that find it impossible to improve their lot in a hostile
society. They are the remnants of a once proud breed that have
over the last few decades become increasingly dispossessed by
puppet governments manipulated by the middle and upper-
middle classes.

For entertainment they choose mass events like dog
racing, fairgrounds, theme parks, street markets, pubs, football,
Royal weddings and, believe it or not, church going (God
knows - they've got little to praise him
for). But the working classes spend
most of their time stuck in front of
their tellies, finding books or
proper newspapers too
much like hard work.
They are, however,
served badly and
cynically by their own
tabloid press that, one
can only suppose,
contrive to keep them in the ignorance they often seem to revel
in. Papers like the *Sun* or the *Daily Mirror* wield enormous
power, chucking out miles of column inches of pure
inconsequential garbage and competing to see how low they can
estimate their readership. Their ability to manipulate their
jargon-intoxicated audience cannot be taken lightly and press
barons like Rupert Murdoch, the media tycoon, have been
seriously suspected of using them to bolster their own political
beliefs and aspirations (see page 13).

Our message might seem light and bland,
but those poor sods eat out of our hand.

Advertisers can and will sell the working class practically anything. If they can't get to the adults directly, they'll attack their kids by buying up all the advertising space between children's telly programmes convincing the poor little nippers that they can't live without: vacuum-formed mutant villages, all-year-round chocolate Easter eggs pregnant with plastic toys guaranteed to choke the average toddler, or hideous teenage dolls with all the interesting bits strangely missing.

' *I never knew the working classes had such pale skins...* '
Earl Curzon of Kedleston

At the top end of this class they struggle unconvincingly, embarrassingly and hilariously to better themselves, often by skipping the middle class and flirting with the upper middles. Hyacinth Bucket from the series *Keeping Up Appearances* captures the breed perfectly.

Ten Principles of the Working Class

1. Always shout at and chastise your kids in supermarkets (never reason, if a slap will do).

2. Always dispose of your litter where it can offend everyone.

3. Take your kids into pubs and introduce them to drinking and smoking as soon as possible.

4. Always settle arguments violently.

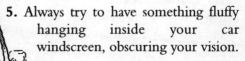

5. Always try to have something fluffy hanging inside your car windscreen, obscuring your vision.

6. Find Jeremy Beadle not quite as offensive as everyone else.

7. Always call your lunch 'dinner' and your dinner 'tea'.

8. Always fill up the back garden with old toys or bits of cars.

9. Always blame everything that goes wrong in your life on someone else.

10. Always hate the police.

Ten Things You Must Never Do If Working Class

1. Never eat anything that isn't fried or boiled.

2. Never say a word against the Queen Mother (just bitch continually about the others).

3. Never kiss anyone on both cheeks.

4. Never give anything whatsoever away or to charity.

5. Never watch documentaries, discussion programmes, or listen to anything with a lot of stupid talking.

6. Never buy dogs that you can't beat, or that won't bite people.

7. Avoid doing anything you're not paid to do.

8. Avoid giving up smoking, gambling or drinking.

9. Never drink wine and avoid places where they do.

10. Never allow your daughter or son to go out with anyone from a higher class (unless there's cash in it).

WARNING: You are now entering a joke-free zone.

The Underclass

There has always been poverty in this country, and many would claim that life's a doddle compared with Victorian times, when a much larger proportion of the population were homeless, and forced to beg for food and sleep on the streets. Since then, however, the fabulous welfare state has come to our rescue, designed to give everyone a basic standard of living - employed or not. Thank God and our politicians for that. Now we have a much better class of homeless beggars sleeping rough on our city streets.

Poverty as we all know, is a relative term. The poverty line is most easily defined as the minimum necessary for survival (by survival we mean - not dying!). In this country, as you might have noticed, we don't have thousands of pop-eyed, swollen-bellied children in rags, literally starving to death, so we must relocate the line, taking into account the overall standard of living in Britain. The Conservative government are renowned for lowering that line, limbo-like, as a rather inspired (I think) way of making us all look better off. Despite what they tell us, however, poverty (and we all know what that means) is becoming more and more rife, and the people caught in the poverty trap, more and more numerous. A recent study by a chap called Oppenheim concluded that in 1979 the proportion of people living at, or below, the supplementary benefit level was 6%. This soared to 17% in a mere ten years. In other words 30% of the population were hovering around the edges of poverty in 1987 compared to 20% in 1979. You can bet it's considerably worse now.

The rich may come and the rich may go, but the number of poor is bound to grow.

Where to View the Underclass

Apart from the more obvious ones, who so inconsiderately get under our feet with their tedious begging when we're trying to do our weekly shopping, or go out having fun in the evenings, the very poor are quite a difficult breed to spot. You won't find them, for instance, at any of the normal working class venues as mentioned before, purely because, being *not* working, they can't afford to go anywhere. You won't see them in supermarkets, with vast trolley loads of grub, because they can't afford to buy more food than they immediately need – tending to feed, sheep-like, as they go along. You won't see them on holiday or at leisure parks, because they don't know the meaning of the word *recreation*; and you won't see them laughing because most of them have forgotten how.

You *will*, however, see them in chip shops, as chips are the only bulky food that they and their kids can afford. You *will* see them in shopping malls, libraries, railway stations or anywhere where someone else is paying for the heating, and you *will* see them hanging around street markets waiting, vulture-like, for any free, or almost free, handouts. You *will* see them, when young, loitering in parks or on street corners, unemployed and with little or no chance of ever working.

You will also see them filling up doctors' waiting rooms and hospital out-patient departments waiting patiently to be treated for symptons of malnutrition, tuberculosis and rickets (not seen for years). And, just like the people who live off rubbish dumps on the edge of the world's poor cities like Rio de Janeiro, you will see a fast-growing sub-group of young men who trail round skips and municipal rubbish dumps sorting out bits of discarded televisions, vacuum cleaners and other outdated technology to sell as spares. This is Merrie England 96, headed by a marvellous government that constantly assure us middle class people that they care, while constantly looking for ways of cutting benefits and changing the goal posts for the poor devils that need them to survive. I think we should all take time out to ponder the views of that nice little Justin something or other, the fourteen year old delegate at the 1995 Brighton Tory conference. His idea for feeding the poor in London was for them to go and catch fish in the Thames and supplement their diet with berries from Epping Forest. Youthanasia? I'm all for it!

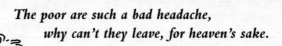

The poor are such a bad headache,
why can't they leave, for heaven's sake.

Ten Principles of the Underclass

1. Always talk in the present tense. You have no future.

2. Only eat cooked food a couple of times a week, it saves on gas.

3. If old and cold, always wear all the clothes you own and stay in bed all day.

4. Only eat food that has little or no nutritional value.

5. Only *promise* your children that they will receive Christmas and birthday presents when things improve.

6. Don't expect your children to get a decent education.

7. Realise that the government have enough on their plates trying to keep the other classes happy without worrying about you.

8. When begging, always say please and thankyou.

9. Be extremely grateful for whatever the government hands you out.

10. Always recognise your place at the very bottom of the pecking order.

Ten Things You Must Never Do if a Member of the Underclass

1. Never ignore the patronising advice of your betters.

2. (But, never expect any real help from them.)

3. Never aspire to a bank account or one of those cards that get money from out of the wall.

4. Never expect to travel on anything but public transport.

5. Never even consider going abroad.

143

6. If a girl, never forget that sex means babies.

7. Never go to restaurants.

8. Never own anything.

9. Never be happy.

10. Die young!

WARNING: You are now returning to a joke-full zone

The Nouveau Riche

Nouveau Riche is the term given to anyone who has, either through hard work or a sudden injection of hard cash, tried to lift himself out of the class he was in. They are despised by the upper and upper middle classes, ignored by the middle classes, cheated by the working classes and wistfully envied by the poverty stricken. I love 'em! Their vulgarity knows no bounds, as their judgement is always tainted by how much things cost rather than any question of aesthetics. If you're a kid and your parents are nouveau riche, you will have the latest computer games, the most expensive trainers, your own bathroom and a mobile phone (and also be secretly despised by all your friends). It usually takes about two to three generations to level out the effects of quick money, and even then it's practically impossible to be accepted anywhere but amongst your own kind.

You've got the money I can see, but don't think you're as good as me.

Where They Can be Seen

The nouveau riche are fairly rare but hilariously obvious when observed. They will never be seen on public transport, tending always to stick to that most obvious of status symbols – the flash motor. They always go for Jaguar XJS's, Rolls-Royces, Mercedes convertibles, and give their teenage kids those horrible little Japanese sports cars that look like partially sucked sweets. One of the conditions of purchase is that these cars are instantly customised with gold instead of chrome fitments, metal-flake paint, and white-walled tyres, to prove that, not only did they have the money to buy them, but there was still enough left over to vulgarise them even more.

A Sad but True Story

A young guy, who recently made a killing in the city, bought a brand new, top of the range, BMW convertible. After adding every possible extra, he decided that he would have the ultimate stereo system fitted. In order to do this, he took out the small rear seats and customised the area to take the ultimate hi-fi that money could buy. When he took the car for a service, the mechanics spotted that he'd weakened the construction of the car so much that it was now dangerous and illegal, and more to the point irrepairable. The car was declared a write-off. All together now – OH DEAR, OH DEAR!

Back to the plot. The Nouveau Riche love private planes and helicopters (Noel Edmonds?) and buy huge mock Tudor-style houses (á la Duke and Duchess of York) with electric gates, near where they were brought up and, if not already installed, put heated swimming pools in their back gardens. They wear the best clothes that you can find in the most expensive, but vulgar department stores (provided they have the designer logos on the outside), wear kilos of gold jewellery and always carry wads of folding cash (if they must use plastic, they make sure it's platinum). They spend a great deal of their time in exclusive golf or country clubs, spending money like it's going out of fashion to impress people just like themselves. Everything they buy has to be slightly larger than life and unashamedly flashy. Even their dogs are big, showy and rather stupid – Afghan Hounds, Great Danes or Old English Sheepdogs, which all die early due to lack of exercise.

But Who Are They?

Sportsmen who make it big (particularly boxers and footballers), comedians and naff TV presenters, lottery and pools winners, car dealers, small company bosses bought out by conglomerates, Asian retailers, Jewish entrepreneurs, Arabs, night-club owners, pop stars and Nigel Mansell.

Ten Principles of the Nouveau Riche

1. Always park blocking others in when visiting a restaurant, so that your flash car can be announced over the hotel or restaurant speakers, and so that you can be seen ostentatiously going to move it.

2. When you've made it big, trade in the wife who supported you through the bad times, for a young model, showgirl or gameshow hostess (and make sure she's taller than you).

3. If black, marry white.

4. Always buy loads of flashy gifts at airports and wear dark glasses at all times (even on the plane).

5. Always buy gold-plated fittings for your bathrooms.

6. Try to gatecrash celebrity golf matches and be photographed next to Jimmy Tarbuck, Bruce Forsyth or Sean Connery.

7. Always wear pastel-coloured tracksuits around the house.

8. Only eat pre-prepared food from Marks & Spencers (as the instructions for the top of the range kitchen equipment are usually in German).

9. Only eat out at those country restaurants named after some fancy French chef.

10. Try to tip more than everyone else (but make sure they know).

Ten Things You Must Never Do if Nouveau Riche

1. Never mix with others whose names aren't worth dropping or who aren't also wealthy or at least upper middle class.

2. Never be seen with your working class parents. Buy them a bungalow at the seaside and give them an allowance to keep quiet.

3. Never worry about world events, poor people, politics or ecology.

4. Never be seen without a suntan (preferably from a sunbed).

5. Never listen to music that other people haven't told you is okay and always be seen on the opening nights of Andrew Lloyd Webber musicals.

6. Never show disappointment when your children aren't invited back to their public school-mates' houses for the weekend.

7. Never allow anyone to buy a bigger gift for your kid's school.

8. If a woman, never ask your husband where he's been if he's home late. Just enjoy the money he gives to keep you in your place (and have a scene with the boy who cleans the pool).

9. Never use an interior decorator who hasn't done a house featured in *Hello!*

10. If featured in *Hello!*, never appear bored (and always look fond of your wife, husband, pets and children).

So, in a nutshell, that was my version of the social structure in Britain, as we nose-dive towards the millennium. Overriding the whole business, however, has been the arrival of a new social splitter that has no class barriers. This, as if you didn't know, is the great *job* or *no job* divide.

Before we go into what's been revealed in this chapter, here are a few questions.

1. Most adults make snap judgements about people based on their accents, jobs, education and whether they come from the north or south. Do you?

2. If you claim you don't, what about more external things like clothes, interests or the sort of house they live in? If you think someone is naff, posh, crude or slightly vulgar, could this be the beginning of the same thing we blame adults for?

3. Do you think papers like the *Sun* and the *Mirror* are common and down-market?

4. Do you think papers like *The Times* and the *Telegraph* are boring and up-market?

5. Do you think your parents have a class bias?

6. Do you think you have a class bias?

CRAP CORNER

These are the main points revealed in this chapter. Again they are only my opinion:

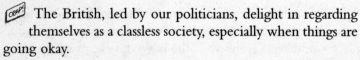 The British, led by our politicians, delight in regarding themselves as a classless society, especially when things are going okay.

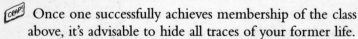 Once one successfully achieves membership of the class above, it's advisable to hide all traces of your former life.

The upper classes can come out to play with us when they choose, but never the reverse.

CRAP! The upper classes deny racism implicitly. Why not? They never meet any blacks.

CRAP! Magistrates, especially those do-gooding upper middle class women, always judge the lower orders as if they have had the same advantages as themselves.

CRAP! The upper classes always treat foreigners as people not fortunate enough to be British.

CRAP! The British change their opinion about capital punishment according to the company they're keeping.

CRAP! The middle classes believed in Thatcher, but only while she was making them money.

CRAP! The middle classes believe that people who live on the streets should shape up and ship out, until one of their sons or daughters finds themselves in the same position.

CRAP! The lower middle classes always claim that winning vast amounts of money wouldn't ruin their lives – until it does.

CRAP! The lower middle class, having struggled to get where they are, believe anyone that talks proper.

CRAP! The lower middles love abroad, but only those locations that allow them to carry on consuming all things British.

CRAP! The working classes continually bleat about their lot, but allow politicians to destroy their unions and manipulate them mercilessly.

CRAP! The working classes always claim to love their children. Who else can they bully?

CRAP! The working class always make the loudest noises about the state of the country, but wait for others to do something about it.

..AND HERE'S ONE FOR THE TORIES

CRAP! The underclass are fabulously harmless, as they have absolutely no power – or even voice, to complain about their tragic state.

CRAP! Everyone hates the nouveau riche, unless they join them.

CRAP! The nouveau riche never buy anything unless it can be seen.

BEAUTY IS IN THE EYE OF THE BEHOLDER CRAP!

❝ Most women are not as young as they're painted... ❞
Max Beerbohm

It's amazing just how much the advertising and magazine industries hit on women. In Britain the fairer sex are dragged out again and again to sell everything from diamonds to deodorants, lawnmowers to lav cleaners. In fact, in a recent survey, London came top of the world polls for using the image of woman to sell on billboards, hoardings and subways (it's nice to be top at something).

But why women? Why isolate them? Simple! In the clichéd, stereotyped (and frequently phoney) language of advertisements, they are connected with secure comforting domestic happiness (where did I go wrong?), images of glamour and, most of all, sexuality. Women from sex goddesses to secretaries or prime ministers to post-persons are interchangeable with these concepts, becoming a currency to be exchanged like money. Just as the images of women are bartered by advertisers, these images could be said to relegate them to just another product on the market like floor cleaners or custard powder.

When you need something to boost your campaign, Fall back on women – again and again.

But not only are images of women used to sell things, they are the main targets of the ad campaigns too. 80% of all shoppers are, in fact, female. Why? Because most men are bone idle. So advertisers tear their hair out trying to think of new ways to trap and exploit what they pretentiously label the 'female identity,' which is that of the ideal wife, mother and homemaker.

❛Advertising is the art of making whole lies out of half truths...❜
Edgar A Shoaff

But there are several more ways of skinning a cat. The other main method is to ease the cash away from those poor deprived souls that haven't pulled in their own hunky, caring, home on time, fabulous in bed, helpful in the kitchen - knight in shining armour. The main idea, therefore, behind a lot of advertising is that fulfilment comes man-shaped, and is that end-of-the-rainbow, pot of gold that all on-the-shelf damsels have been yearning for. To score that winning goal women must live up to all the images of perfection that are constantly being shoved at them. The very magazines that set themselves up to speak for women are the most guilty of making their readers continually aware of how far they fall short of perfection. There is a whole industry churning out production lines choc-full of products designed specifically to cash in on every spare inch of the female body (yes there too!), and articles telling women over and over again where they've been going wrong with the rest of their lives.

The main group targeted are adolescent girls through to young women in their mid-twenties, stopping apparently, just short of the thirty year olds (when, one can only suppose, women come to their senses and recognise rubbish when they see it). How do you fancy being constantly told that your chest's too small or too big, too droopy or too firm, your hair too thick or too fine, your body too thin or too fat, your legs too short or too hairy? The result can only be to make the reader continually screwed up as to whether they're wearing the right clothes over the right body and whether that body smells okay and is covered by the right make-up. By continually changing the goal posts every month these 'women that know' - the journalists - find easily enough garbage to fill any amount of magazines ten times over. It's all crap! But do women really believe all the stuff they dictate about their bodies? Does Dolly Parton sleep on her back?

' *Journalists write because they have nothing to say, and have something to say because they write…* **'**   *Karl Kraus*

But who are these flawless people who women are persuaded and cajoled into aspiring to. It certainly isn't the journalists themselves, they usually look like funeral parlour salespersons (black, black and more black). It must therefore be those scrumptious, untouched-by-human-hand models that beckon from the glossy pages. I'm afraid if you ever have the good fortune to meet one of these perfect beings on her day off, you'll be struck by just how imperfect (and dim) they really are in real sometimes spotty - sometimes blotchy - make-up free - often exhausted - life.

Just because we look so pretty, don't go thinking we can't look shitty.

But everyone on the profit side of the beauty biz is onto a winner. Survey after obvious survey has told them that amongst girls (and some boys), looking good to attract the opposite sex overtakes everything else, especially at school. So much so, that a recent study showed that if the careers fairy were to wave her magic wand and grant three wishes, most young girls would ask to be either a hairdresser, a beautician or a model, all of which require so few qualifications that total brain amputation would be very little hindrance (and often an asset). Unfortunately, so many girls want and have wanted to be hairdressers (before settling down to a hubby and baby production) that supply has overtaken demand making it, for decades, the worst paid career around.

If you want a wage that's fair, don't have nuffink to do with hair.

This is the sort of thing you're up against. These are sample headlines from one issue of one fairly typical magazine.

☞ How to look like Barbara Cartland at 94. (*Live twenty years too long?*)

☞ I'm so fat, but I look so good.

☞ Underwear. From The Sublime   to the Ridiculous.

☞ Fakes progress. Ten simple ways to achieve an all over tan. (*Set fire to yourself?*)

☞ Miracle jeans that uplift the sagging jeans market.

☞ Six ways to keep cool. (*Die six times?*)

☞ Five reasons to love the summer.

☞ Wake up the youth of your skin.

Most amusing of all are all those magic ingredients that our frail bodies apparently can't live without. Here's a sample taken from current magazines.

☞ *Freeman Botanical shampoos and conditioners*: not tested on animals. Simply bursting with fruits and flowers, nuts and berries, gathered from around the world *(Christ, it sounds like you could feed your animals on 'em)*.

☞ *Boots Life Source Range*: You can experience the forces of nature at work in your bathroom (especially after an Indian take-away) when you use Boots Life Source range. Named after the Elements – Earth (pink) *(pink earth?)*, Sun (orange) and Water (blue).

☞ *Botanics*: Science + nature = botanics *(who says?)*. Clean away Rinse-off mousse with active Natural Extracts, Hypo-allergenic. Containing extracts of cornflower and honeysuckle.

☞ *Thalassobath*: £16.50 for four bath sachets. One of the Thalgo range (sea based). Contains an algae obtained from cold-water plants in the North Atlantic. *(Is that why cod have such good skin?)*

☞ *Ponds Fresh Start Daily Wash*: With AHA *(see totally obscure terms)* and Gentle Micro Beads.

☞ *Palmer's Aloe Vera Formula*: Our laboratories have developed the solution for the summer skin by blending the natural healing properties of Aloe Vera (sounds like a Coronation Street greeting) with Vitamin E and rich emollients.

☞ *Tesco's Moisture Mist Skincare*: Containing Ormagel – extract of seaweed. Ormagel was first discovered a few years ago after studies were carried out amongst Brazilian seaweed pickers *(why?)*, who were found to have remarkably smooth, moist, lustrous hands and arms *(Perfect! There must be thousands of you out there trying to look like Brazilian seaweed pickers)*.

☞ *Lancaster Skin Therapy Vital Oxygen Supply*: £39. New powerful moisturiser. Pure oxygen molecules – A.O.C.S.

Asymmetric Oxygen Carrier System – patent pending *(blimey, that sounds scientific)* and natural extracts infuse the fragile skin around your eyes with intensive moisture *(that's much wetter than normal wet)*.

☞ *Clarins of Paris (mmm - French! Must be good!) Gel Multi-Actif Anti-Capiton Super Raffermissant Formule Suractiveé Body Shaping Gel - Ultra firming*: In other words, to continue in French mode, merde de taureau.

☞ *L'OREAL Plenitude Clarify - A3*: radiance revealing cleansing milk with triple AHA *(aha! AHA again)* Fruit Acids. Dermatologically tested.

One is tempted to ask whether this could conceivably be pure, fresh as a mountain stream, vitamin fortified, bollocks. I'm sure the most complex scientific breakdown would reveal that one shampoo (basically mild soap) is much the same as another, and the only way to improve these and all the creams gels and God knows what else that we plaster our perfectly adequate skins with, would be to leave out all the cheap scents and bogus additives. Anyway, if we are to believe this clap-trap, providing we start early enough, the normal progression of from baby, to child, to teenager, to grown up, to old can be stopped whenever we choose. I think somewhere around twenty four's about right. That's a boat I unfortunately missed years ago.

Beauty gets Serious
And what about all the companies dedicated to changing what that great plastic surgeon in the sky originally supplied? This is far more interesting and often more sinister.

*However good you think
your body,
we'll convince you that it's
rather shoddy.*

If you'd have been a model in Ruben's time nobody would have given you another glance if you didn't have a huge bum and tiny boobs. If you'd been a woman in the nineteen twenties or even the early seventies, any surplus flesh would have been seen as uncool and very unsexy. The Victorians, who liked a bit of both (though never admitted a bloody thing), preferred their women huge at the top and even huger at the bottom, torturing them, by forcing their waists into tiny corsets. Since time began, the shape of women has changed even more than male attitudes towards them.

Some would have it that this paranoia with shape is, and was, caused by the whim of man. But it could be said (and I'm walking a shaky plank here) that if this were true it must take a pretty stupid species, firstly to care a jot, and secondly to try and do anything about it. Imagine a male zebra turning down a female zebra because he'd gone off stripes, or an elephant who suddenly preferred little noses.

Hurrah for Bras

We're a long way from the sixties, when women were invited to burn their bras as a way of telling men where to shove their stereotypes. Nowadays the image of women as sex objects has never been stronger, but at last it is them that are calling the shots, and using their femininity as a power-base instead of the very reverse. Just look at all the sexy underwear and body contouring ads in just about every paper and magazine. Indeed the latest *Wonderbra* poster campaign featuring the spectacularly endowed, blond haired, moist-eyed (due to the garment in question being a little on the tight side) – you know, that one responsible for a measurable increase in urban road accident figures (male) – could be seen to set back their campaign twenty years. One could ask why most men get excited about the size and shape of the two swellings that every woman in history has grown on her chest, or the article of clothing that holds hold them in place – but that's another book. The *Wonderbra* campaign, far from being lampooned by women on the grounds of exploitation, has been an enormous 38DD success, probably because at long last they are enjoying the new experience of having the choice to be what *they* want to be, when they want to be it. Yes, women can be sex objects, so can men (even David Mellor), blow up dolls and bonny sheep come to that.

Principle: We thought our movement would go far, ever since we burned the bra.

What do Men Like?

I believe the answer to this rather pointless debate lies somewhere in the centre. Women, despite all those previous arguments, do try to second guess what men really find most attractive and then attempt to push, pull and cajole themselves towards that image. And this again is where those women's magazines come in. Article upon article is served up by the aforementioned gurus, either attempting to tell their too short, too tall, too fat, too thin, too spotty, too pale sisters, what they should do to put themselves right, and almost as many telling them that it really doesn't matter anyway. Dodgy 'doctors' in even dodgier 'clinics' who, having sold out to blood (or silicone) money, now devote their lives to reducing cellulite, removing wrinkles or pumping up boobs, feel the need to pass on their expertise. Advertisers claim, between them, to be able to transform anyone into anyone else they feel like, with products that have been tried and tested from Tulse Hill to Timbuktu (but that no-one's ever heard of).

If you want your life to be fab, give us your money and we'll fight your flab.

Here are some of the thrilling things that can be purchased to improve our slightly less than perfect bodies:

☞ **'The Cartilade Success Story'** which claims to be 'three hundred years old but still a secret'. Here's the rest of the copy. 'Sharks have no bones but a skeleton composed almost entirely of cartilage. It's this cartilage that's attracting interest in the US health market. Cartilage Technology Inc. is now importing Cartilade, 100% pure shark cartilage, directly into the UK. Try some today. US Cartilade Shark cartilage is obtained only from sharks that have been harvested for food.' *(Which must make the poor bastards feel a lot better.)*

☞ **The Clay Company** 'has a home body wrap treatment with pre-treated cotton strips that are moistened and secured with cling film (supplied). For intensive cellulite treatment, you can combine this with their Anti Cellulite mask and detoxifying Body Scrub. Cost only £22.95p'.

☞ **Fluvoxamine**: 'A wonder drug developed by psychiatrists in the States to treat compulsive disorders like excess shopping *(true!)*. £72 for one month's supply'. *(That's a lot of shopping, folks! Perhaps this wonder drug induces amnesia so that you can't find your bloody credit card.)*

☞ **Niplette**: (For the permanent correction of flat or inverted nipples). 'Through gentle suction the Niplette pulls your nipple into a small, plastic, thimble-like cup. In a matter of weeks of continuous wear your nipple will stay permanently erect.' *(Hmm! I wonder if it works anywhere else?)*

☞ **Forcythe Cuticle Therapy Gel:** 'Get into the daily habit of softening cuticles to stop them cracking' *(just think, people are starving in Africa).*

☞ **The Vinegar Book:** '308 uses of vinegar including: – protecting and beautifying *(and pickling)* your skin – stopping hiccups – banishing dandruff – fading age spots – calming nausea – fading headaches – shining car chrome – dissolving chewing gum and repair wood scratches'. *(And is rather good on your chips.)*

☞ **Ginkyo:** It's good sense. A natural source extract backed by £3m research *(oh yeah!)*. Recent research indicates (notice *indicates*) that Ginkyo tablets could *(notice could)* help maintain peripheral circulation and in particular the blood flow to the brain. Ginkyo Concentrated is one of the strongest Ginkgo biloba supplements available *(well three cheers for that)*. The cost of a four week course is little more *(notice little more)* than you would spend on a month of body conditioning or yoga *(any amount is a little more than I spend!)*.

☞ **The Poultney Clinic:** 'Britain's leading hospital dedicated exclusively to cosmetic surgery.' *Specialities:*

• *Refining the shape of the nose*: 'Each nose is different *(really?)* and the experienced surgeon achieves a harmonious balance with all facial features'.

AT LEAST IT MATCHES YOUR EARS MR SMYTHE

• *The Classical facelift*: 'Restores a firm jaw line, smoothes the cheeks and revives a pleasing youthful appearance' *(even if you didn't have one before?)*.

• *Liposuction*: 'Stubborn areas of fat that refuse to respond to diet or exercise' *(but respond brilliantly to money)*.

• Also: eyebag and eyelid improvement – chin tucks – neck lifts – lip improvement– breast enlargements (*try one first and see how you like it*) – uplifts and reductions – wrinkle improvement (*who wants better wrinkles?*) – 'bat ear' correction – receding chin correction – cheek implants *(where?)* – 'tummy tucks' – mole and tattoo removal (***I love cosmetic surgeons***) – male baldness.

Consultations are held only with highly-experienced, caring (*and bloody pricey*) surgeons.

...BUT
All the stuff advertised above is just one tiny part of a huge industry. Actually I don't have that many problems with it; if saddos want to spend their money on patching up a machine (their body) which will eventually wear out and end up on the scrap heap anyway, who am I to ridicule them. If women want to look like a replica of Joan Collins (who, poor dear, will one day turn, Dorian Grey-like, into a wrinkled old soul like everyone else) so be it.

❛ *Beauty is truth, truth beauty...* ❜ *Keats*

❛ *Bullshit is bullshit ...* ❜ *Farman*

What bugs me is that in 1996, with the most advanced technology available, kids can literally die being ferried from pillar to post in an ambulance because there isn't a hospital to take them, or old people are made to wait for ages because they haven't the cash to pay for surgery that might make their lives a little less painful. All because the government of the day refuse to put the right amount of hard cash into OUR heritage – the National Health Service. It's all going the same way as

SORRY, BUT YOU'VE NOTHING LEFT IN YOUR ACCOUNT

America. If you've got the money to pay, then you can have what you want or need when you want or need it. If you haven't, – then tough!

Having said all that you might be interested in a little product I've developed.

☞ **Bayboil from The Farman Laboratories:** distilled from the tearducts of the Patagonian tree skunk, this brilliant balm, which is supplemented with essential squeezings from the Hindustan bogwort and fortified with B75/793/249, will transform the ugliest woman into a Baywatch babe after 23,000 applications. Money back if not completely satisfied (*and if you can find us*).

Send £753.50 for a sample one-application pack.

The Great Diet Debate

❛ *A dieter is one who wishes that others wouldn't laugh at his or her expanse...* ❜
Al Bernstein

Whether they do or not, 59% of women believe that they weigh too much, compared to 63% of men who think they don't. A recent Gallup poll showed that most women believe that men fancy thin women, whereas only 18% of the men agreed.

This, as you might realise, is manna from heaven to all those dedicated to making money out of women's paranoia. If all the dietary preparations, pills, books, magazine articles and exercise equipment were put on one side of the scales and all the fat they were trying to remove were put on the other, there's no doubt where my bet would be as to the heaviest. Here are a few of the myths about dieting:

☞ The American Cancer Society discovered that users of artificial sweeteners are more likely to gain weight than non-users.

☞ Those who don't drink milk are three times more likely to develop cancer than those who drink a couple of glasses a day.

☞ The poor are more likely to be fat than the rich. As the Duchess of Windsor used to say 'you can never be too rich or too thin.'

☞ Women who consume alchohol 7-13 times a week consistently lose more weight than those who cut it out.

This is brilliant. Just as the food industry returns higher and higher profits, constantly inventing new-fangled foods guaranteed to make us fatter; a new little sister industry grows alongside selling stuff guaranteed to take that extra weight that we've just put on ... off. The master touch is that it seldom dawns on your average Sainsbury's trawler that many of these make-you-fat foods and slimming preparations come from the same manufacturers.

We'll make 'em fat, we'll make 'em thin – either way we're bound to win.

Actually, who gives a damn? If we want to fall prey to all those wolves tugging for a share of our surplus fat, so be it. More fool them. If they want to be robbed blind by snazzy suburban fitness centres (that con you into parting with a grand a year to struggle into a pink leotard and step up and down for half an hour a week), then so be it. If they want their fat sucked out through their very skin or to be pummelled and pushed at poncey rip-off health farms, then let them.

But I can save you all that trouble. I will bet anyone any money you like that my two word remedy for overweight will work on most people. It's cheap to do, it requires no special equipment (or poncey leotards), it will make you feel on top of the world and you don't have to go out of the house to do it. Send £5,000 and a stamped addressed envelope to **The John Farman Weight Loss Clinic Inc.**

Just in case you didn't guess,
the answer's simple –
JUST EAT LESS!

Or as Harry Secombe put it:

' *My advice if you insist on slimming: Eat as much as you like – just don't swallow it.* '

CRAP CORNER
Just to sum up:

CRAP! Women are becoming a form of currency to be used and abused by advertisers.

CRAP! Women's magazines continually put women's appearance down and then build them up to justify their own existence.

CRAP! Most of the models that women are forced to aspire to, look almost as crappy as any one else when not in front of the camera.

CRAP! Advertisers love using quasi-scientific words to fool and fuel the public's insecurity.

CRAP! The actual shape of women's bodies is manipulated by fashion.

CRAP! Any one can have anything done to them on demand provided they can pay.

Very often the manufacturers who produce fattening foodstuffs also produce low calorie slimming foods.

BRITAIN IS A PACIFIST COUNTRY

6 Jaw jaw is better than war war... 9   *Harold Macmillan*

☞ Six times as much public money goes on weapons research as it does for research into health protection.

☞ The government spends nearly ten times more on promoting arms sales than it does on ordinary exports.

☞ In 1989 the government set aside £234 million from our total aid budget to go towards Malaysia's Pergau dam project. Very nice of us. And in return we got the £1.3 billion arms deal that was under negotiation.

☞ In 1985 Maggie Thatcher signed a stupendous 'arms for oil' deal with Saudi Arabia worth £2 billion a year. There were reports that allegations of 'kick backs' (bribes to you and I) were hushed up.

☞ In the same year, the Iron Lady signed a humungous arms deal with Jordan (£270 million) at a time when the government were well aware that Jordan was passing the arms on to Iraq who were notorious for the disgusting way they treated the Kurds.

☞ No other sector of UK industry is as successful in the international marketplace.

☞ British tank makers Vickers have negotiated orders worth $2.5 billion with five Middle Eastern states.

☞ Britain is the fourth largest supplier of arms to the developing countries.

☞ There is a huge bill, paid by us British taxpayers, for British weapons exported to countries which are either really rich or have appalling civil rights records.

☞ At least £384 million a year is paid by us, the British taxpayer, because the guys we sell 'em to don't pay up.

Is Arms Manufacturing a Necessary Evil?

In a country where there haven't been as many people living on the streets since the Second World War, it's interesting to note that we as a country could have saved ourselves a cool more than £12 billion a year in 1991 (last figures available) by simply reducing our spending on arms to the same level as all our European NATO brothers. I'm sorry, but it really looks as if we've been shuffling along in the shadow of big daddy America for it is there that the full effect of an economy dominated by military spending can be observed.

For years it was thought that making loads of weapons was rather good for a country's economic well-being. Relatively recently, however, your common Yank-in-the street has been getting restless, demanding more homes for the poor, rather than more parking places for more nuclear battleships. New York's Mayor Dinkins, while overlooking a city that makes London look like the Emerald City (at the end of the Yellow Brick Road), remarked that the price of just two B2 bombers could eliminate the whole of the city's astronomic 1991 deficit. Between 1947 and 1989 the US government spent more on the military than the value of all US industrial plants and equipment and all the country's civilian infrastructure combined. Blimey, you only have to look at the state of Russia these days to see how silly the whole thing can get. A fat lot of good it was having the largest army in the world, when you couldn't even get a can of Coke.

How strange to view the mighty bear, with not much to eat and nothing to wear.

We know now that a military-industrial complex is actually inefficient and damaging to the economy in which it operates. Firstly, arms manufacturers tend to care only about the end product and not about economical methods of manufacture or minimalising costs. This attitude of cost-maximising has a habit of creeping into all sorts of other methods of civilian production. Secondly, making guns, planes and bullets does damn-all good to a country's productive capacity, as there tend to be few useful by-products like roads, education or machine tools. Bringing this into our own backyard, this often means that, like America, British firms are often hard put to produce civilian goods as cheaply (or well) as their competitors in Japan or Western Europe.

With the terminal sickness of consumer manufacture, the Americans have had to borrow from abroad to pay for their foreign shopping. They now, poor dears, have the largest national debt in the world and, as they always say, what America does today – as sure as burgers is burgers – Britain will do tomorrow.

But we're veering away from the lucrative business of civilised countries making arms for uncivilised countries to kill themselves with.

Who Does What?

Before we get onto the big players, it's interesting to find out who the individuals that trade in arms on our behalf actually are. You may well ask. Trying to find their names and the companies they work for, is like trying to find who fired the first bullet in Bosnia or how much of Elton John's hair is actually real. In fact, it is well known that the whole nasty business is shrouded in thick clouds of secrecy and that's not only extremely difficult to penetrate, but even dangerous to try. Rumour has it that there are lists held in very high places of the names and addresses of anyone who even gets close.★

You might well find the going tough,
if you try to source who sells this stuff .

How Does It All Work?

Like all huge industries there is a network of operatives employed to satisfy the customer. In the arms business, these are the key players:

1. The Rep

First off there's the sales rep. Not some Essex lad with a Ford Orion and his suit jacket hanging in the back, but some ex-public school, ex-RAF type who cynically keeps a beady eye on where trouble is about to break out in the world in order to shift some gear. He spends his time flying hither and thither in first class, five star luxury, searching out potential customers. His job is to inform these customers as to what his merchandise can do and whether it's been 'blooded' (used in an actual war) or not. The recent Gulf War was fab for this, as it meant that a whole lot of new toys could be tested on real soldiers (even our own!). The rep makes a lot of money salary-wise, but not nearly as much as he can doing private deals with all those countries that his government have told him not to deal with.

2. The Fixer

A very nice job if you can get it (main qualification - total unprincipled bastard). He acts as go-between between the foreign buyers and the aforementioned rep and makes his ill-gotten gains by creaming off a percentage on any deal he sets up. Needless to say, with the sums involved, it doesn't have to be that high for him to make a huge

★ Make sure no-one is watching you read this book.

killing. Everyone involved in the deal despises the fixer but, just like a prostitute's pimp, he's a necessary part of the transaction.

3. The Skimmer
The skimmer doesn't actually have to do anything to earn his chunk of the action. He is someone who usually works high up in some tin-pot, Mickey Mouse 'defence' ministry, and has the ability to promote or stop a deal going through if he so desires. He will base his 'reward' on what the fixer gets.

4. The Runner
The runner gets the goods in and out of countries. His main expertise is in the business of 'sanction busting' (flogging things to governments his country's not supposed to deal with). He knows people in embassies who are prepared to sell false 'end-user' certificates, which make it look as if the arms aren't going where they are going. The real destinations could be places such as Iraq or South Africa, terrorist organisations or, bless'em, all those nice drug barons in South America who run fully-equipped private armies.

And the Government?
In a way nobody should be that surprised that big business is involved with armaments. After all, money is the root of all evil. But what about the people we have elected to act on our behalfs? Surely they must be above all this. Oh, that it were true. Throughout the years after the Second World War there have been a trail of veiled scandals that simply prove that the boys from Whitehall, and indeed the governments of most other western countries, are in it up to their greasy necks.

Don't go thinking we're above it all, but if questions get asked, we're bound to stall.

Arms to Iraq
You need look for no better example than the Gulf War. That charming Saddam Hussein, the self-styled dictator,

who'd been murdering his own people for years (and terrorising anyone and everyone else) suddenly turned on little neighbour Kuwait. It goes without saying that the fact that Kuwait supplied a large amount of the west's oil had nothing to do with the 'we-must-be-guardians-of-oppressed-little-nations' that America trots out every time she feels threatened. It all became rather daft when the big question emerged. Where did that Hussein get all the sophisticated armaments that he was about to fight with?

Plane Sale-ing

In 1975 Iraq was becoming a bit pissed off because the weapons supplied by Russia were looking a bit old-fashioned. Although a considerable improvement on crossbows and Tommy guns, anyone who's ever seen a Russian car or tried to listen to Russian pop music will understand why. At this time the British and the French were making a snazzy jet fighter that was better than any other in the world. A certain Mr Said K Aburish, an arms dealer living in London, became rather interested when he realised that the Iraqis were after buying 60 planes (worth a cool $400 million) and that he could pull a six percent commission for him and his Iraqi mates if he could deliver. He rang the company that made the plane and spoke to John Hannay the director of the military aircraft division who perked up considerably when he realised how much loot was floating around. He assured Mr Aburish that he'd meet with the Foreign Office and see how they felt about supplying the beastly Iraqis with weapons. To nobody's real surprise, the reply came back that the British government would 'view with favour' the supply of arms to Iraq. Moral dilemma – forget it. Easy peasy.

Then the Iraqis demanded an uninterrupted supply of spare parts 'under all conditions' which put our poor government into a bit of a quandary. Surely this meant that they could get into a situation where we could be sending spare parts to repair planes to attack us back with? Typical of our representatives, they painfully straddled the fence and said that they would 'endeavour' to guarantee such a deal. This wasn't good enough, however, and the Iraqi delegation jumped on their magic carpets and hi-tailed it back home. Either you guarantee the things or you don't, they cried. Then they went to the French, who everyone knew would sell their almost-as-good Mirage-F1 fighters to shoot their own grand-mères with. Those tricksy French, however, in typical Gallic style, hitched up the price on each plane by $4 million. The Iraqis, not used to being cheated themselves, began to look wistfully back towards the Russians. Their planes might be crap, but at least they were cheap crap. The French foreign minister, Jacques Chirac, stepped in, realising his lads had been caught with their pantalons well and truly down, and promptly dropped the price back to what anyone else could buy them for (he also bagged the commission for the French). A little later France had the embarrassment of having to send 4000 extra troops to Saudi Arabia, when their precious 'client' Saddam Hussein sacked their embassy in Kuwait.

If you deal with dogs,
you're bound to catch fleas.

In a nutshell, this illustrates how the whole sorry business works. Countries falling over each other to sell arms to whoever wants them, and for whatever they are wanted for. Net result? Saddam Hussein bought over $31 billion worth of weapons from several countries, including all the five permanent members of the United Nations Security Council (including us).

Gun? What Gun?

The British government ended up with a jolly red face in April 1990 when eight huge bits of tube labelled 'petroleum piping, bound for Iraq' were stopped by British customs.

Remarkably, when all these tubes were joined together they looked rather like a gun, a 'Supergun', in fact, capable of launching rockets and huge three-foot wide nuclear 'bullets' at Israel. The makers, Sheffield Forgemasters, pointed out that they had full permission from the government to send them. The government, in typical fashion, refused to release the information that could have proved this, for fear of showing their hand in the matter.

A Nice Day Out

I'll tell you what. How about taking the family to the Birmingham Exhibition Centre. Not to *Cruft's Dog Show* or *The International Gift Fair*, but to *The Defence Components and Equipment Exhibition*. Unfortunately, you won't actually be able to buy any actual planes, battleships, guns or bullets, but it's just the place for all those components that go to make them up, a sort of weapons-fair for khaki-anoraked kit assemblers. GEC Aerospace, for instance, offer 'intelligent power control and generation systems' and 'remote thermal control' all designed to kill and maim people far away where you don't even have to witness the aftermath. Brilliant! Everything at the exhibition is so new, and clean, and clever, and bright, and shiny that it seems rather indecent to mention those careless and perverse foreigners who seem to go in for collecting up the limbs of their dismembered wives and children, just so's they can get on telly.

Just like the way we like to buy our meat, these exhibitors prefer to contemplate the results of their endeavours in the form of super-clever technology rather than their flesh-ripping, clothes-burning, building-trashing capabilities. Bastards, I call them.

All's Fair in Love and War

Serge Dassault is a powerful industrialist and head of one of France's top aircraft companies. He has always had an excellent relationship with the British, but when the Falklands war kicked off he happily supplied the Argentineans with Exocet missiles to fire at us. When asked if he saw anything vaguely hypocritical in this course of action, he replied pleasantly, "The British are friends. The Argentineans are customers. I have the highest regard for both of them."

CRAP CORNER

So what's so terrible about trading in weapons? If we didn't do it, everybody else would. Anyway, isn't it nice to make money out of something we're good at? These are the double standards as I see them.

CRAP! The government always seem to put the discussion of arms sales at the back of every agenda.

CRAP! They like to think, and be seen to think of themselves as peace-lovers, but are prepared to make hard cash out of other people's disputes.

CRAP! The government are very good at publicising aid to third world developing countries, but seldom remember to mention that they are also flogging them arms.

CRAP! The government is inextricably linked with the shady businessmen who sell weapons of destruction.

CRAP! Countries only fly to the aid of other countries if there's a chance that the conflict could backfire on *them*, either strategically or financially.

CRAP! Weapons salesmen only talk cause, never effect.

POSTSCRIPT

Junk food and too much telly are making a major contribution towards pacifism. A report in May 1996 stated that the armed forces, who need to recruit 15,000 young people every year, were finding it difficult to find any one fit enough to begin the arduous training. Tee-hee!

ONLY NICE PEOPLE GET MARRIED

❝ The wedding cake is the only cake that once eaten can give you indigestion for the rest of your life...❞   *Anon*

Ever since we were children, we have been led to believe that a worthwhile member of society is one who should strive for a good secure career, a decent standard of living, a fairly new car, a fitted kitchen and marriage to a suitable person (preferably of the opposite sex). In most societies marriage symbolises society's rubber-stamp of respectability and also a sort of emotional handing over of children from parents to the future spouse. The last twenty or so years, however, has seen a 24% decline in marriages, and the duration of those that do happen is getting shorter and shorter. This, of course, begs the questions (a) whether the whole shebang is on the way out, and (b) whether the membership of the hallowed institution is worth the paper it's printed on.

It seems to be beyond reasonable doubt,
That conventional marriage is on the way out.

Here are a few more statistics:

☞ Only 29% of girls are still virgins at 16, but their average age for marriage is 26 years.

☞ At this point in history, just over half of marriages break down before death doth them part or, put another way, double the number of married people split up in 1992 (the last time anyone counted) compared to 1971.

☞ The offspring of divorced people are 50% more likely to divorce than others.

☞ Britain has the highest divorce rate in Europe (it's good to be top at something).

☞ An almost unbelievable 60% of all married men are apparently having a sexual affair with someone who isn't their wife (from Mary Westmead's book *The Trouble With You*.) I heard this statistic when listening to *Woman's Hour* on Radio 4. When I questioned the producer on its accuracy, she said that it was in the book and that they therefore didn't question its accuracy. Well that's fine then.

☞ The highest percentage of these blackguards come from the professional or should-know-better classes.

Couldn't Be Better

Every Saturday, churches and registry offices groan with bushy-tailed youngsters who commit themselves to each other for life in front of their nearest and dearest.

Mothers weep, guests go "ooh!" and "aah!" and gaggles of old ladies (wedding groupies) swoon at the church gate at these visions of happiness. Fortunes are spent on receptions, presents and honeymoons (what a stupid word) to the point that the whole thing has become a humungous rack... business. Richard Branson, for instance, who seems literally to trip over ways of making money, has started an offshoot company with the intriguing title *Virgin Brides*, which handles and supplies everything to do with your wedding day and night, presumably from the pre-nuptial carnations to the post-nuptial condoms (*Mates* of course).

Marriage or Not?

Like it or not, marriage is still the usual way for people of opposite sexes to rationalise living together. Not only that, but youngsters are actually getting married earlier than ever. But certain aspects of marriage have come under the spotlight. The first is that marriage lasts for life, the second is that it gives a woman a secure, settled income and status and the third that marriage is the setting for all child-bearing and sexual co-habitation. If all the wedding presents that I've given, had been returned on the happy couple's divorce, I could probably open a department store (albeit a very naff one).

Baby Alarm

But what happens to mothers who have to bring their kids up alone?

The now rather shagged-out stork is delivering more nippers to unmarried mothers than at any time in history: 4% of all births in 1900 and 28% in 1990. The number of one-parent families has, therefore, nearly doubled in twenty years and it has to be said that the lion's share is headed by women who are more than likely to be working class. Up to quite recently the man has walked away Scot-free (who's Scot?) as society's efforts to force them to support their children failed, but the recently set up *Child Support Agency* has been doing its best to redress the balance, by hunting down errant fathers and at least trying to force them to dip into their pockets (no father is ever required to pay more than 30% of his net income). It won't surprise you to know that a high proportion of these women who are not supported by the 'impregnator' (sounds like a Schwarzenegger movie) live on or near the poverty line due to a bizarre, if not cruel (and horridly hypocritical), government policy that means that if you do find some work (even if it's not necessarily permanent) or are given the *occasional* handout from the daddy, it's not worth declaring it because those heartless penpushers will dock your benefit. Fair enough, you might say. But if you are unskilled, the money you receive by working is often less or hardly more than the benefit, which makes one ask the inevitable question – why work at all?

Baby Blackmail

If that isn't bad enough, our all-caring government, who seem to believe that children should be seen and not had (unless middle class), have what appears to be a sleazy pact with the gutter press to hound and ridicule these poor girls by claiming that they get themselves pregnant merely to pick up benefit or get housed. C'mon! This is about as daft as someone sending themselves to prison because they're into free food and lodging, or an animal putting its foot in a trap to make some hunter's day.

Some cash and a flat, that's as maybe,
But it isn't a reason for having a baby.

And What Does God Think?

Religion is a conceited effort to deny the most obvious realities...

H. L. Mencken

The whole subject of sex, marriage and faithfulness-within-marriage is a minefield which only the most well-adjusted can traverse safely. The Church, God bless it, with its pale, boney finger continually searching for the pulse where contemporary life is concerned, is continually blowing itself up. It frowns on sex before marriage and co-habitation by hankering after that bygone age (which never really existed) when nice girls and nice boys dutifully pattered out of their nice parent's homes on their wedding morning. The poor dears practically swooning with anxious anticipation at the imminent prospect of a bit of real action, instead of all that nervous struggling on the sitting room sofa while Mum and Dad were out walking Rover. Although there are no figures to prove otherwise, it must be said that most couples, certainly in *my* parents' day, probably weren't virgins when they got married and that this fact was (and is) the best kept secret of all time. Another fine example of adult to offspring deception.

God Knows

It must be said at this point that many might think that the Church has a cheek giving its opinion about anything, let alone sex, when you consider that church attendances are the lowest in history. How would they like it if a couple of mates and I eased round the Archbishop of Canterbury's palace and told him how to run *his* business? And how come so many adults state their religion as Church of England and insist on a Christian marriage, when one in ten haven't been near a church since they were Christened (apart from going to someone else's wedding)? Come to that, should you be *allowed* to be one of the 70% who get married in church if you haven't even stuck your head round the door for years? Worse than that, the Church has absolutely little or no policy (since 1957) on marrying someone who has actually been married before, leaving the whole decision to God and the individual priest at the individual church. Things have certainly changed since poor old Princess Margaret tried to marry divorcé Captain Peter Townsend in 1955, when it was made perfectly clear that a Christian marriage was indissoluble (holy water?). Presumably God needs the business these days.★

One is tempted to put all this in the same bag labelled *Mindless Convention* that insists on parents having their nippers

---

★Isn't it surprising that when someone Royal is thwarted, the rules miraculously change almost immediately?

Christened (given guardians whose job it will be to oversee their spiritual upbringing until confirmation), having religion taught as a compulsory subject in school when most of us remember it being a joke or rest period, or pitching up, slightly inebriated, for Midnight Mass at Christmas (giving it the same significance as the fairy on the Christmas tree or the hapless turkey).

Doing It Right

British society, I'm sad to say, is founded on the bedrock of a need to be seen to do the right thing. They go along with marriages, Christenings and even religion-based funerals because, for as long as anyone can remember, it has been the way that respectable members of toytown do things. Even those who might be regarded as quite progressive and free thinking, seem to go gooey over flouncy dresses, three-tiered cakes, bridesmaids, confetti and soppy hats. Don't get me wrong. Weddings can be jolly nice, and a better than average way of spending a Saturday afternoon (unless you're into football, shopping or a short romp in the long grass).

A Helping Hand

To help this institution along, the government give away the Married Man's (notice 'man's') Tax Allowance, an underwhelming £1790 per year (per couple) off their tax. Actually they only get 15% of this, so ending up with the princely sum of £268.50, which is why lots of people don't even bother to claim it. It's worth noting that this amount is reducing every year so it could be said that even the powers-that-be no longer have any faith in marriage. This is strange for a party that is continually banging on about the merits of family values (albeit in a pathetic and sadly obvious effort to catch votes).

I rang my accountant the other day, to find out if there were any other advantages moneywise in getting hitched, but after an hour of pure financial gobbledegook, I hung up and had to lie down in a darkened room. To be fair there are a few other rather obscure tax benefits but (a) they are far too complicated for my half-baked brain and (b) they hardly amount to a cupful of beans when you look at the overall picture.

Pension Perils

Another area where the government could be seen to be shooting themselves in the foot relates to the new rules splitting a husband's pension with his wife on divorce.   This actually seems fine and dandy at first glance (and only fair) – until you realise the implications. Any woman with her eye on the main chance, could marry a well-pensioned guy, then run off with her lover and take half the retirement income for which the poor sod had worked his whole life. If you combine this with the other new law that refuses to consider blame when a separation occurs, then you realise what a rat's nest of problems are about to be created.

DON'T FORGET HIS POLICIES

But Why Should Anyone Want To Get Married?

Could this be the crux of the matter? When two people are really into each other (notice how I avoid the 'L' word) they need to make a promise that goes way beyond simply asserting that they think their opposite number is the best thing that ever happened to them. They (and this once included me) then seem to need to broadcast this commitment (that there will never be anyone else till death doth them part) to the whole world. This obsession with owning, being owned, and being seen to be such, still seems fundamental in quite a large proportion of mankind, womankind and apparently gaykind. I have no problem with this. It's a free(ish) country after all. But surely, with a near 50% divorce rate, you stand just as much chance of going the distance without committing yourself to a costly, time-consuming ceremony as with one.

> *Love and marriage*
> *go together like a horse and carriage.*

But What's the Alternative

Back in the forties when my parents got hitched, it was practically unheard of for couples to live together (unless they were arty or in show business). To have a child in that situation was even worse, not only for the parents, but for the child. That horrid word 'bastard' was a common taunt in the playground and often kids would be hounded into near breakdown. These days, thank God (or should I say 'no thanks to God'), nobody cares any more, and the middle classes often regard it as rather trendy, modern and 'in-your-face' to not only regard marriage as a rather primitive institution, but actually celebrate the lack of ceremony by having children outside its professed protection. Furthermore, anyone using the term 'bastard' in its true dictionary meaning is more likely to be persecuted himself, as such a huge proportion of kids these days have unmarried, separated or divorced parents. Usually the child of an unmarried liaison takes Dad's name, but recently, with the current vogue for poncey double-barrelled surnames, Mum and Dad sling theirs both together (metaphorically speaking).

It is important to remember, therefore, that the opposite to marriage isn't 'the one-parent family' as some would have us believe. Although statistics don't exist, many think that a relationship held together because those involved actually prefer it that way, is better than one held together by some daft vow made years ago and now recorded on a scrap of champagne-and-cake-stained paper.

But Beware! Marriage and the Law

It seems on the surface that it might well be a toss-up as to whether there's any point in getting married or not, but – as always – the law trails mournfully behind the path that society has chosen. Here are a few examples that could cause a load of grief:

1. Many people use the term 'common law marriage' to identify a relationship where two people co-habit outside wedlock, and believe that it offers the same protection as the term 'married'. It doesn't. It might surprise you to know that no such arrangement exists in law, and for that reason a couple have few legal rights whether they've been together for ten minutes or fifty years.

2. If two people share a house, for instance, but the property is only in one of their names, the house doesn't go by right to the remaining partner on death, but reverts to the next of kin of the deceased. They can then give it to their tortoise if they want. This also happens if two people share a council house or flat. The tenancy cannot be passed on as a matter of course, which means that if the partner whose name is on the contract decides to leave, the other one has to pack his or her bags as well.

3. On the breakdown of a marriage, a wife is entitled to support from her ex if she can't be independent. No such arrangement is available if the couple never got married.

4. Good news. Contracts can be drawn up to handle the distribution of property should such a situation arise. Bad news, the law, in its wisdom, refuses to recognize such contracts.

Why Not?

Surprisingly, taking everything into account, I still have no problem with people getting wed if they want to. But, if truth be told, I do find the whole churchy side of marriage primitive and hypocritical. It seems that, by doing it 'Under God's Roof', there is an awful assumption that some kind of cosmic angel dust sprinkles from on-high to keep the loving (at that point) couple together for eternity. This is, quite honestly, as daft as believing in flying saucers or Mystic Meg's lottery predictions.

> ‘ *The Church exists for the sake of those outside it...* ’
> *Frederick Temple*

Just like the family car, a marriage (as we are told by those that know) must be taken out every now and again, inspected and

serviced regularly, if it's to run smoothly. I, sadly, have never had a car (or a marriage come to that) that didn't break down eventually – through neglect or, dare I say, failing parts.

I once met a couple who thought they were clever,
Because they managed to stay married for ever.

CRAP CORNER

This whole subject is buried under a pile of semi-truths and hypocrisies. Here are some of them.

CRAP! The wedding ceremony says 'till death do us part', but a lot of remarkably alive-looking people manage to receive a blessing in church for a second or even third time.

CRAP! Getting married earlier seems to indicate that you can get divorced and on to another spouse much sooner.

CRAP! Many people in Britain get married because they are frightened of what other people will think if they don't.

CRAP! Although the church decrees no sex before marriage, there's an awful lot of terribly tubby girls to be observed walking up the aisle.

CRAP! Weddings, just like funerals, are a huge financial racket.

CRAP! Despite what the older generation tell us, few were virgins when they got married. They just kept quiet in those days.

CRAP! Most young people who haven't been near a church since they were christened, wouldn't dream of being married anywhere else.

CRAP! The establishment still believes that young women get themselves pregnant to cash in on benefits.

CRAP! The government reduces financial incentives to get married every year.

CRAP! The law offers little or no protection to couples who have not got married.

CRAP! A contract drawn up to protect unmarried couples, should they split up, is not recognized by the law.

What do you think?

• Do you believe that marriage as an institution is on the way out?

• Do you reckon that, once married, a couple should stay together simply because of the children, even if they can't stand each other?

• Do you think that society or the Church has a right to tell people how to rule their lives?

If you have strong views on this, or anything else in this chapter, let me know (see back page).

SEX SHOULD NOT BE SEEN AND NOT BE HEARD

CRAP!

> **Whatever else can be said about sex, it cannot be called a dignified performance...**
>
> Helen Lawrenson

There is something about the word sex that causes mothers to clutch children to their bosoms, respectable adults to shuffle uncomfortably and puzzled little kids to ask awkward questions. Sex has been a constant since the first little frogs hopped out of the primeval soup, but for some reason, we humans are still embarrassed about it.

The showing of mature specimens doing what, let's face it, has always come naturally, remains a subject capable of raising the highest passions.

It's most odd. We can watch all kinds of animals and bugs screwing themselves silly (when not eating each other) any night of the week on 'let's-snoop-on-nature' telly, but I've never heard of anyone asking *their* permission (another case for Animal Rights?).

> **If S-E-X ever rears its ugly head, close your eyes before you see the rest of it...**
>
> Alan Ayckbourn

Sex on the Shelf

Forty years ago girlie magazines, as such, were almost unheard of. Admittedly, some of the more shady newsagents might have had a couple of copies of *Spick and Span* or *Blighty*, featuring wholesome looking women with airbrushed erogenous (making them androgenous) lower regions, tucked away under the counter; but times have changed. These days, practically every corner shop and petrol station from Lands End to John O'Groats has a top shelf groaning with mags that cater for all known sexual proclivities. Women with appendages the size of footballs, men with big moustaches sporting exceedingly uncomfortable underwear, disrobed and decidedly matronly looking suburban ladies (readers' wives) of all shapes and sizes, looking like they've just sauntered out of the local launderette – all available for our perusal. Some of the more explicit ones (apparently labelled American style) are reminiscent of gynaecologists' instruction manuals, while others show fat, middle-aged couples trussed up like oven-ready turkeys in rubber and metal – enough to make your eyes water just thinking about it.

We've found a way to hide our blubber,
dress from head to toe in rubber.

The most amazing aspect of this whole jolly business, however, is that no one ever seems to buy them. I mean, have you ever noticed a copy of *Rubberwear Weekly* or *Razzle* being sneakily slipped in a bag with *Exchange and Mart*, a packet of Rolos and ten Silk Cut? I haven't. Do you ever see them on someone's coffee table between *Hello!* and the *What's On Telly* mag? Me neither. Do you ever come across them in dustbins between the potato peelings and Coco Pops packets? Never. But surely, all these countless publications must have vast circulations (a) to justify the huge costs of printing and circulation and (b) to make soft-porn king Paul Raymond a multi-millionaire and practically owner of sleaze-centre Soho. So where, in the name of Mary Whitehouse, do all these blasted magazines go, and where are they now? The answer must be that, like single socks and biro tops, they don't go anywhere – they're just hidden from view. Throughout the length and breadth of the land must be secret caches of girlie mags, tucked away at the back of pant and sock drawers, under the stairs, mouldering in garden sheds or under that bedroom floor board that squeaks when you tread on it. And nobody who buys them ever admits their existence. Bizarre or what? A whole industry that relies on consumers that deny consuming.

What the eye doth not see, the heart doth not grieve.

Question: Why do people (mostly men) deny buying them? What's so wrong about publications that concentrate on what should be a totally natural function in our lives? *Answer*: Because society contrives to make us ashamed. In a country that has sex rammed down its throat (whoops!) at every opportunity, more and more people, even though they might be in stable, loving relationships still fantasise about something (or someone) different, just like the head chef of a posh French restaurant might sometimes drool over the idea of Chicken McNuggets. The joke is, most of the average man's fantasies are the same. To be honest, and with no disrespect, the girl kitted out in silly, impractical underwear in *Escort* or *Razzle* isn't the girl you marry or take to tea with Mummy. Nor is she the girl you set up home and have nippers with. She is your pretend mistress. More often than not, these models are just normal people, often married, often with proper day jobs, who simply cash in on having a good bod. But try telling all this to your local vicar or the leader of the Penge Townswomen's Guild.

The arguments *for* soft pornography are fairly simple to understand. Some sociologists and shrinks believe that the incidence of rape and sexual deviation would be far greater if these magazines were not freely available. The arguments against are, for me, far more difficult to comprehend.

Boys' Toys?

But, to be fair, arguments *for* are primarily a man's view (and I'm primarily a man). Women generally see the whole thing somewhat differently. Some believe that the girls who pose for these pictures are merely being used as sex objects, and that they let down the whole cause of women in their quest to be taken seriously as equals.

A quote from the Leeds Women's Liberation Newsletter: "We are protesting and fighting back against images portraying women as sexual conveniences for men to abuse, hurt and degrade. Pornography in films, magazines and sex shops incites men to treat women as instruments solely for their use. Porn is a big money-making business, based on the suffering of women."

In America there are whole covens of anti-pornists who are linked with the much more frightening rightwing extremists and dreaded Christian Fundamentalists. They're the sort of people who have had Jane Fonda's workout videos removed from sale, because there is too much heavy breathing, revealing exerciser clothes, too far apart legs and stares that can only mean one thing.

Ordinary women often react equally strongly, believing that if their other half needs to buy these mags, it means that they are, in some way, not coming up to scratch, particularly in the bed department. Many also believe that, instead of bringing their fantasies to the bedroom (where they should be), men find it easier just to open a girlie mag (making sure no one's around first).

My theory, for what it's worth, is that if more men did talk openly about these magazines, and therefore their fantasies, with their partners (as many are beginning to do) instead of bedding their secretaries or worse, (a) their sex life might get much better, (b) the mags might get a lot better, and (c) there'd be less incidents of twerps like David Mellor or H-H-Hugh G-G-Grant feeling the need to get their jollies elsewhere.

*A bird in the hand
can be had on demand.*

The powers that be, bless 'em, have taken it upon themselves to make the owning of material featuring human love-making legal, but the selling of such material in a public place, not. Okay, so if you can't buy porno films from shops, how does anyone come to own them? The answer is that they can be, and are, obtained through mail order ads in the dirty mags and even some newspapers. The only problem with this is that the sending of pornographic material through our postal service is illegal. Ummm!

Do Unto Others as You Would Have Done to You

Everything we've described so far has been, how can I put it, relatively straightforward. Sex between man and woman, woman and woman or man and man, though still 'not quite nice' as a topic for dinner table talk is not nearly as 'not quite nice' as the subject of sado-masochism or bondage.

*Talk sex over meals if you really must,
as long as the chicken's the only thing trussed.*

In December 1990 fifteen men stood in the dock accused of gross immorality. They came from all walks of life from an ice cream salesman, to lay preacher, to pig breeder, but belonged to a much larger ring of 'friends'. Some home-made videos had been found that contained scenes of such a bloody nature, that the jury practically fainted on viewing them. A restaurateur (Happy Eater?) for instance, was observed doing eye-watering things to the private parts of an antique dealer while dangling from a home-made scaffold (the antique dealer not the restaurateur). Another involved a willing participant being lightly tortured to the strains of a Gregorian chant (how pleasant) while a missile engineer was observed to be enjoying his own 'missile' being honed down with sandpaper (ouch!). Yet another involved a fireman signing a lawyer's bottom with a *Stanley Knife* (I bet *Stanley* won't use that in their ads).

I could go on, but I'm feeling a little queasy. In each case, the 'doer' and the 'done to' were accused of the same crime; one as torturer and the other as the aider and abetter (or helper). The fact that everyone was a willing participant was ignored, even though the defence pointed out that a crime's only a crime if the one that something's being done to actually *minds*.

...And the Hypocrisy?

Needless to say the press were beside themselves with abject glee. This one had the lot: homosexuals, people in ordinary jobs, kinky violence, genitalia, you name it. Needless also to say, the police were beside themselves with equal glee. If there's one thing macho cops hate it's gays, and the idea of catching them red-handed (or better) in perverse sexual practices was beyond their wildest dreams. Their hypocrisy was plain for all to see for only two years earlier they'd broken up a series of wild but 'straight' bondage parties in a hotel in sleepy Cumbria and the participants had got off with small fines and large warnings. Most of the guys in the aforementioned ring received prison sentences ranging from two to five years.

Don't get me wrong. What these guys did defies belief. Happy Families it certainly ain't. But, if this is the free country we are always told it is (and nobody else gets hurt) then it means that authority has taken it upon itself to decide what we should or shouldn't do.

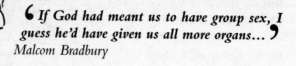

' If God had meant us to have group sex, I guess he'd have given us all more organs... '
Malcom Bradbury

The Hunt for What's Dirty

We live in a country which is supposed to have laws to protect us from those nasty men who make money out of something we all do (given half a chance). I decided to track down the actual words on paper which tell us what those-that-rule-over-us regard as obscene, and it turned out to be like finding the source of the Nile or the origin of a well-known joke.

I first rang the Law Society. Let's face it, I thought, if they don't know, nobody will. A rather snooty lady answered the phone and, obviously thinking I was some sort of pervert, swiftly recommended me to the Public Information Office of the House of Commons. They in turn suggested a load of weighty gazettes that would tell me of all the convictions in the last hundred or so years. Not having a hundred or so years to go through them, I tried my local Citizens Advice Bureau. The adviser was very helpful and somewhat intrigued and asked me to come to her office (I think she wanted to meet a real pornographer). She lent me a copy of *Butterworth's Police Law*. Now, I don't know who Butterworth was, but these are some of the rules that the cops work to.

☞ Under the Obscene Publications Act of 1959 an offence is committed by anyone who publishes an obscene article whether to make money or not; or possesses an obscene article for publication to make money. *(This means you can sit at home and write a stream of complete filth, but if you as much as give it to someone else to read you're breaking the law).*

☞ An article is deemed to be obscene if its effect is to corrupt or deprave anyone seeing it. *(This definition must be nonsensical because it's like saying 'how long is a piece of string?' What is likely to deprave and corrupt one person, might be all in a day's work for another.)*

☞ The decision as to whether something is deemed to deprave or corrupt, must be down to a jury.

☞ It is down to the police to decide what they will or will not send to the courts *(and what they keep to take down the pub).*

☞ Publishing means any attempt to distribute, circulate, sell, let or hire, give, lend or project in front of others. *(In other words, anything that involves the passing of something from one person to another.)*

☞ If it can be proved that the 'obscene' article is for the public good on the grounds of art, science or literature, or other matters of general concern, a person may not be convicted. *(It's interesting to note that huge framed photographs of the American artist Jeff Koons, literally doing 'IT' with his wife, in explicit detail, can be seen in exhibitions or in practically any art section of any bookshop.)*

The book went on and on describing in a hundred different ways how obscenity is anything that is indecent, offensive or likely to corrupt, but still didn't remotely say what these terrible things could be.

Brainwave!

I'll call the police themselves. They must know what they're looking for – it's their job. I started with my local police (always charming when you're on the other side of the counter) who put me onto Scotland Yard's Public Relations Office. They couldn't help me either, but gave me another number to try. It turned out to be the Paedophile Unit, and, having sworn I heard the click of a tape recorder, I quietly asked in a strong northern accent (I'm from the deep south), about the definition of obscenity and indecency (apparently they're now two different things). Having assured them that I wasn't just seeing how far I could go with gerbils, they gave me another number, saying that these chaps would definitely be able to help. When I finally asked who I was talking to, the gentleman on the other end said 'Bob'. Though it was nice to have a new chum, I pressed a little harder and found out I'd finally got hold of the Metropolitan Police's Obscene Publications Unit. Brilliant. It was like finding the Holy Grail (well almost). At last I was about to find the secret of filth from the very men who track it down. His answer, I'm not exaggerating to relate, was "Search me, guv, we only wish we had a few hard and fast rules to go by".

Conclusion

The bottom line seems to be that the whole business is a complete and utter cock-up (in every sense of the phrase). All we know is that in the circles that matter sex is still regarded as rude and something that should be kept metaphorically under the counter. As Mr Butterworth had said, it is down to the actual police officers themselves (and we all know how well-balanced they are) to decide what might be obscene and then send it to the courts for them to make a ruling. This would be okay and it should mean that a proper code could be written – but, and this is the stupidest BUT of all – what one court might decide is pure filth, another might find totally acceptable.

' *Obscenity is whatever happens to shock some elderly and ignorant magistrate* '   Bertrand Russell

In the Dark

Your poor local newsagent, therefore, can be prosecuted for selling obscene material (sale or return to the distributors), even though there is absolutely no guideline for him to follow (and it's probably against his religion anyway). Although it is generally accepted that sexy mags are put on the top shelf of shops, there is no requirement to do so, children of any age may buy them and the newsagent is perfectly at liberty to sell them to anyone he wants.

For instance, although you can see a woman's nipples in practically every newspaper, TV play, film or woman's magazine, you will never see them on the cover of a girlie mag in a shop (just you check!). One would assume that this

is because there is a law against it. There is none. It's just a funny little convention that's built up in the trade. Just as I'm writing this chapter, WH Smith, who wholesale magazines to 20,000 newsagents, have given their customers the right to refuse to accept all the rude 'top shelf' stuff.

What do you think?

1. Do you believe that anything that two consenting people can do to each other that doesn't involve violence, children, pets or librarians can really be rude or bad?

2. Do you think that watching people having sex on television should be banned?

3. Do you believe that people who have no access to sex, and suffer often unbearable levels of frustration, should be able to get relief from 'obscene' material?

4. Do you think women are exploited by girlie magazines and/or rude films?

CRAP CORNER.

Let's look at the main points again.

CRAP! Nobody ever admits to buying 'dirty' magazines but they do have a huge circulation.

CRAP! Although sex is shoved in our face at every opportunity, be it the newspapers, telly or advertising, it is presented in such a coy way that we often feel ashamed of our natural urges.

CRAP! In America the situation has got so bad that even exercise videos are regarded as soft porn – and this from the country that produces junk like *Baywatch* (or is it *Boobwatch?*).

CRAP! Sado-masochistic behaviour between people of opposite sexes is rewarded by a slap on the wrist by the courts, but if it has a homosexual slant, they throw the book at you.

CRAP! Everyone's opinion of what is or isn't obscene is as valid as everyone else's. This could well be because the actual details are not written down anywhere.

CRAP! Obscene material is down to what any policeman decides to send to the courts and what any court, on any day, regards as illegal.

CRAP! You can get away with practically anything, provided you label it ART.

CRAP! Even the Obscene Publications Unit of the Metropolitan Police have no written guidelines to go on.

WE REALLY DO CARE ABOUT AIDS VICTIMS - HONEST

CRAP!

' *Illness is in part what the world has done to a victim, but in a larger part it is what a victim has done with his world, and with himself...* '
                                                              Karl Menninger

In 1981 Acquired Immune Deficiency Syndrome - AIDS was identified for the first time in Los Angeles - the birthplace of everything new and trendy. We'd heard vague rumours of this mysterious disease but didn't take it too seriously. Funny really, not long after that it was predicted to be humanity's ultimate threat and, amongst those Holy Joes that think they know (and tell us with tedious regularity), God's final revenge on our permissive ways (hallelujah!).

What Was It?
AIDS was a little cracker of a disease, as tricky as a jigsaw puzzle with half the pieces missing and - just to give it that extra fizz - it came in two acts. Act One was rather innocuous and as passive as ... a dozing Rottweiler. You went to your doctor, had a blood test and were told you were HIV positive. Okay doc, so what? You didn't feel any different to how you felt last week or even last year. Hey! That's my kind of disease. But the virus was like a slow ticking time-bomb that threatened to blow up and transmute into the full-blown AIDS anywhere and at any time - and there was absolutely nothing you could do about it. That was Act Two. So what was so dreadful about AIDS? Why all the fuss?

Whatever it is, (and no one's really any closer) it has a nasty habit of eating away at the very immune system that prevents us from ending up gift wrapped, boxed and six feet under from every common cold, cough or athletes foot. Consequently, an AIDS carrier is a bit like poor old Salman Rushdie - never knowing where to look for the next threat to his life.

So How Do You Catch It?

Just to get everyone in on the act, the press, with the same hot-potch of half-baked theories and uncorroborated reports that they use to kick-start any scare, led us to believe that anyone could be infected by anything from sitting on public toilet seats to swapping spit through snogging. Suddenly all of us who didn't have a regular partner looked at each other with quizzical, side-long glances. Most of this hyped-up junk was soon discredited however, like most of the ill-informed crap the tabloids try to flog us.

Where Did it Come From? Who Can We Blame?

ARE YOU SURE YOU'RE NOT GAY?

Those bloody homosexuals, came the quick reply. We always knew that all that kind of behaviour would come to no good, said all those people who'd been dying for any excuse to start another witch-hunt. We always knew that sex between the same gender malarkey would end in tears. Actually the timing turned out to be a bit of a drag, as it arrived when gays were becoming far more acceptable and were even beginning to enjoy the 'coming out' process. This, however, was the excuse society needed. "Good riddance," cried all the 'angrys of Tunbridge Wells'. "We didn't beat those Krauts just so's a load of pansies could take over the world," they bayed. "By Golly, we always knew that the good Lord would seek revenge on such perversion."

' *This sort of thing may be tolerated by the French, but we are British - thank God...* '   Viscount Montgomery

But then reports came in of 'normal' people, ie heterosexuals, contracting the disease, mostly from bisexuals (those that bat for both sides) who'd fibbed about what (or who) they'd been up to. In the past the worst you could get from an unprotected heterosexual bonk was a dose of something rather itchy and unpleasant, and a trip to the doctor's which, though somewhat embarrassing, was fairly easily treated and certainly wasn't going to kill you.

Out of Harm's Reach

But then reports came in from black Africa that thousands of heterosexual couples were contracting AIDS and were passing it down to their children. "Oh well," Mrs Average-Britain thought, "Africans don't have the same attitude as us - life is cheap; and, let's face it, they're a long, long way from 24 Chestnut Avenue."

Its simply a case of cause and effect,
What else can those natives really expect.

But then reports came in that intravenous drug users were passing it on to each other through infected needles. "Oh well," Mr Average-Britain thought, smugly, "who cares about that lot? We don't know anyone that uses hard drugs, and they would probably die before their three-score-years-and-ten were up, anyway."

But most of all, the AIDS scare was a wonderful opportunity for the telly and mass media boys to jump on the 'concerned' bandwagon and show how much they cared for their public's welfare. Showbiz personalities fell over themselves and begged to be used to educate us in the ways of the condom (and yet again boost flagging careers);

instructive programmes showed us how to put them on (please!) and how easy it was to get into compromising situations (pleeease!). Never was more patronising crap ever ladled onto the British public, and never was anything more calculated to scare the pants ON us. Britain went AIDS crazy and fortunes were made by sleazy, opportunist clinics in places like Hampstead and Harley Street doing 'confidential' tests. Why confidential? Because, if you chose to go through your local GP, it would go on the record. So what? Surely it's better to be safe than sorry and not infect anyone else?

Old News

As sure as the weather forecast's always wrong and kids get fed up with their toys by Boxing Day, the media, with the attention span of a dim kitten with Alzheimer's, eventually became bored with AIDS (when did you last see anything about it on the telly?) and simply trailed away. Eventually, the government realised they too could get off the 'caring' bandwagon and cut the money they were putting into research and the funding of AIDS charities.

Of course we're concerned and we realise it's tough,
But we really believe we've done quite enough.

Fortunes were still being spent by those huge dedicated pharmaceutical companies, however, to find some vaccine to prevent, and a drug to cure, the disease. But not, as you might have supposed, due to some altruistic desire to help their fellow man, but to be the winner of the most fabulous pot of gold at the end of the longest and most convoluted rainbow in the history of medical research.

Better Sorry Than Safe: The Insurers

Hypocritical? That's nothing. The all-caring, see-you-all-right-in-your-old-age insurance institutions, run by little grey pen-pushers called Norman and Brian, who'd been squeezing cash out of us for donkeys' years, refused (almost understandably) to take on any more business from anyone who was HIV positive, but then made sure they checked with all of their future clients' doctors as to whether they'd simply had the test or not. Thousands of people who wanted to put their minds at rest, were prevented from either getting the okay - or getting the treatment, purely from fear of being blacklisted, and remained free to infect others in their ignorance.

❛ For almost seventy years the life insurance has been a smug sacred cow feeding the public a steady line of sacred bull... ❜
                                                            Ralph Nader

And so it went on. We, the Great British Public, returned to brushing the whole nasty business under our carpets, safe in the knowledge that if we didn't know anyone who actually had it, then it couldn't happen to us. Likewise, if we weren't gay, bisexual or a smack addict and didn't even know anyone who was, then what was the big deal?

JANET AND I CERTAINLY WOULDN'T KNOW ANYONE LIKE THAT

The jury's still out as to whether AIDS will be the scourge that was threatened ten years ago. Reports are coming in of children, born with the disease, who are throwing it off. But the current complacency is more than dangerous - like fiddling (or rather bonking) while Rome burns. Until our elders and betters REALLY take this on board, and spend proper money on research, we are all condemned to walking the there-but-for-the-grace-of-God-go-I tightrope.

Statistics

In the meantime it wouldn't be that daft an idea for the government to set up a proper committee to study all the thousands of contradictory reports, doomladen or otherwise, in order to publish the one statistic that really answers, once and for all, a question that really needs to be answered: If you are an average, heterosexual, British person, what are the real, no-bullshit chances, percentage-wise, of catching AIDS?

Summing up, this is how I see the whole sorry business.

CRAP CORNER

CRAP! Aids, like rabies, is fine as long as it stays abroad.

CRAP! Aids is God's way of rewarding promiscuity.

CRAP! If you want to blame anyone, blame homosexuals.

CRAP! People in the Third World are used to this sort of thing. They're brought up to expect it.

CRAP! Insurers believe that it isn't enough to be free of Aids if you look like the sort of person who *might* catch it.

CRAP! The only thing the popular press could do when concern for aids became yesterday's news was to hound the poor devils that already had it.

CRAP! If you don't know anyone who's actually got AIDS or is HIV positive, then you can safely assume that it doesn't exist.

Stop Press

The government, in a sudden rush of blood to its withered brain, has decided to target gays in future AIDS campaigns. Only fifteen years late! It's nice to know that they're so on the ball.

POLITICIANS KNOW BEST

' *A politician is an arse upon which everyone has sat except a man...* '

e. e. Cummings

To really understand how Britain has got to the position it is in today, it might be worth looking at the politicians who have unselfishly strived to get us there. On one hand, the word *politics* can refer to anything to do with our lives where we can recognise an inequality of power between two or more people – and the efforts that are made to make the whole business fairer. I suppose if you follow that line, it makes any kind of social jiggery-pokery political.

The word *political*, refers to all those set-ups or institutions that have made it their business to organise and keep us from pulling ourselves apart – which we call 'the state'. These are: parliament – which makes up the laws; and the civil service and local government – which make sure we follow them. They also organise the public services (drains, parking meters, cemeteries etc), the police (who make us do as *they* say) and the army (who go abroad and make foreigners do as *we* say).

But can politics be dragged out like a laboratory rat and studied on its own? Or, when we think of parliament, the civil service and political parties, do they simply show all the social divisions (like class) that are seen within the rest of society? Assuming the state (and therefore politics) are there to do society's bidding, how does society tell it what to do? (Answers on a postcard.)

Well, for a start, the ability to even think of the state

and society as different things hasn't always been possible. Back in the dark ages, before the eighteenth century, they were all rolled into one – the state *was* society and vice versa – all being breathed on hard by the king or queen, who, in those days, had far more clout than today. Times have changed and even by the nineteenth century it was the House of Commons that had THEM by the short and curlies. Political parties, with differing views, had begun to develop in the late 18th century because people (being people) couldn't agree on anything, and – following them – elections, enabling the common man to decide which one he preferred (that was the theory, anyway). Once this particular party, and therefore view, was decided on, it simply remained the job of the winners to carry their promises out. And that, my friends, is where the whole bloody shooting match went horribly wrong.

Politics and Class

The political system and the class system are, and always have been, inseparable. Ever since the 1680s, when they first arrived, the Tories always sprang from the loins of the top end of society, who, until relatively recently thought it their *duty* to rule over us poor serfs and show us how to live, by example. Back in 1965, the mother of the extremely aristocratic, if somewhat skeletal, Sir Alec Douglas Home (Eton and Oxford and Transylvania) actually made the classic comment about her lad, "How kind he is to *do* Prime Minister". Presumably she thought her son, and the upper classes, were doing the British a favour.

Somewhat later, dear old bushy eye-browed Dennis Healey of the Labour Party, saw it slightly differently. He reckoned that the ruling classes, who, bless 'em, had thought they had certain moral and social obligations, were losing the plot. And whose fault was that? You've guessed it. He claimed that dratted grocer's daughter Margaret Thatcher (the Mrs Bucket of Downing Street), despite her ludicrous pretensions to upper classdom, had taken the Tory party *away* from the toffs and landowners.

> **To you she might seem rather grand,**
> **but not to us who own the land.**

The Best of the Bunch?

Times have changed a bit since then but, despite having an acrobat's son as our current Prime Minister, it's safe to say that most of the Conservative MPs are still born with silver spoons in their mouths (though sometimes plated and often tarnished), having gone to expensive public schools and top universities. The Labour Party, though headed by a similarly educated chappie (Tony Blair), are mostly the sons and daughters of working, or lower middle class stock (or claim they are). Having said that, you can't help noticing how much the Labour Party seems to be drifting further and further from those roots, as they wallow in all the perks of a middle to upper middle class life.

We've already established that all the top positions in society (including politics) are held, and have been since time began, by the upper classes and that as far as they're concerned, it's the way it should be. Here's a quaint but illuminating quote from Sir Ian Frazier in 1938:

❛ England has gained much by having a class of people not compelled to earn their living, who have been able to devote their ability and time to developing our art of government, free institutions, etc. Our parliamentary system, local government, public work generally, has benefited enormously. ❜

This was fine in the past, when everyone knew their place, but these days, when the edges have become a little blurred, and we get whole sections of the community trying to squeeze into the class above, things are beginning to look a little different.

In order to know where exactly you fit, it's important to know where dividing lines split.

Vive La Difference

Many people these days have completely forgotten what Socialism or Conservatism really stand for and, when it gets right down to it, what the difference is. This is it (in theory):

Socialism

In essence, Socialism is the provision for those with less by those with more, with shared ownership of all the utilities (transport, gas, water, etc.) and the pursuit of equality for all (where have we heard that before?). They believe that workers should share in the profit of their employers and have a say in the way the companies are run. They believe that any child from any background should have the same shot at education (and that Father Christmas should leave them all the same presents).

❛*Socialism is only workable in heaven where it isn't needed and in hell where they've got it...*❜ *Cecil Palmer*

Conservatism

Conservatism is the belief that any form of State manipulation of the economy is wrong but believes it *should* set moral standards. Conservatives hate any form of change by intervention that rocks the steady boat, and believe that market forces should influence change naturally. By and large a Conservative believes in the survival of the fittest, that men are not born equal, and that nothing should ever be put in the way of the entrepreneur. It is the rich and powerful man, for whatever reasons, that creates the opportunity for a decent standard of living for all those less able (which sounds jolly good when you say it quickly).

I BET YOU'RE A LOT MORE EQUAL THAN ME

> *6 When a country's young men are Conservatives, its funeral bell has already rung... 9*   Henry Ward Beecher

So?

Why aren't we given that clear a choice? Why does it sometimes seem difficult to see where Conservative policy ends and the Socialism starts? How come the Conservatives, who have only ever got as much as 44% of the vote in recent years, have been allowed to sell off, to those that can afford it, all those essential parts of British life like the telephone service, the gas industry and the railways, that used to belong to you and me? How come the workers allowed their trade unions, that gave them some defence (admittedly abused) against bullying by their employers, to be defused. How come the Socialists seem now to believe in a free-market economy, resulting in whole industries like coal-mining being scrapped because some pen-pusher in Whitehall believes it to be uneconomic? AND HOW COME TONY BLAIR SOUNDS POSHER THAN JOHN MAJOR?

How It All Works

Before I go into my all too predictable rant about the state of politics today, let me explain briefly how it all fits together.

Britain works largely on the two party system, which means that the Conservative Party (the Tories) and the

Socialist Party (Labour) take turns in being either the Government or the Opposition (the doers or the done to). Basically the Government decides what it's going to do and the Opposition tells them they are crazy, dishonest, unfair, hypocritical or any other adjective they can dream up. This pisses off the other party, the Liberal Democrats, no end, because they always come third (or lower) and therefore never get a look in at anything. For years they've batted on about *Proportional Representation* (a parliament populated by MPs of each party, the number of which is decided by the number of actual votes cast throughout the land), and to a degree they have a point. At present our system's a bit all or nothing and desperately unfair (especially if you're a Liberal Democrat - tee-hee!).

Stand and Deliver

Before a general election each party presents its manifesto - a flash word to describe a document laying out what each party plans to do should it either stay as, or take over, government. This is usually a work of the purest fiction, comparable with the most fanciful fairy tales. All the parties, including the Liberals (who never get a chance anyway) promise the earth to get we voters in their bed, rather like a playboy chatting up a bimbo at a nightclub. Often there is no way they can ever carry out these promises financially but, like the glassy-eyed girl, once we're all hooked, it's usually too late.

If half truths are told at this point, however, they're nothing compared to those super-porkies that politicians of all nations tell once they've got their feet under the table. For example:

☞ Our Tory government were found to have stepped sideways from their policy of not supplying arms to the combatants in the first Gulf War and turned out to know all about the *Supergun* business. They lied through their teeth when found out (see page 173).

☞ The same Government got into extremely hot water following the trial of three executives of a company called Matrix-Churchill, who'd been called up in front of the beak for trading arms with those dratted Iraqis prior to the second Gulf War. British intelligence colluding with a few ministers in order to skate round the arms embargo on Iraq – without telling parliament. It turned out that the defendants had had government backing and MPs were furious that, not only had the ministers done an about-turn policywise, but were prepared to see the three defendants get banged up rather than own up. The Scott Report on the whole affair was pretty damning but, as always, the ministers concerned managed to get away without even a slap on the wrist.

☞ In May 1996 Dame Shirley Porter and her gang of five councillors and officials were ordered to repay a cool £31 million over the 'homes for votes' scandal. They were accused by the district auditor of 'wilful misconduct' in masterminding a sneaky vote-gaining exercise. They had, over a few years, cynically moved council tenants (Labour voting) out of their homes (and the voting catchment area) and sold those homes to largely Tory voting punters at a substantially reduced rate. This blatant 'gerrymandering' showed 'a blatant indifference to right or wrong'. The whole business is due to come up before the beak in 1997.

❝ *A lie can be halfway round the world before the truth has got its boots on...* ❞ *James Callaghan (nicked off Rev. C. Spurgeon)*

Telly Time
The televising of Parliament in 1989 was a bizarre idea and badly timed. A classic example of MPs shooting themselves

in the goolies, in pursuit of an ego boost. Just as all those loyal Thatcherlings were beginning to smell a rat, it showed us in no uncertain terms what a load of braying, lazy, often inarticulate old tossers our leaders really were. It also showed what a meal ticket they were on - the House of Commons being as empty as their promises, most of the time, often not being able to reach a quorum of 40 members out of a possible 650. The others (admittedly mostly Tory) were out and about feathering their personal nests with all their undeclared private directorships and consultancies. Putney MP David Mellor, for instance, dashed round a dozen or so companies, including British Aerospace and Shorts of Belfast, as well as being on the telly and radio every five minutes (though God and his agent know why). In fact, at the time of writing, he's just been offered £100,000 a year to join the advisory board of the Kuwait Investment Office. Bugger Parliament!

***We must make all the cash we can,
in case they kick us out again.***

To make it even worse, members of the two opposing sides even make sleazy little pacts not to go to work on certain days, so as to make the voting fair, though heaven knows what fair's got to do with politics or the price of jam. As for the House of Lords, the few shaky old codgers that do manage to get away from their nurses for the day, look like the victims of a sleeping-gas attack whenever the powers that be are daft enough to televise them. They, like Terry Wogan, Jimmy Saville, The Flower Pot Men or all those others whose style belongs to the distant past, should be buried gently and with little fuss.

❛ A severe though not unfriendly critic of our institutions said that 'the cure for admiring the House of Lords, was to go and look at it'... ❜   Walter Bagehot (1826-77)

The Chop

Two of the features of parliament that have always astounded me are the 'guillotine' and 'whip' systems. The guillotine is the term for a time limit set on all debates of new Bills. This effectively means that if something hasn't been properly discussed, a vote must be taken anyway, presumably so that the lazy bastards can get home early. What a daft way to make decisions about the things that will affect the lives of us all.

JUST ONE MORE POINT I'D LIKE TO MAKE QUICKLY.

The Whip

The whip is even worse. This is a system by which party 'heavies' lean on the relevant members to vote for whichever government is flavour of the year, over various important issues. Can you believe this? These whips, as they are called, hold immense power and can influence the whole career of each individual member, from jobs in the government to knighthoods. This means that there's no such thing as a vote based on what an individual member actually thinks (if he wants to get on). He must always be seen to follow the party line. This strikes many people as pure crap and about as democratic as a Red Indian ambush. The guillotine and the whip, I believe, make a total mockery of the House of Commons, but as one just-retired minister commented, "It wasn't until I joined the government that I realised just how irrelevant parliament was."

❛ You cannot adopt politics as a profession and remain honest... ❜   Louis Howe

Europe Ahoy

It must be said that both major parties have an extremely
woolly attitude to Europe. The European Community (or
extremely Common Market), was formed in 1967 and we
British joined in 1973. We've been bitching about it ever
since. It was widely held to have been developed to form the
world's largest trading bloc, but it didn't take a committee of
dictators to work out that, when push came to shove, Europe
would be the biggest boy in the playground if ever a global
scrap broke out again. Hugh Gaitskell, the sometime Labour
leader, back in the sixties, claimed it would end a thousand
years of history. Whether this is true or not, Britain does seem
to be teetering on the edge of a situation where all major
decisions regarding its past and future will be in the hands of
faceless European bureaucrats. Mind you, if you've seen the
faces of some of our home-grown bureaucrats, you'd be hard
put to see the difference.

Call to Arms

If you believe a country should make its own decisions on
points of its own law then the European Court of Justice
should have you raking through the attic for your grandad's
army uniform. This court, with its thirteen international
judges, can override any decisions made in any of its member countries – from whether we should hang our very own
murderers or whether or not our budgies need a licence –
and has severely got up the nose of Tories and Socialists
alike. Again, however, if you look a little closer at some of
the whacky decisions our judiciary make, it might be no
bad thing. As yet the European Parliament, which meets for
one week every month in Strasbourg, has not nearly the
same power as national governments, but the much talked
about (to the point of total apathy) Maastricht Treaty threatens to sharpen its teeth considerably. This treaty, signed in
1991, claimed to simply aim at tighter political and economic union between the member countries, but shows all

the signs of whipping even more power away from each one of 'em.

ECUs or Not

We Brits, surprise, surprise, well versed in the fine art of fence-straddling (and we've never been that thrilled about being Europeans anyway) wouldn't swallow the whole pill, backing out of the *Social Chapter* and refusing to accept a move to make our money the same as everyone else's. Well, at least till we'd discussed it in our Parliament. John Major, who wins the faceless prize hands down, was predictably all for it - despite protests from Grand Puppeteer Thatcher - well miffed as she believed he'd feed out of her clammy hand (see! he can't be all bad). Even so, like it or not, it looks as if we'll all be paying for our Euro-burgers and Euro Disneywear with exactly the same money (ECUs) as all the rest of 'em by 1997. Yet another decision your elders have made for you for which you'll probably spend the rest of your life suffering the consequences.

Life Before Major

Talking of Maggie; since she got shafted by those she herself had dominated more than any other Prime Minister since the Second World War, everyone from the middle class down became suspicious that the Tories could well be *only* interested in power, and that they conceivably might *not* have their best interests at heart. When Nigel Lawson, her Chancellor of the Exchequer, cut super-tax, he basically built a damn great wall round the super-rich and told them that the gravy train could flow round it once more. If they stayed with the Tories, he claimed, their position was unassailable. Because of the average Briton's lunatic trust in anyone in a pin-stripe suit and with a cut-glass accent, we in the middle let him (and them) persuade us that they would protect us too. We now know they had their fingers crossed. Britain has slid down the economic helter-skelter to such a degree that the standard of living for the average man throughout most of the industrialised world has long overtaken ours. Why is this so? Didn't Britain invent practically everything worth inventing, and show all those ungrateful savages how to wear proper clothes and use knives and forks (while robbing them blind)? By Jove, they should be horse-whipped!

Having said that, it is only the average man that's feeling the pinch. Things are different at the top. Britain's rich became £15.5 billion richer in 1995, and the average wealth for the top 500 is £140 million. In 1988 there were around 18,000 millionaires. These days there could be double that – and that's without the lottery.

National Frump

Well, before you get the Union Jack out and start goose-stepping up the street, picking on foreigners, it might be interesting to note that in terms of gross domestic product (that's the amount each individual contributes to the economy) we are eighth in Europe alone, just above Spain and even Ireland (and they've had a bloody war on!). So, working on a basic rule of economics which goes – if you don't make the money, you've got no right to spend it – it's no surprise that all those countries above us will seem, in varying degrees, damned expensive to the poor (literally) Brit abroad.

Just to cheer you up even more, the value of our dear old British pound has dropped to a phenomenal seventh of its value since 1971, which is roughly when we joined the European Common Market, and not long after the discovery of almost limitless oil – both of which were supposed to make us all jolly rich. Whose fault is it? Work it out for yourselves. During that twenty-four year period the Labour party have been in power for only five years, so you could say the Tories are nearly five times more to blame. Having said that (and so as not to seem too biased), the Labour party made a right cock-up of their bit (between 1974 and 1979). But that *was* twenty years ago.

❛ Socialism is a boring way to speed up the mess... ❜
                                                          Buckminster Fuller

How Did We Get to How We Are Today?

Most political journalists spent April 15th, 1992 wiping the copious amounts of egg from their alcohol rouged faces, following a fourth election victory by the Tories. They'd got it all spectacularly wrong. The British, silly fools, with nobody else to blame but themselves, could now look forward to yet another four years of Tory rule, making a staggering seventeen in all. The rich (who were richer than ever) sighed with relief. London was to remain the greatest tax haven on earth, the left (or opposition) appeared to be a spent force and Attila the Hun (as Clement Freud labelled Thatcher) could absolve herself from any responsibility for the economic shit that the country was in.

But to many of us who were politically somewhere in the middle, it was an inky black day. We hated HER, we loathed the YUPPIES, we couldn't stand Tory elitism and were ashamed of the fact that whatever this sick government had done, we - the Great British Public - seemed to settle for the devil we knew rather than *any* kind of devil we didn't. Even the Tory intellectuals (a dying breed) were sorry. They knew what a balls-up they'd made of running the country and actually looked forward to a short period in opposition, during which they could sharpen up their policies and come up with some more radical ideas (or *any* ideas, come to that).

Hard Labour

The sad old Labour party had blown it completely. Never, in all those Tory years, had they been presented with such an open goal. There was the country lying at their feet, like a defrocked nun, waiting to be taken, and all they could do was squabble amongst themselves, over well-past-their-sell-by-date socialist dogma that should have been committed to *Room 101* with flat caps, lace-up boots and Arthur Scargill. In their way, they let the class system rule their policies in just as near-sighted and stupid a way as the Tories, failing as ever to realise that a lost-the-plot society cannot be rectified overnight. Poor old Neil Kinnock, their figurehead, though admittedly well-meaning and sincere (though red-headed and freckly) looked as much like a leader as Mr Bean and couldn't even beat his unpopular opposite bean (John Major) at the general Election.

Having said that, it wasn't just his fault. Okay he'd gone soft on selling off all the nationalised industries, but the rest of his colleagues, in their clamour for power, forgot what opposition really meant, and what their party really stood for. This, as I see it, was to bridge the gap between private enterprise and the needs of the ordinary man; to take all that ridiculous amount of money wasted on defending a country that nobody could be bothered to invade anymore and spend it on education and therefore the future; to keep the amazing power of the corporate from squashing the individual; to stop increasing power being centralised and try to give it to more representative local government; and to let the British public know, in no uncertain terms, that democracy itself has been severely endangered by one of the most selfish and up its own arse governments in history.

Libby in the Middle

As for the middle ground, we had the Liberal Democrats, a hotchpotch of anoraks with lily-livered, straddling-the-fence, designed-not-to-upset-anyone ideas, headed by the totally one-colour (beige) Paddy Ashdown, who looked as if he'd be more at home running a suburban garden centre than a country. He's one of those infuriating people who, having no strong opinions of their own, try to score points off those who at least believe in *something* (the two big parties) by claiming that we, the British people, deserve better. Everybody knows, however, that he, just like his weaselly predecessor, David Steele, would jump into bed with either of them (he's currently nibbling Blair's ear) if it meant getting fifteen minutes of power.

THE LIBERAL PARTY ALWAYS REFLECT OUR VIEWS - WHATEVER THEY ARE

❛ *A Liberal is one who is too broad minded to take his own side in a quarrel...* ❜
Robert Frost

Many people (25%) did however vote for the Liberals or nationalist parties at the last election, but most of us have realised that voting Liberal, is like buying an extra lottery ticket to make sure of winning the lottery.

❛ *Liberalism is the first refuge of political indifference and the last refuge of Leftists...* ❜   Harry Rosholenko

The Result?
We, the disillusioned, did what we thought to be the only thing possible and buried our heads under the sand. We didn't want the tried and tested Tories, we didn't want the plot-lost Labour party and we regarded the others with no more credibility than the Raving Loony Party (and some a lot less). The result was that the Tories, God bless 'em, got in with substantially less than 50% of the total votes cast. So we, the British, simply followed sheep-like as we slipped back into an age reminiscent of the Edwardian era before the First World War - a privileged class wafting between the country and London, propping up a regime based on the serving of a few by many, and every one knowing their place. But now it was all a paper-thin sham. Under all that Porsche-driving, champagne-swigging, property-hoarding jollity was a

C . R . A . P .

growing underclass who didn't like it up'em one bit. Single party politics are all very well, but it doesn't take Machiavelli to realise that given their head (and what a big one Maggie had) the country could well end up with a dictatorship, which is what has happened in so many Third World countries. Recent history now reveals that a lot of those very Tories that were in charge realised the danger just as much, but like a conductor trying to stop a runaway bus, felt they were at the wrong end to do anything about it.

It's hard to work out what to vote, so we'd all better stay with the sinking boat.

Help Yourselves

And this wasn't just a British phenomenon. Throughout Europe equality and a fair deal for all, was losing popularity, symbolised by the merciless trashing of the British trade unions. Socialism was having a bad time and, when communism collapsed throughout the Eastern bloc, it seemed to be game set and match. The poor would have to fend for themselves because, as sure as hell, no-one else would.

But the fat, conservative cat was out of the bag. All that eighties rubbish was built on straw and *with* straw; for when that big bad wolf called *reality* came along and merely prodded our inflated, yuppie-led economy, it burst and deflated like a pantomime dame's brassiere. So why did Thatcher and her Tories get voted back in? Because the voting British simply didn't have the balls to try anything else. It was the same blind devotion to strong leadership that allowed Hitler to dominate the Germans, Sadam Hussein to lead his sad little country to near destruction and Bluto to walk off with Olive Oyle.

John the Caring

❛ A politician is an acrobat (or acrobat's son). He keeps his balance by doing exactly the opposite of what he says... ❜

Maurice Barres

The humble, but rather chummy, John Major (cynically brought in to win the working class vote) and his sidekicks proved much the same as their predecessors – as all their policies carried that glossy 'Made by Thatcher' label. Sure they made all the right noises, but when it came right down to it, one could hardly spot the join. Their attitude to the ever-increasing number of financially crippled and homeless, for example, has been predictable and well publicised. Having watched his predecessor trash the rented property sector in Britain overnight, by offering landlords home improvement grants if they made their houses into one again, he found their presence on the streets of our capital an embarrassment. But let's face it, they said, there weren't enough of them to influence votes (Major's well known obsession) and half of them wouldn't bother anyway.

Okay they're jobless and have nothing to show,
But I do wish they'd find somewhere different to go.

❛ There is no poverty in Britain... ❜

Peter Lilley (Tory Minister 1996)

Marie Antoinette stirred in her grave. It was the 'let them eat cake' syndrome all over again. The fact that the Tories had caused the shit we were in, and therefore the massive increase in unemployment and running down of the welfare state (which had caused their predicament in the first place) seemed to have been forgotten. Tory ministers were notorious for their 'on your bike' attitude to employment.

They'd all succeeded as self-made men (having been to good public schools and universities), so why shouldn't everyone else? If there was no work in one place then the working man should go and find it elsewhere, or set up in business on his own. This arrogant presupposition that everyone is self-motivated, self-confident and competent to go solo, typified their holier-than-thou-attitude to the working man. For God's sake, most people have absolutely no desire to run their own business and why should they? They just want to go to work and earn enough for their families to live the lifestyle that they have chosen. It is up to the progressive governments to make sure that this is possible.

I'm All Right

Having said all this, why should the government worry? Major and his cronies hardly noticed the increase in their BUPA contributions or gentlemen's club memberships, so didn't give a toss about the growing discontent in the country. Even so, history might be tempted to wonder if the financial boom of the late eighties ended due to the government's conscience over how unfair it was that the old us-and-them gap was expanding as fast as Margaret Thatcher's ego.

6 She only went to Venice because someone told her she could walk down the middle of the street... 9
Neil Kinnock

History must be joking! At least we know *that* wasn't the case. If they'd had their way, the middle classes and above would now be having champagne delivered instead of milk and servants living below stairs once more. The sad thing is, we middle classes would probably have let it happen, to the detriment of all below, had not circumstances changed so dramatically.

...And the Future

40% of those between 18 and 24 (5.2 million), who were eligible to vote at the last election, didn't. Unless something unexpected happens, the percentage could be far greater next time. The politicians comfort themselves by thinking that young people these days are simply apathetic - they just can't be bothered to cross the road to vote. Recent surveys have shown, however, that far from this state of affairs, a huge amount of today's youngsters are quite well aware of what's going on. They choose not to vote because they see the whole sorry bunch, Labour and Conservative, as at best a load of out of touch wrinklies and at worst a group of out and out prats. They appear to them to be more interested in their own personal careers, and perfectly prepared to do and say whatever is necessary to achieve, and stay in power.

Politicians today would be well advised to consider the faint possibility that their young potential electorate do see them for what they are. Why can't they wise up to the fact that they're all totally pissed off with big party politics and the men who run them, preferring to involve themselves with issues that they feel they might be able to influence, like the environment, exporting of animals and protests about the Criminal Justice Act.

Politics Goes Pop

It doesn't take a panel of those parasitical political gurus like Jeremy Paxman to work out that having a sizeable proportion of the floating voters not even prepared to stay on the surface must make the big party players somewhat uneasy. "Crikey! If the other side was to manage to haul 'em in, it could well influence a complete election. If we can't actually bully, bribe, or - heaven forbid - change our policies to help them, what can we do?"

The answer to this poser, which we are forced to witness all too embarrassingly often, is for the actual main players - the politicians - to try to make themselves more user-friendly to young people. They seriously believe that by wearing department store jeans with their brightest cardigans and by being seen at every opportunity, bobbing up and down (why do people lose their sense of rhythm at forty?) to pop music, their 'prey' will be lured into believing that they're one of them. Some of the consequences have been hilarious. Who could ever forget that freckly Welsh groover, Neil Kinnock, jigging about like a demented puppet on a Tracy Ullman video, or much, much worse, that sad little Lib-Dem ex-leader David (Mr Hip) Steele's 'I feel Liberal Alright?' rap, accompanied by his own Steele-Step dance routine. Oh please!

> ❛ Politics is developing more comedians than radio ever did... ❜
> Jimmy Durante

Just like humans at a chimps' tea party, MPs also like to be seen at events where one normally wouldn't expect to find them. There's always a healthy smattering mixing with the rich and trendy 'coke-set' at the pop industries self-masturbatory Brit Awards ceremony, though our poor Heritage Secretary, the Julie Andrews-ish Virginia Bottomly (a regular attender) always looks as if she'd be much more at home at one of those turgid Tory cocktail parties with a glass of sweet, South African sherry in her mit.

Don't Rock the Vote

The latest whacky thing to try to get the little would-be voters into the booth comes from, you've guessed it, America, in the form of a campaign called *Rock the Vote* (doesn't that make your toes cringe?) which apparently helped Bill Clinton to make President (as bad a reason as any to do anything). The poor old Tories are understandably getting very nervous, for although *Rock the Vote* pretends to have no political bias, it has been organised by an ardent leftie record company owner. Not only that, but it's a well known fact that if anyone could persuade young people to vote, there's an overwhelming probability that, because all the idealism hasn't yet been squeezed out of them, they'd plump for Labour (in the hope that all the idealism hasn't been squeezed out of them).

❛ Any man who is not something of a socialist before he is forty has no heart. Any man who is still a socialist after he is forty has no head... ❜
Wendell Willkie

CRAP CORNER

It could be said that we get the government we deserve. This might be true, but that doesn't excuse the following hypocrisies and double standards.

CRAP! Politicians, like double-glazing salesmen or investment brokers, will promise anything to clinch a sale or achieve power. Unfortunately, they all suffer amnesia when required to come up with the goods.

I'M SURE OUR BROCHURE WILL CHANGE YOUR MIND

POLAR DOUBLE GLAZING

CRAP! When normal people bend the truth, it's called lying. When politicians do it, it's called 'being economical with the truth'.

CRAP! Labour ministers believe that everyone should have the same education and therefore the same chances in life – but while they're waiting, send their own kids to upmarket, fee paying schools.

CRAP! The middle and lower middle classes have a tendency to trust anyone who speaks with a smart accent.

CRAP! Posh Socialists like Tony Blair and Harriet Harman, though Tories at heart, realise that they've far more chance of power within a largely working class Labour Party.

CRAP! The Great British Middle Class, terrified of any change in case it affected their well-being, voted the Tories in for a fourth term and have regretted it ever since.

CRAP! John Major found the presence of people sleeping rough on our streets an awful embarrassment, even though his government had practically forced them into it.

CRAP! Politicians of both parties believe that by simply trying to prove that they like pop music, they will attract the youth vote.

THE BRITISH ARE NOT A RACIST PEOPLE

❝I am in favour of the race to which I belong having the superior position . . .❞   Abraham Lincoln

Out of an adult population of over 58 million there are 583,000 black, 616,000 Indian and 456,000 Pakistani or Bangladeshi people. Other ethnic minorities account for 489,000. Overall these account for 4.9% of the adult population. Over 33% of ethnic minorities are under 16 compared with only 19% of whites. Now I'm not very good at sums, but I don't have to dive for my calculator to work out that the stork must be delivering little ethnic minors almost twice as regularly as the rest of us. This also means that if we don't learn to rub along with this minority before it becomes a majority, we could be heading for some heap big trouble.

What Race?
A hundred or so years ago the actual populations of different countries were called 'races'. Daniel Defoe (of Robinson Crusoe fame) once described the English as a 'mongrel half-bred nation'. These days we use the term 'race' to describe a people who all come from roughly the same place and who look alike (and who, as scientists say, 'share a common gene pool') wherever they have chosen as their home.

For some fairly obscure reason, we British like to think of ourselves as fair-skinned, of average to tall height, with pleasant regular features and medium build. Where we get that from, heaven knows. Anyone who's ever walked through the average British shopping precinct on a Saturday afternoon will soon realise what a load of old cobblers that is.

A fair cross-section would have trouble getting past the door of that alien bar, full of mutants, in *Star Wars*.

The British, we think, are a marvellous race,
tall and handsome and fair of face.

Having come to that conclusion you'd think the populations of the four nations, (England, Ireland, Wales and Scotland) who now all look vaguely similar due to mass cross-nookie, would get on pretty well. But we know that just isn't true. We really don't need to look much further than our own islands to find people who have trouble co-habiting, so heaven help anyone from further afield.

'All those who are not racially pure are mere chaff . . .'
A. Hitler (Mr)

The truth is (as I see it) when we think of ethnic minorities, we really mean people of a different colour. The Italians, Spanish, and Scandinavians etc. might be minorities too, but because they don't look that different (actually Scandinavians can be recognised by their blond hair and terrible clothes) nobody seems to notice (and let's face it we've been conquered by most of 'em at some time or another). And the Jewish community, having been on the wrong end of the shitty stick for most of their history, are these days having a relatively stress-free time in Britain.

In 1968 a dangerously eccentric and outspoken MP, Enoch Powell, came out with the unforgettable and maybe unforgivable words:

"Those whom the gods wish to destroy, they first make mad. We must be mad, literally mad, as a nation to be permitting the annual inflow of some 50,000 dependants who

are for the most part the material of the future growth of the immigrant-descended population. It is like watching a nation heaping up its own funeral pyre . . . As I look ahead, I am filled with foreboding. Like the Roman, I seem to see "the river Tiber foaming with much blood".

This speech could be interpreted in two ways. Either it was a sensible (if somewhat unsubtle and flowery) warning to an overpopulated island, or one of the most overtly racist statements ever made. Makes no difference really, because it became a rallying call for some 100,000 proper racists who'd been champing at the bit to rally round a leader. They wrote (somewhat embarrassingly for Enoch) in support, and virtually ended any political ambitions he might have had.

The fact that racism is an issue in Britain at all has a lot to do with whether or not our black minorities fit into our established class structure (see page 117). To be honest, at this point in time they don't! (Whoops, there goes another politically incorrect statement.) For a million reasons – religion, culture, dress, food, music – you name it, black people, in this country will probably remain outsiders from the mainstream of British society, however much they earn, however much they learn, and whoever they marry. This doesn't necessarily mean that this must always be so, but you can't force such things. The supposition of the late sixties and early seventies, illustrated by that sickly sweet pop song *Melting Pot*, by the mixed-race group *Blue Mink* (1970), was that eventually, due to more and more cross-pollination (pardon the metaphor), the whole world would become one huge, coffee-coloured community (heaven forbid). It was a nice, if somewhat sick-making, sentiment (if you like that sort of thing) but the crystal ball seems to have been faulty as, more and more, the various ethnic races, for whatever reasons, are choosing to stick together (whichever country they happen to be in). As a matter of interest, four years later, *Blue Mink*, tired of trying to make money out of harmony, split up.

It is now thought by those that 'know' that a people's access to its own cultural roots is essential, and to expect them to abandon them just because they live in someone else's country is stupid★ (actually, it's quite easy to prove that most of us Great British came from abroad anyway). In fact, the risk that individual ethnics take by assimilating our way of life completely is to be ostracised by their own, who often see them as having sold out. If you've ever heard the American term 'Uncle Tom', you'll know what I mean. Anyway, why should ethnic minorities worry about our class structure, when they've got perfectly good or bad (depending on which way you view it) ones of their own. It has to be said that educated blacks will have literally *nothing* to do with their uneducated counterparts, and lighter black people often look down on darker ones.

Recognising a race's right to exist is one thing. But unfortunately the British who, believe it or not are reckoned to be one of the more tolerant nations in the world, catch their breath at the mention of all–ethnic schools, English being taught as a *second* language, whole families not even bothering to learn the lingo at all, or – worst of all – foreign families being on our income support scheme.

People who come from far far away,
Should abide by our rules and do as
we say.

Where this whole business gets beyond a joke, however, is

★This, quite rightly, works exactly the same the other way round, when a Briton takes up residence in a black country (except he's usually running the show).

when we examine what has happened to non-achieving ethnic minorities (particularly those of West Indian origin) who can easily be identified by skin colour. It's not unfair to say that, for whatever reason, they have become a category parallel to the underclass described earlier, with as much chance of achieving fair deals, or equal job opportunities as I have of winning the lottery (especially as I've never bought a ticket).

All's Well in Tellyland

The odd thing is that the media, and particularly the more visible ones - like television, would lead us to believe that there really isn't a problem. Every other presenter, newsreader, or weatherperson (if they are actually humanoid) seems to be from an ethnic minority which, if you too had just come from outer space (or Norwich), would give the impression that Britain is now fully integrated and that everyone is getting on like a house on fire. Would that it were so. In all my years in advertising (and now in publishing) I rarely, if ever, see or saw a black face, unless in the typing pool, the mail room, the canteen or cleaning up afterwards. Come to that I've hardly ever met a black illustrator, journalist, architect, designer, bank manager, or insurance broker, let alone racing driver or jockey (neither of which I've ever met anyway). Why could that be? Is it because those particular jobs are beyond their capabilities, or is it because they are excluded?

How to Change Your Colour Overnight

The Ford Motor Company, in a recent recruitment brochure illustrating the assembly-line staff at one of their truck companies, took an existing photo sporting an obviously healthy mix of races, and retouched all our coloured brothers to make it look as if they only employed whites. If this wasn't bad enough, it later turned out that it was virtually impossible to become a lorry driver for Ford if you were black or Asian.

Why?

We British are notorious for not really trusting foreigners, especially if they look different. Any black person who's made it big will tell you that they had to work twice as hard to get where they did. The higher up the social scale you go, the harder and more slippy the path. Yes, you do get the odd token black person who's often become (or had to become) more English than roast beef (like Trevor MacDonald), but he or she's often just for show, and usually knows it only too well.

It's such a difficult nut to crack, making it big (if you are black).

We're All the Same

Most people like to think they're not racist, especially those who have no direct contact with black people. My mother, a regular churchgoer, always used to point to those sticky-backed pictures that we used to get at Sunday school, of dusty folk in far-flung foreign lands and tell me that everyone was the same under the skin and that we should love all foreign folk as if they were our own. She would tut-tut at racists' remarks, especially her father's (my grandad), who could have taught that nice Mr Hitler a thing or two about fascism. That was until an Asian family looked as if they might buy the house next door. Suddenly all the old, six-times-round-the-block, racist claptrap started to flow. 'I'm sure they're very nice people really, but you must have heard how they fill their houses up with all their relatives,' or 'As soon as one lot go out to work another lot come in and sleep in the same beds. I hear some of them even share shoes,' or 'They keep those curries bubbling away day and night until the whole street smells like Delhi or Southall High Road.'

Mr and Mrs Patel did buy the house next door to my mum's, in our leafy North London suburb, and soon dispelled all her stupid fears. 'They keep their house beautifully,' she cooed patronisingly, 'and look how well the children are turned out.'

The hilarious sting in the tail came a few years later, however, when, due to extremely hard graft, our neighbours started to show signs of wealth. Their house became the best in the street, Mr. Patel had a nice new Merc and Mrs Patel a shiny red Datsun. The little Patel-lings were now being driven off to private schools. One day, to the surprise of all, a *For Sale* board went up. They were moving on, to a bigger more expensive (and detached!) house in a much smarter suburb. 'Not good enough for them, I suppose' was my mum's peevish, and somewhat dismissive response.

> **It's oh-so-important to know
> your station,
> Especially if you're black or Asian.**

Racism is about fear. Fear of the unknown. My mother's attitude was simply an exaggerated version of the attitude of a large percentage of the middle-class population. Black people are fine, upstanding and worthy as long as you don't actually have to have anything to do with them. In a way I think I prefer the attitude of the average working-class man, who at least wears his John Bullish racism for all to see. It might be hateful and ignorant, but at least it ain't hypocritical.

But are *you* racist? Let's play a little quiz:

1. What do you think if you see an Asian driving a Rolls-Royce? Do you assume they work in a corner shop – or do you imagine all sorts of ways that the wealth could have been built up? Are you jealous?

2. Have you ever laughed at a joke or comment which highlights any particular part of a black man's anatomy?

3. If you see a black man driving a big flash car do you ever think he's nicked it or deals in drugs?

4. If your mother or father are divorced, would you feel okay if either of them came home with a partner who's a different colour?
5. If someone from an ethnic minority does something unkind or dishonest do you ever refer to their background?

If you can hold your head high and say 'not me!', then good for you. If, on the other hand, like most of us, you do have the odd, sneaky racist thought, usually when things aren't going too well for you or your family, then it's back to the drawing board. We can only change ourselves and our viewpoints if we face up to them first.

Reverse Racism

❛I am not going to promise a Cabinet post or any other post to any racial or ethnic group. That would be racism in reverse at its worst. . . .❜
John F Kennedy

Like always, there is another side to this issue. Among the educated liberal middle-classes there is a phenomenon that I label 'reverse racism' and it can hack you off almost as much as the other kind. Have you ever met those people who bend over backwards to excuse anyone from an ethnic minority when they behave badly, purely because they like being seen to be 'right on'?

Late in 1995, the police's head 'guv' - Sir Paul Condon - happened to mention that most street crime in inner-London was carried out by gangs of black youths. In a way it was a bit like saying that most of the birds in Trafalgar Square were pigeons, and most of the tourists foreign. Simple, to the point, and based on statistics and his officers' observations. Okay, he should have qualified the remark by stating the social reasons that go to cause this state of affairs. He should also have referred to the many other crimes that are predominantly caused by white people. But the police were never much good at diplomacy (or subtlety for that matter). The hue and cry that followed defied belief. True, most of the police I've ever come across have been racist, anti-Semitic and homophobic (not to mention thick), and true, your average law-abiding black person gets a

pretty unfair deal at their hands, but it still doesn't make an over-simplistic statement of fact a racist statement.

Let's Get Correct

Many people believe that the solution to all these problems is legislation based on a form of sloppy political correctness. *The Times* newspaper reported in January 1995 that a social services inspector who had just visited a church-run children's club in rural Lydbrook, Gloucester, got his government issue Y-fronts in a twist because none of the dolls or Lego characters that the kids played with were black. The Reverend Michael Foster, who ran the club, insisted that Lego figures only came in yellow (which must have pleased the Chinese) and that if you were going to insist on black ones then what about white ones as well (nice one vic!). The inspector said that their policy was to reflect a multicultural society and seemed to think it was even more important in an area that didn't have any black kids. I suppose it was beyond his reasoning to imagine that these kids

watch telly and read books and just might have some inkling that there are black people in the world. Anyway, why did these busy- bodies try to remove black jelly babies from the rest of the pack several years ago? You can't have it both ways.

People of all colours *can* rub along together pretty well, be they black, white, yellow, blue or green. But for

God's sake, it would take centuries before the world's population were to level out linguistically, culturally, and everything else-ally. Anyway, who wants that? Sounds jolly boring to me.

What we need is RESPECT (man!) . . . not legislation, and as soon as the powers that be recognise that they cannot legislate respect, the better it will be for all. The answer lies in the hands of parents - pure and simple. (Not mine - I hasten to add!) Not teachers, not police, not politicians, not vicars, not social workers, not soppy, over-opinionated pop stars - just parents. Until British parents show, by example, that there is good and bad in everyone, whatever bloody shade they are, we'll carry on shooting ourselves in our multi-coloured racist feet.

If a mixed race society is to prosper and win,
We simply must make it a terrible sin,
To judge fellow folk by the colour of skin.

CRAP CORNER

But what do you think? Have I been unfair to black people, white people or anyone in between? Turn to the back page and then extract your pen. But first, let's just recap on the main points.

Despite our desire to appear racially pure, it's very difficult to find anyone who isn't, in reality, of mixed race.

It isn't just ethnic minorities who suffer inequality and persecution, it's *coloured* ethnic minorities.

Wanting to restrict immigration, doesn't necessarily make you racist.

Black people often forget that they are just as capable of being racist as white.

The telly and films would have us believe that there are just as many coloured people in good responsible jobs as anyone else.

CRAP! Your great British middle class are fine about black people as long as they don't have to know any.

CRAP! The further you go down the social scale, the less hypocritical people become regarding race. They're just plain prejudiced.

CRAP! That goes for the aristocracy as well – except they should know better.

IT'S A FREE COUNTRY

If you go down in the woods today you're sure of a big surprise. It won't be bears that will get you, but the 'sign police'. *Don't Pick Flowers, Don't Go Off the Authorised Paths, Don't Climb Trees, Don't Picnic, Don't Light Fires, Don't Litter, Don't Lurk, Don't Breathe, Don't Smile,* or simply – *Don't.*

And what about parks? *Don't Skateboard, Don't Roller-skate, Don't fly Kites, Don't Walk on the Grass, Don't Walk on the Water (for saviours), Don't Ride Bikes, Don't Carve Your Initials on the Benches, Don't Fish in the Ponds, Don't let your Dog off the Lead, Don't Loiter, Don't Feed the Ducks,* or *Don't Feed the Winos.*

And what about public buildings? *Don't take Photographs, Don't Run, Don't Touch, Don't Snog, Don't Sit, Don't Eat, Don't Go That Way, Don't Go This Way, No Entry, No Exit, Private, Go Home.* The list goes on.

The clearest sign that we have won,
is when you simply can't have fun.

The whole world is turning into a 'no go', 'no do' area. A nanny state. An environment of small signs, designed by small people whose object is to make our lives as bland and boring as theirs. Anorak and cardigan wearers who've never had a sexual encounter in the open or with the light on, have never swum starkers in the sea at night, never even tried a cigarette (and certainly never anything stronger), never sneaked a drink out of the drinks cabinet when little, and certainly have never got pissed. And people who are determined that you or I shouldn't either.

They're the ones who think anyone from drug takers to prostitutes should be executed, that homosexuality should be banned (until their Neville turns into one), wouldn't give anything away if they won the lottery, cause egg industries to collapse at the first hint of salmonella poisoning, cause the beef industries to collapse at the first hint of Mad Human Disease, vote Liberal, think Cliff Richard's an example to young people (or even think about him at all), love pop classics played by nauseating Nigel Kennedy, and pop selections by Michael Ball, *really* like Harry Secombe, agree with fascist taxi drivers so's not to cause a fuss, and love anyone who thinks remotely like Mary Whitehouse.

Phew that's better!

' *Believe me! The secret of reaping the greatest fruitfulness and the greatest enjoyment from life is to live dangerously . . .* '
                                                        Friedrich Nietzsche

Safety Kills

Control of the masses' freedom to live dangerously if they want, is creeping into every aspect of our rounded-off, no-sharp-edges, seat-belted lives. For instance:

☞ Pill bottles and domestic cleaning containers with tops like Christmas cracker puzzles, that only slightly backward three year olds (the ones they were designed to protect) can open.

☞ Family cars that won't allow you to drive them and bleep at you unless you do as they say. (Actually, how come most modern cars go nearly twice as fast as the speed limit?)

☞ Cigarette packets with grizzly health warnings bigger than the brand names. SMOKING SENDS YOU TO HELL AND DAMNATION.

☞ The tidying up and de-emotionalising of sport, causing footballers to go to prison for merely taking a swing at each other (instead of for simply having bad haircuts).

☞ Constant tut-tutting when you eat white sugar, white bread, or red meat or drink tap water, alcohol, ordinary milk or non de-caffeinated coffee – in fact practically everything that you actually like!

I think it really is polite,
to let you know we're always right.

Here are some of my proposals to make life safer.

☞ Cut all branches off trees to prevent climbing.

☞ Make all vehicles (including planes) out of bouncy rubber.

☞ Ban anything sharp.

☞ Ban being cross.

☞ Exterminate all animals that bite and aren't fluffy with big soulful eyes.

☞ Forbid swimming, climbing, running, hopping and jumping.

☞ Forbid sex unless between people with current government licences.

☞ Forbid religion (cause of more strife than anything else).

☞ Ban this book.

The Great Anti-Hurty-Things-in-your-Pocket Campaign

After the terrible murder in December 1995 of headmaster Philip Lawrence in London's Maida Vale there were several news features to illustrate the danger of knives. It showed some police 'expert', in a white lab coat, demonstrating the qualities of what looked like the ordinary kitchen variety, by plunging it into a bag containing something soft (baby hamsters perhaps). Golly, I thought, *knives must be dangerous!*, and I have lots of the horrid things in my house. If I'm not careful I'll be going to go out and kill someone. Better throw them all away and get sliced bread in future, buy all my other food cut into small pieces, make sure we get rid of all pins and needles and only have plastic scissors in the bathroom. I then came to wondering if the whole of the Swiss Army might soon have their little red penknives taken away?

Strangely enough police statistics don't seem to justify the hysteria that ended in the *Daily Mirror's* thinly disguised reader -pulling gesture to have a 'put-your-knife-in-and-no-questions-asked' box in the lobby of all police stations for one month. Scotland Yard told me the following facts:

☞ Between 1993 and 1994 there were 2,332 crimes in London involving sharp instruments (knives, swords, beaks etc.) and the following year 2,550.

☞ Between 1993 and 1994 there were 3,823 crimes involving blunt instruments (iron bars, clubs, cellos etc.) and the following year, 3,502.

(I'm no statistition but this looks to me as if a hundred or so thugs with blunt instruments, sharpened 'em up.)

☞ Between the years of 1985 and 1994 the proportion of murders caused by sharp instruments as opposed to other methods has risen by only 2%.

Seriously, the new ban on carrying knives, though obviously an attempt to solve the problem, is as pointless as taking the points off compasses, blunting saws or having all animals' teeth and claws removed. A knee-jerk reaction to a much bigger and unaddressed problem. Unless I'm mistaken, a knife - like a rock, a stick or a toy train for that matter - is only as dangerous as the intent of the person holding it. One of the best (sorry - worst) murders was the subject of a story by the great Roald Dahl. He described a murder committed by some woman who bashed her husband over the head with a frozen leg of lamb which she then fed to the cops (the leg, not the husband). I suppose if you were to take that seriously, it makes a sheep a potentially dangerous weapon! I've heard of the beef ban, but this is ridiculous. Anyway, how would you get all those sheep in those amnesty boxes in police station lobbies?

We need more understanding of human nature, because the only real danger that exists is man himself...   Carl Jung

It's all total, undiluted CRAP. The only reason the great British public, or the sleazy media that represents it, got their corporate knickers in a twist over the poor headmaster's death, was because Philip Lawrence WAS a headmaster - a highly respectable member of the establishment, second only to a doctor or bishop (and that's leaving out policemen★).

All of us have, at one time or another, had headmasters or mistresses (head that is), and because of their awesome position of authority we believed they were invulnerable. It was all too scary for the respectable masses. If it could happen to someone like him it could happen to anyone. Let's face it, proper nice people don't usually get

---

★I'm always amazed at the pandemonium when a policeman gets hurt. Isn't it their job to place themselves in dangerous situations?

murdered or attacked - only criminals, drug addicts, loose-livers and people who stay out after eleven o'clock.

But we all know this is not actually true. Only five years ago I was beaten unconscious by two teenage thugs with iron bars because I rather unwisely intervened in an attack on a neighbour. They thought his flat housed a member of an opposing gang who had injured one of their brothers. Despite being caught red-handed by the police (weapons in hand) they only got 40-days community service (that'll teach them) and the incident didn't even reach the back page of the local paper. I got £200 compensation and twenty nice new stitches in the top of my head.

Just to strengthen the point, here's a few more statistics kindly sent by the Home Office Research and Statistics department: Between the years of 1984 and 1994

☞ Attempted murders went up nearly four times

☞ Threats or conspiracies to murder went up seven times

☞ Woundings doubled

☞ The number of firearms used in robbery nearly doubled

☞ The number of offences using firearms in the street trebled

While all this is going on hardly any money is spent trying to solve the problems of the huge and growing urban community of bored, out of work, often penniless youngsters who group together and get into serious trouble for want of something better to do. They're not in the right, we know, but neither is some priviledged wally like Fergie spending millions of tax payers' money, symbolically showing the *under*priviledged two freckly fingers. As for judges, most of them are so shut off from real life (and soon to be boxed and shut away for good), that they are as much use as a blind person judging a beauty contest when it comes to understanding modern life.

*There's so much they could do
with their time,
That doesn't involve getting
mixed up in crime.*

Street gangs do, have, and always
will, fester and multiply in deprived urban
conditions, just like bacteria in a dirty pond.
The worse the conditions, the more violent the gangs. It
doesn't take a school of sociologists to work out the
connection between a whole section of our community to
whom employment isn't even a possibility and the unleashing
of rage against the society that doesn't seem to give a toss.

E for Exaggeration

It reminded me of the tragic case of the ex-policeman's
eighteen year old daughter who died after taking Ecstasy. The
moral majority once again pulled its massive high horse out
of its pristine stable and galloped around making as much
noise as possible. The facts that, statistically, this young
woman (old enough to vote, get married, have kids etc), was
more likely to be run over on the way home (ban cars after
eleven, we cry!) than by popping a pill, and could well have
been killed by drinking too much water (so thinning her
blood), gets forgotten in the scrum to find who can be seen
to be the most self-righteous. Again, one would have to be a
sandwich short of a picnic not to see the connection between
this huge outcry and the fact that she
was the daughter of a an ex-
policeman (the very ones trying to
wipe the problem out).

Warning To Dweebs

Just in case anyone thinks that nasty
John Farman's recommending
weapons and drugs, don't bother –
I'm not – and never will. Drugs can

be (and often are) real nasty, and they can, in certain circumstances kill you. But, just like Paracetamol (which, believe it or not, is just as dangerous if misused), they are becoming, like it or not, part of modern life. What we need is more REAL, non-sensationalised knowledge (and then still more!). If the press and even parents refuse to see the difference between a spliff or a shot of heroin, or an E and a lump of crack, then they're just plain head-under-the-sand stupid. As I write, it has been reported that Ecstasy is no more dangerous than aspirin AND that tests in America have shown that it causes permanent brain damage. See the problem? If these ill-informed parents tell their kids, for instance, that all drugs kill, and those kids find out that *actually* they don't, they are in severe danger of chucking the baby out with the bath water, and never being believed again.

Here's a few real facts from Andrew Tyler's *Street Drugs* which should be an essential in every teenager's Christmas stocking (and maybe their parents' as well). For instance did you know that:

☞ Smoking cannabis appears to be worse for the lungs than cigarette smoke, and hashish smoke is more dangerous than herbal. There is some evidence that the tar from cannabis could increase risk of lung cancer.

☞ Smoking dope can severely muck up your driving ability.

☞ The latest evidence now shows that cannabis smoking CAN become mildly addictive.

☞ The most dangerous aspect of Ecstasy or methylenedioxymethamphetamine (try saying that while chewing a toffee) is that you can never be sure what you're getting. It can be manufactured to all kinds of formulas and will almost certainly be mixed with anything from antihistamine (great for curing hay-fever while getting out of it!) to ground glass to lav cleaner.

But on the other hand:

☞ Methadone, the much cheaper substitute drug that is given to heroin addicts is more addictive, less effective, and kills more people through overdose.

☞ In its unadulterated form, cocaine provides all the vitamins that the hard working, undernourished South American Indians need. The greenery is rich in thiamine, riboflavin, and vitamins and two ounces a day should do you nicely.

☞ Cocaine is a drug of much lower toxicity compared to alchohol, barbiturates or heroin. Deaths from overdose are rare, though the jury's still out as far as deaths from cocaine related incidents are concerned.

Six Ounces of Cannabis, Please

If there ever does come a point when everybody is in possession of all the hard facts drugswise (through a *serious* government information drive) then many people who are actively involved in the problem, believe that we should legalise the lot - cannabis, ecstasy, speed, heroin - you name it. Not only could the quality then be strictly controlled, but there is a strong argument that de-criminalising all drugs would take away their mystique and 'let's-do-something-really-naughty' appeal overnight.

Nothing makes me quite so hot
As talk of legalising pot.

Mine's a Double (standard)

We all know the dangers of cigarettes, and the government's ludicrous attempts to make smokers into neo-criminals, and we all know that all narcotics are horribly evil and a passport to hell and damnation, but there's a much more powerful drug that can drop a grown man in half an hour, causes uncontrolled violence, is quite easily addictive, promotes loads of suicides and kills thousands of people every year either from its use or by being hit by vehicles being driven by people using it. It can make you horribly fat or cause severe malnutrition, give you stomach ulcers, trash your liver, shrink your brain (and your willy) and can cause certain kinds of cancer. It can damage the heart, cause numbness throughout most of your body, and cause miscarriages if you're a woman But that's the bad news.

The good news is that its great to take, makes you instantly funny and really attractive to the opposite sex. You can get it anywhere relatively cheaply, administer it in public and the dealers now stay open all day. It's widely advertised as a jolly conduit to a good time, earning the government (and therefore you and me) a huge fortune due to their cut. Britain is one of the top producers of this wonder drug and is one of the five biggest exporters. What is it called? You only get one guess (unless you're pissed out of your brains when reading this).

'One of the great disadvantages of wine is that it makes a man mistake words for thoughts...'
Samuel Johnson

CRAP CORNER

Much of the content of this chapter, I confess, has been slightly tongue in cheek to make a point. It would be ridiculous to suggest that our fair land should be turned back to a state similar to the Wild-West with gun-toting, knife-throwing, law-flaunting yobs (see football supporters when their team loses) refusing to accept any of the rules that a society imposes as part of the process of becoming civilised. But:

When you get an authority that plasters public places with anti-smoking propaganda, but is still willing to accept billions in revenue from their sale, you realise that things are not quite right.

[CRAP!] When you get an authority that covers our beaches in signs telling us not to do this, that or the other, but is willing to condone human excrement being pumped into the very sea that laps against them, making some of our shores a serious health hazard, you must start asking questions.

[CRAP!] When you get an authority that allows notices everywhere telling young kids not to fish in country rivers unless they're friends of the owners or have an expensive permit, when all the 'public' rivers are polluted by industrial effluent and are all but fish-free, you realise that things aren't quite fair.

[CRAP!] When you get an authority that puts up signs telling youngsters not to use their bikes on country paths for fear of making them rutted, but is willing to sit back and watch vast areas of the countryside be gobbled up by urban development or pointless by-passes that put money into the pockets of the rich and powerful, you must scratch your head and wonder where it's all going.

[CRAP!] When you get an authority that sheds hugely publicised crocodile tears over the horrific murder of children by some maniac that was allowed a permit to own guns, but is reticent to consider banning the nasty things because they have their own gun club in the basement of the Commons, you must come to your own conclusions.

[CRAP!] When you get an authority that dedicates itself to making the roads (and therefore us) safer, but spends practically nothing on inner city public transport or developing an alternative to a method of propulsion (the internal combustion engine) that is positively pre-historic in concept, you wonder who's protecting what. (Could it possibly be that the fuel used, the by-product of which is planet-threatening pollution, makes a fortune for successive governments who are merely puppets of the super-rich oil companies?) Answers on a postcard (recycled of course).

To sum up, however, society must protect itself from those who want to ruin public amenities and everyday life for the rest of us, but in doing so, the powers that enforce these rules MUST be seen to keep their own personal noses squeaky clean. The balance between this and the obvious flip side – the creation of a nanny state, should be down to pure common sense. Something that is often in very short supply. What do you think?

WE ARE NOW ALL SEXUALLY LIBERATED

(CRAP!)

> **Sexual intercourse is a grossly overrated pastime; the position is undignified, the pleasure momentary and the consequences utterly damnable...** *Lord Chesterfield*

Now this really is a tricky topic. One that has been argued about since the first man asked the first woman to go to his place for a little prehistoric, back of cave, nookie. It's rather odd when you consider that the sexual act is something that nearly all of us will have a bash at sooner or later – so why the big deal? For some reason humans have been embarrassed about sex from day one, and it's difficult to put one's finger (or anything else) on why. After all, animals, whether weasels or wombats or tigers or tortoises seem to have no prob. They simply sidle up to someone they fancy (hopefully of the same species) sniff them in a most personal manner, and then, if the other party's up for it, simply do the biz and return to what they were doing before (usually sod all).

FANCY A FROLIC?

> **Is sex dirty? Only if it's done right...** *Woody Allen*

It is purely because grown-ups *do* get so embarrassed or over-sensitive about the subject, and the fact that parents find it so difficult to talk about 'it' with their 'innocent' offspring, that the problem slides down from generation to generation. Why should this be? Most adults, and practically all parents (except Jesus's – by all accounts), have done IT at sometime in their lives. Come on, don't you, whenever you see a coach-load of highly respectable, silver-haired senior citizens, relish the concept of them having done it at one time or another? I do! Don't you ever stare incredulously at some pompous old peer on the telly, trying to imagine him doing IT? I do? Or don't you ever ponder on the bedroom activities at Buck House? Did the Queen *really* do it? I do (ponder that is).

Many believe that sex is dirty (especially if you're over thirty).

For as long as I can remember, parents have told their horny youngsters "Don't do it" and while they're not doing it "Be careful". Parents, when I was young, maintained that they stayed in with their stamp collections or *Searchers* albums, waiting for the joyous sanctity of marriage before going 'all the way' (see page 176). If you believe that, you might as well believe that the guy in the bad cotton-wool beard and carpet slippers putting presents in your Christmas stocking really was Santa Claus. Teenagers these days, thank God (or AIDS) are probably less promiscuous, but far more honest.

But why all the fuss about sex? Why is society so obsessed with it? The problem is that parents find it so difficult to face the central and simple fact that doing what comes naturally feels better, and can be more of a thrill, than just about anything else (short of the *Nemesis* ride at Alton Towers). Add the fact that (unlike Alton Towers), it's absolutely free (which is why mean people could well turn into sex-maniacs) and you've got a very alluring pastime.★

Not only that, but masturbation (first practised in the ancient Chinese province of Wan King) has only just come off the '100 things you must never, never do on pain of eternal damnation (and blindness)' list.

★ Women's magazines often try to tell us that to do it properly requires advice and training, but that could be because they've often got precious little else to write about.

> *Masturbation? Don't knock it, it's sex with someone you love...*
> *Woody Allen*

It's still something that, even in these liberated days, most adults would not admit to, even on pain of finger-nail removal. It beats me. We don't get uptight if someone rubs their nose or scratches their head a lot, so why get so uptight about any other part of the body?

Whether you're a tramp or a banker,
you should never admit to being a...
person who goes in for self gratification.

Back to the plot. How does all this hypocrisy about sex manifest itself?

The Sexy World of Advertising

Sex shifts product. This is not theory – this is fact. If you've ever giggled knowingly at that TV commercial starring a beautiful babe teasing and nibbling, licking and sucking a long, cylindrical (if somewhat flaky) chocolate bar, and thought it was just your filthy mind working overtime, fear not. Yes, you have got a filthy mind, admittedly, but so have all the people involved in making the thing. But Hold On! I hear you cry. This is 1996 and women are no longer seen as sex objects or exploited for profit. Oh yeah – and foxes are no longer seen as sport, and bears never shit in the woods!

Exploiting women must be wrong,
unless a huge budget comes along.

Advertising, it must be admitted, is one of the more subtle exponents of the sexual message. But not that blinking subtle. For instance, do women really run their fingers lingeringly and longingly across their naked bodies when scrubbing those intimate places in soap ads? Of course they don't. Do they really toss their hair provocatively (and in slow motion) every time they wash it? Of course they don't. Do they really clean their teeth simply so that they'll be more alluring to kiss? No way! And do they really make little tick marks on their perfectly bronzed bodies to show where the sweat - sorry perspiration - isn't? Not on your nelly (or theirs). But before we nod our heads and put our *Men are Shits* tee-shirts back on, maybe you should consider for a second that it isn't only the women who get used for their physical attributes. What about all those terribly tedious deodorant and shaving ads using dishy guys with bodies that make the average man look like John Major's weedy brother, or extremely well 'built' guys unself-consciously dropping their jeans in launderettes. C'mon, if the average man dropped his strides in public, he'd be on a charge before he could even say Levis. And what about that ad in which all the office girls rush to the window at the same time every day to watch this hunky construction worker taking off his shirt and downing a Coke?

❛ *Sometimes I think if there was a third sex, men wouldn't get as much as a glance from me...* ❜   Amanda Vail

❛ *I'll drink to that...* ❜   John Farman

So why do we swallow all the guff that's shoved at us? Why can't we see we're being manipulated? Could it be that those oh-so-clever ad men (and women) have sussed, through years upon tedious years of market research (that privileged view of the bloody obvious) that they believe that by using certain products, the world that encloses the beautiful people of Adland will become available to them. It's weird, the very most you're likely to get out of chocolate bars is a spotty skin and a few, very un-alluring inches of blubber round the waist. And bucketfuls of oil of jojoba* won't make your hair thick and bouncy if it's as thin and weedy as mine.

Honesty's all very well,
but not if you've got a product to sell.

In a world where one product is practically the same as any other for a given purpose, the only way the manufacturers can use muscle on the competition is in the way they present it to us, the public. That's why they don't feature that many dear old senior citizens going about their ablutions or trying to get their National Health dentures round a candy bar. And that's why we don't see our dear old wrinklies dabbing their liver-spotted bodies with their essence of pomegranate-zest sun lotion, while languishing wheel-chair bound outside their twilight homes. The wonderful world of advertising is a world of glitzy perfection. No one ever farts after eating baked beans, no one ever pees in the bathroom wash-basin when the loo's busy, and no one who isn't drop-dead gorgeous ever gets picked up, or does the picking up, in all those tedious and predictable boy meets girl ads. Actual sex: all that heaving, panting and sweating, is only suggested, but never seen. In Adland, sex (of a mystical and beautiful nature) always happens off-camera, behind billowing muslin curtains to the sounds of a crescendo of strings or the crashing of waves. It isn't that it's all a ridiculous, misleading, fatuous hype that gets me; it's the fact that we all seem to not only accept it, but be drawn into it, which we prove by buying the crap that they sell.

---

* Yet another by-product that manufacturers can't find any other use for.

'Implication's always safer than penetration...' Me

All the Fun of the Fairs

But that's just mainstream TV advertising. What about all those areas that employ real live women to sell products. Pretty, if somewhat bimboid, girls have for years been used at commercial trade fairs. Say you're a company selling left-handed grommets or gold-plated lavatory fittings and you're located in a huge hall alongside all your competitors selling practically identical kit. Doesn't it stand to reason that you will look for something to drag the punters to your stand rather than the others. What do you do? You take a leaf out of the fisherman's book. Just as he casts a lot of tasty extra bait to attract the fish to his hook, you, using exactly the same principle, employ tasty babes with wide smiles and short skirts to grab their eye. Nothing to do with lavatory fittings (apart from the fact that these girls just might go to the loo as much as anyone else) but a lot to do with men's (particularly salesmen's) willy-led attitude to life.

If you want to shift your gear,
girls are best – never fear.

It is interesting to note at this point that 95% of mammals are not monogamous, and that the male of any species, according to Roger Short (an Australian reproductive physiologist) especially if he is generally larger than the female, is the culprit. If any credit can be taken, it must be said that the human male is practically the only species able to keep it in his trousers, so to speak, and stick with one partner (on the other hand it could simply be that other species don't wear trousers).

Optional Extras

At motor shows, the manufacturers go even further and employ scantily-clad girls draped across the bonnets of their new models. That potential buyer from Ruislip or Ostletwistle doesn't, for one minute, think she comes with the car, or, as one might be forgiven for supposing, believe that the ownership of said product would necessarily lead to the capturing (and owning) of this kind of accessory. After all he knows he'll still be driving his somewhat less-than-showroom-shiny missus down to the shops every Saturday as usual, whatever bloody car he buys. Modern motors might look great in professionally-lit showrooms, or in ads careering through the Nevada desert, but in a wet Saturday afternoon Tesco's car park, containing identical men in fur-collared car-coats and knit-backed driving gloves, they all look much the same. But it is the *fantasy* that draws the potential punter in. Whichever way you look at it, middle-age men (the only ones who can afford new motors) prefer young girls (certainly to look at), and anyone that tells you otherwise is fibbing. (Luckily, young girls tend to prefer young men, otherwise countless women would be traded in when past their peak.)

A Small Deposit

It's not only women that run the risk of being traded in. A doctor's report was published recently that claimed that business was booming at the sperm banks. Not really surprising. We're always being told that the sperm count (much like the hair line), in we poor men, is receding owing to the stress of modern living. But this, my friends, is not the reason. On closer investigation, and interrogation, it turned out that the women were childless, *not* because of lack of lead in the male pencil, but because they SIMPLY WEREN'T BONKING. Apparently they'd rather their husbands went down the sperm bank, make a deposit (so to speak), simply so that they could, at a later date (between Sainsbury's and the hairdresser), be impregnated in the comfort of a nice warm, impersonal surgery, even though it costs copious amounts of readies. The implications of this are astounding. For years generations of women have been dying for the sex bit, but lived in constant fear of becoming inhabited by small alien beings, but these days many are dying to get pregnant, but can't face nature's way of attaining it. Get your head round that one.

We need you men to sire our kids,
but sex as such is on the skids.

Sex at the Movies

Sex sells movies: yet another earth-shattering fact. Just about every film you see these days (short of Bambi or Babe) has something, usually irrelevent to the plot, which finds an excuse to include the oldest participant sport in the world. I'm sure if they made a movie of the life of Mother Theresa, they'd try and get a bit of the old between-the-sheets into it somewhere (even if it did only involve her mum and dad). Forget God, and forget art. Any bright-eyed young drama student must realise, that if she or he wants to hit the big time they must be prepared to get their kit off at some point along the road to fame and fortune; and any embryonic script writer must save some space for a sex scene of some description.

Whatever you're playing, be it peasant or toff,
the message's the same – you must get 'em off!

Again, I have no problem with this. Sex is a part of life, after all, so why not allude to it if you want. The snag is that there are a load of other parts of life that aren't alluded to, so the 'sex-is-something-naughty' scenario is continually being pushed before the public's, ever-widening eyes. When for instance, do you ever see cowboys, (or Indians, for that matter) stopping in the middle of a gunfight, or round-up, to go to the lavatory? How often do you see characters like Superwoman desperate to get to the chemist at that vital time in the month? On an even more trivial level, when, in an age when auto-thieves are poised on every pavement, do you ever see a movie star lock his car door?

Every day things on the silver screen,
are never heard, and never seen.

But all this is fairly unimportant. After all, we all know that people in movies don't function like normal folk - so why expect them to? But there is one aspect which is a tad more serious. Why in an age when we are told, every five minutes, that sex with anyone without a 'full service history' is the equivalent to home-testing an electric chair, is one particular stage of the sexual procedure never shown? Lets examine the scenario.

Action! Boy meets girl; dreamy music and loads of body language; boy invites girl (or vice versa) back to his place; girl's outer garments slip to her ankles; boy's follow; underwear explodes. They fall onto the bed; standard aerial view showing mass limb entanglement (carefully avoiding showing the 'rude' bits); girl falls asleep with head (sporting contented smile) on boy's chest.

Never - ever, do we see either participant halt the proceedings and reach for the rubberwear. Why? Because in Movieland everything has to be seamless and beautiful - and relatively fast! Imagine hunky Brad Pitt, while leaping around the motel with that naughty, and newly met, Thelma (or was it Louise?) in the movie *Thelma and Louise* (or was it *Louise and Thelma*?), suddenly halting the proceedings and routing through his heavily advertised Levi's pockets. He'd then have to struggle with the condom packet (not easy in the height of passion), squeeze into the contents, and return to the plot hoping everything was just as he left it. It's all a bit like a racing driver must feel when dashing into his pits to have *his* rubber (tyres that is) changed before rushing out to hopefully regain the same position.

Actually, in Thelma's case, it would have made no difference anyway, since she and her mate ended up driving over a cliff (which is as good a way as any of avoiding sexually-transmitted diseases).

Sex on telly

As I'm writing this book, news is coming through of a code that parents can programme into their tellies to make the watching of rudeness impossible for their children. Nice one in theory. Nobody wants their six year old watching bonking in Birmingham or porn in Purley. The idea falls flat, however, because a) you are never quite sure when some couple in the most innocent-sounding of programmes is going to drop everything (literally) and do it over the Zanussi, and b) because some parents, by trying to protect their offspring from hard reality as long as possible, are likely to go bonkers censoring everything from *The Countryside in Spring* to *Carry on Camping*.

Having said that, I'd make sure nobody in my house (or anyone else's) could watch crap like *Pyjama Party* or the *Girly Show*, as they're so obviously an attempt by the TV moguls to cash-in, in the most down-market, crass, shoddy and blatant way, on teenagers' new sexual honesty.

❛*Feminism infuses my every waking and sleeping moment...*❜   *Katie Puckrick (presenter Pyjama Party)*

❛*Crap...*❜   *John Farman*

Censorship's one thing, but certain aspects of modern life like hairdresser jeeps, *The Sunday Sport*, drinks like *Malibu*, trendy vicars, pot-noodles, shell suits and pathetic TV programmes should be disposed of on the grounds of being a waste of space, time and raw materials.

Sexual Harrassment in the Office

Over the last few years, there's been a huge hue and cry, involving a mass twisting of the knickers, about an age-old but recently recognized inter-office sport called *Sexual Harrassment*. The rules are quite simple. Take one girl, preferably pretty, and if possible, slightly naive, and one (or numerous) lecherous male member of staff. (The game can be played the other way round, but it's not nearly as common.) The male then harrasses the female with numerous sexual innuendos until she either gives him what he's after - after work - or leaves the company. Usually the male member (pardon the expression) is in a far superior position company-wise and can use this power as a form of ill-disguised blackmail.

Countless girls have been underpromoted, moved sideways, or even fired by frustrated unsatisfied bosses over the years. But now it is a crime and these horrid men are dragged protesting into court and given the third degree (women involved in the law, by the way, suffer greater sexual harrassment than any other profession). Feelings, as usual, run pretty high on both sides, the flames often fanned by our inimitable holier-than-thou press (that's the same press that splash naked women across their pages to up the circulation - amongst other things!).

Exploitation of women is the pits, but here's young Tracy with the enormous ... grin.

v. Sex in the Office

Quite a different issue, but one with its own hypocrisies. 60% of all couples meet at work. If you think about it, it's a damn sight easier than most other venues like pubs, clubs or parties where, as a rule, if you do see someone you fancy, you either strike there and then, or stand a fair chance of never seeing them again. Men carry the greatest burden in the old chat-up stakes as most women can be rather prehistoric about it. Although not exactly favouring the earlier mentioned old club-on-the-back-of-the-head-and-back-to-the-cave school of seduction, they do generally like the guy to start the ball rolling. Any woman who is observed to be actually making the running stands the risk of being branded a slag by her chums (when men do it, they become an object of admiration among theirs). Unfortunately, despite pleading for equality, loads of women of the old school *still* demand the door being opened for them, their coat put over their shoulders, or their chair being pulled out in a restaurant, and some I've known would practically give up smoking before thinking of lighting their own cigarette. Thank God teenagers today don't bother with all that crap.

Men, being the simple organisms that they no doubt are, where matters of courtship are concerned, have problems working out what is above the acceptability line and what isn't. What seems like a great chat-up line can fall flat on its face if mistimed. On the other hand, women label men who don't make clear their intentions, as wimps. Most women find the sexual (for that's what it is) approach offensive, ONLY if they find the presenter unnattractive (well that's my opinion anyway - another politically incorrect one to put in your trousers!).

Some women say they like it lots
But like it less - when it stops.

261

CRAP CORNER

All a bit confusing, eh! Summing up:

CRAP! The human race are obsessed with sex, but at the same time, when compared with animals, are unbelievably repressed.

CRAP! Most parents try to con their kids by giving the impression that when they were young they waited for marriage before having full-blown sex.

CRAP! The one thing that parents and sex educators fail to inform you is that sex feels better than just about anything.

CRAP! Most people still believe that masturbation is 'not quite nice'. That's why it's still referred to as self-abuse.

CRAP! Admen have no interest in reality, preferring to con us by presenting the world of wrinkle-free, spotless, ageless, smell-less perfection.

CRAP! Women are still used as bait to bring potential male customers in for the kill.

CRAP! Car manufacturers sell sexual fantasy when fighting for their share of the market for their almost identical piles of metal, rubber, plastic and glass.

CRAP! A movie without a sex scene is as rare as a policeman with a degree, even though other far more common natural practices are hardly ever alluded to.

CRAP! No one ever uses any form of protection in movie or telly sex.

CRAP! The gutter press are always on some sexual campaign or other, either exposing promiscuity or accusing men of using women for their own ends. Meantime they fill their pages with women in various stages of undress.

CRAP! Some women find men's sexual advances offensive in direct proportion to how much they fancy them.

IT ISN'T THE WINNING, IT'S THE TAKING PART

CRAP!

6 *Serious sport has nothing to do with fair play...* 9
George Orwell

It was once said that soccer was a gentleman's game played by ruffians and that rugby was a ruffian's game played by gentlemen. Despite claims that sport is society's great leveller – an oasis of innocent pleasure in a desert of cynical commercialism – any closer examination might tell a completely different story. The sports people play, just like the newspapers they read, or the people they try to get into bed, are a dead give-away to where they fit in that much bigger and complex game called *The British Way of Life*.

My Team's Better Than Yours..Or Else!
Some 'sports' tend to attract the sort of fans that exhibit the kind of fanaticism only seen in wars or Tom Jones concerts.

Why, for instance, is a Newcastle United supporter prepared to practically die for a team formed from players who've probably never even been to the city before signing? Why doesn't a Man United fan, when kicking the head of a West Ham supporter, realise that he's maiming the same species (*Hooliingus Thickus*) that in any other circumstances he'd probably down gallons of lager with? Or boxing. How can a Chris Eubank fan watch his hero bashing his opponent into wheelchairdom, without realising that he's maiming

HANG ON A MO! AREN'T WE ON THE SAME SIDE

263

practically a mirror image? It all comes down to a need to proclaim 'my whatever-it-is is better than your whatever-it-is'. A need to find an association with a tribe of like-minded people, however tenuous the link. In some ways this could be regarded as quite acceptable, and almost commendable, but support for a team and patriotism for your country can (in my view) lurch into aggression and the worst kind of nationalism. Mind you, on reflection, it might be better for a hundred or so quarter-wits to kick eight bells out of each other after a footie match (and then go home satisfied) than on a newly prepared international battle ground. Whether you agree with me or not (and please let me know) it can be argued that there is a whole separate agenda going on which has absolutely nothing to do with sport.

Sex Free Sport?

The ancient Greeks, bless 'em, not only invented public sport but, better than that, sport without any clothes on (save the odd laurel wreath to keep their hair – yes, their hair! – from jigging about). In those days half of the fun must have been drooling over the magnificent physiques of the participants. But that was then and now is now. Ever since those times, we've been led to believe that sexuality plays absolutely no part in sport and this has been largely true. Right up to only a few years ago, athletes were an extremely unsexy bunch. There's no doubt that the harder the two sexes trained, the more there was a tendency for them to look alike (bums and boobs being somewhat superfluous to high performance), whether it be the pale, skinny, androgynous distance runners or the vast gargantuans that threw heavy or sharp things in the field events. Often the most complicated of tests (the mind boggles) proved inconclusive in separating the female of the species from the male. In fact, some of those huge Eastern-Bloc 'women' looked as if they could eat men alive (and back home probably did!).

And what was the single factor that made this change? It's very simple. Money!! In 1989 a well-gorgeous,

American, black sprinter called Florence Griffith-Joiner turned up at the Seoul Olympics, looking like she'd arrived for a casting for a fashion magazine. The fact that she won the gold in the 100 metres dash was irrelevant. Suddenly the press and multinational advertisers had something new and concrete to latch onto - sex appeal and charisma. The personality machine was kicked into life and fair play or sport for sport's sake had to line up at the start in order to compete. All the old baggy shorts, drab singlets and yellowing plimsolls went down to the local charity shop in favour of slinky lycra cat-suits and shorts brief enough to make hot pants seem positively voluminous (and that was just the men).

In relatively few years sport on any level has became big business and big business attracts the sort of people who, not interested in the pursuit of physical perfection themselves, see gold in them there stadiums. The female athletes especially have transmuted, Eliza Doolittle-like, from being the skinny and rather unfanciable sorts of yesteryear to displaying the kind of lithe bodies the average couch-potato like me can only dream about. I reckon the

longest time spent at an athletics meeting these days, is that spent waiting for the girls to touch up their make-up in the dressing rooms.

Just before you start a race,
Tease your hair and do your face.

...and the boys?

It was hunky athletes like Daly Thompson or Carl Lewis who first caught the attention of the women viewer. All those rather sinewy, chaps with sensible haircuts, like old-timers Roger Bannister or Gordon Pirie, or slightly later, Steve Ovett and Brendan Foster have almost disappeared. Natural selection has thrown up black and nearly black athletes who, though up till recently, were only known for running fast, now regularly outclass all-comers in the long distance events.

Linford Christie, our most famous sprinter became almost as famous for his there-for-all-to-see 'equipment', as for his staggering abilities on the track.

> *If you run it – win it!*
> *If you've got it – flaunt it.*

Gladiators

This emphasis on appearance has resulted in a strange phenomenon that threatens to be more popular than all the established sports put together. The current fad for plush gymnasiums and over-priced keep-fit centres has spawned a breed of fake-tanned super-mutants who, having honed their bodies (but unfortunately not their brains) to the peak of almost cartoon-like perfection, found there was nothing to do with them. Some clever Stateside TV exec. found the perfect solution. Get them to fight each other!

Every week, for no reason that I can establish, over-fit members of the public subject themselves to being beaten black and blue (or blacker and bluer) by a posse of glistening freaks renamed with banal titles like Flame, Sahara, Vulcan, Wolf or Fury (why not Bruise, Sweat or even Plonker?) to the hysterical baying of their friends and loved ones.

Promotion Goes Mad

The press love this cross fertilisation of sex and sport. Suddenly they're able to take the stars from the back sports pages and shove them into the gossip columns. Sport merges with show business as much fancied tennis heroes like Andre

Agassi are linked to female singing stars like Barbara Streisand, or Martina Navratilova with female singing stars like kd Lang. Jackpot of all jackpots, the ex-rugby star, Will Carling was reported to be scrumming with the ex-future queen of England.

Others for some obscure reason, were snapped up by several diverse areas of show business, in a sadly obvious attempt to cash into their temporarily high profile. Sebastian Coe, the runner, went into politics, rugby players like Jeremy Guscott brought in lucrative modelling contracts and swimmers like Sharron Davies or baldie Duncan Goodhew advertised everything from breakfast cereals to shampoo (well maybe not the latter!). Most recently, Damon Hill, the brilliant racing driver (who certainly doesn't need the money) blew his cool completely by promoting pizza with squeaky commentator Murray Walker. I bet his poor dad, ex world-champion, Graham, turned in his grave.

Boxers Frank Bruno and Nigel Benn became everyday media and showbiz personalities despite hardly being able to string an intelligible sentence together. In fact, our Frank, when not punching the lights out of someone (or having his own punched out) could be seen featured in that other antiquated expression of British eccentricity - the pantomine (Widow Twanky with attitude). There's so much dosh floating around that most top sports persons now have managers, like the incredible Mark McCormack, who guarantees to make his charges into megastars (while taking a large slice for his trouble).

If in sport you've made a splash,
Sell your soul and make some cash.

Noble Art?

While on the subject of boxers: one quick peek behind the ring itself will reveal a coven of heavies and gangsters that would make twenties Chicago seem like Never Never Land. The whole lucrative business is controlled by half a dozen or so neo-hoods who invent championship titles at the drop of one of their punch drunk boys purely to jack up the prize money. At present there are four versions of the world heavyweight title: the World Boxing Organisation, the World Boxing Association, the International Boxing Federation and the one supported by Don King the convicted ex-gangster and murderer (whose hair looks as if he's touched a live rail).

Heads In The Sand

Most of the TV sports pundits, like that salt-of-the-earth, cockney sparrah Jimmy Greaves or the 'isn't-everything-and-everyone-wonderful', Sue Lloyd, lead us to believe that they still hanker after the glorious innocence of sport (while making a small fortune telling us). But try as they might, all that old 'play up and play the game' crap or 'it's not the winning, it's the taking part' is showing severe signs of disappearing under a pile of contracts, commercial endorsements and non-sporting behaviour. It was almost funny to watch all these 'experts' after having praised the English fans for so nobly getting behind their team in the recent European cup semi-final against Germany, being forced to watch herds of them rampaging through central London witch-hunting anyone with a vaguely foreign accent, simply because they lost.

Go Faster Pills

As early as the fifties those that cared were beginning to wonder if the pressure to win was becoming too strong. The first major drugs bust was in 1960 when Knut Jenson, a young Danish Olympic cyclist (are all Danes Knuts?), fell off his bike and died. The autopsy detected stimulant drugs in his bloodstream. The added incentive of money, spawned more drugs in sport than the average teenage rave and random tests have now become two-a-penny. Weight-lifters get busted for containing the same sort of steroids as oven-ready turkeys, footballers get suspended for sniffing as many white lines as they run between, and some field athletes seem to spend as much time at the medicine cabinet as they do at the track. As for 'high'-jumping!

Probably the most famous case of drug abuse in sport was in 1988 when the seemingly jet-propelled Canadian sprinter Ben Johnson broke the 100 metre world record at the Olympics. He apparently was so 'up' he hardly touched the ground, and after a random test showed what he'd been on, he was sent home in disgrace.

❝ From hero to zero in 9.79 seconds... ❞

graffiti at Olympic village

Logoed Up

The other new aspect of modern sport is that sportsmen and women have become walking billboards. The names of everything from condoms to chocolate bars are plastered over much of their surface area, to such a degree that they'll soon have to change their kit mid-event to satisfy all their hungry sponsors. I wouldn't be surprised if, before long, the advertiser's name will be announced along with the actual competitor: 'Please welcome, ladies and gentlemen – Coca Cola's very own Linford Christie'. Not possible? In show jumping they are already naming some of the horses after the sponsors.

The problem is that the stakes have all rocketed. Instead of a naff cup or trophy to put on your mum's mantelpiece, or a slap on the back at some crashingly boring TV Awards dinner, thousands of pounds can now be won on just one race, one throw or one hop, skip and jump. Sports millionaires are now two-a-penny and promoters vie to get the big names to compete at their events. The aforementioned Linford Christie, at his peak, could earn 10,000 quid a second, if he could find time between opening sports shops and making commercials. Germany's leading girl swimmer (hitherto a very unsexy sport) is reported to have a personal fortune of over £4million. It's now got to the point that certain sportsmen (no names mentioned) refuse to even represent their country in an unpaid international if there's a few quid to be made elsewhere.

Self-worth and patriotism?
Don't be funny.
See my agent and let's talk money.

Cash for All

Although it's a bit sad, I think I can live with all this. After all, why shouldn't rugby players, cricketers or swimmers, for instance, start to pull even a fraction of the booty that soccer or tennis players enjoy? And why shouldn't they become media stars like pop singers or Great Train Robbers? If the whole sports business has become tacky already, why shouldn't they be able to join the same lucrative band-wagon.

Amateurism or Shamateurism?

We in Britain seem still to be confused by the whole business.

It's a well publicised fact that compared to other countries, our young athletes are hopelessly underfunded. Our training facilities are laughable besides those of other developed countries. The problem is that we still tend to hang on to the rather quaint concept that the main function of sport is to strengthen character and team spirit and that naked professionalism and the resulting money should never come into the equation.

❝ In love as in sport, for better or worse, the amateur status must be strictly maintained... ❞   Robert Graves

Unfortunately, the net result of hanging on to all this joyful amateurism is that for better or worse, the British have turned out to be third rate at many sports and in sports like tennis, our youngsters have about as much chance of coming out on top as OJ Simpson being offered a chairmanship of the Anti-Violence Against Women League.

Play up and play the game we say,
And watch us losing all the way.

So ... if money and professionalism are the new names of the new game, *please, please*, let's accept it, live with it, and keep all those holier-than-thou lectures on loyalty, team spirit, sport for sports sake, for the primary school field.

CRAP CORNER
Here we go:

The press and media are always the first to take the mickey out of our undertrained athletes for never doing anything in major sports like tennis or skiing, but are seldom seen putting their hands in their pockets to sponsor their training.

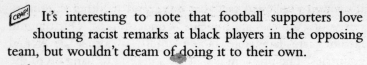 It's interesting to note that football supporters love shouting racist remarks at black players in the opposing team, but wouldn't dream of doing it to their own.

Though loyalty to one's own team is praiseworthy, sport often creates a partisanship similar to nationalism.

Though everyone in sport is supposed to be equal, the prizes for men are still substantially more than those for women.

The whole dream that was the Olympic ideal, man testing his physical perfection against man (and woman against woman) has now totally disappeared. Sport is now big business, and the Olympics are just another way for sponsors to get their name in front of a huge multinational audience.

HONOURS AND AWARDS - ONLY THE BEST PEOPLE DESERVE THEM

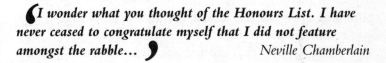

> *I wonder what you thought of the Honours List. I have never ceased to congratulate myself that I did not feature amongst the rabble...* — Neville Chamberlain

Have you ever wondered what you have to do to become a knight or a dame or have letters like OBE or CBE after your name? A couple of times a year, when there isn't a war, a cup final, or some sleazy development at the palace, our illustrious press has a little flutter when the honours lists are published. How did this all come about, we ask ourselves?

Before the 1880s, the dishing out of peerages and knighthoods had been fairly above board. If you had created a pile of wealth and had, in doing so, coincidentally improved the lot of a large number of people, or had done great service to the country or the Government, you might well expect to get the old tap on the shoulder from the Royal sword.

After this date, however, the rot set in and wealthy men openly bribed government establishments by offering hodloads of cash in return for the odd baronetcy or knighthood. A fine example was American millionaire, William Waldorf Astor, who arrived in 1890, promptly became a naturalized British citizen (as they don't have Honours in the States) and systematically bought up palaces, mansions, newspapers and even a seat in parliament. He then chucked money at most of the large British institutions. By pure coincidence he was made a baron in 1916 and, the following year, a viscount.

An even quicker way into a title was to dish a load of loot into party funds and, because political parties of either persuasion are, by definition, always strapped for cash, a title for money seemed a relatively painless trade. By 1910, the backhanders were not nearly so obvious; but all the same, it was fairly clear that if you backed the winning side, you could expect something fairly grand in front of your name. Summing up, if you had it (cash that is) like most other things you could buy it.

By 1922, the money for title business was so established that there was even an under-the-counter price list – ten grand for a nice knighthood, thirty a brill baronetcy, and a proper peerage a mere snip at fifty. It became such a racket that it was common knowledge that even out-and-out crooks could buy whatever title they could stump up the money for.

But by 1925, the outcry by proper sirs, peers and dukes, who hated all these common upstarts joining their ranks, was so loud that an Honours Act was set up to prevent the trading in titles. Nice idea, but all this did was to drive the trade underground and from then on the negotiations had to be done far more discreetly in bars, boardrooms and even bedrooms. And that's how it remains to this day.

Keeping the Natives Quiet

Every now and again a Prime Minister will shoot himself in the foot by giving a title to someone so inappropriate that words like nepotism hit the headlines. Back in 1976, Labour premier, Harold Wilson, not only made his old mate, Joe Kagan, a northern manufacturer of naff raincoats and later convicted crook, into a Lord, but in the same disastrous list his political secretary was elevated to 'Lady' for services rendered. It later turned out that it was Marcia who drew up the list. Quel bon chance!

Most of the time the totally outdated honours system is just a way of buttering up (or quietening down) mad old colonels, gin-sodden naval commanders, those who give money to the party in power or those lucky people who've done brilliantly out of the system already – thank you very much!

These days it's generally accepted that the whole thing is a lamentable joke. Anyone from sweaty snooker players to second-rate chain store owners can expect some sort of reward, whether it be a peerage, knighthood, CBE, OBE (or even GCSE), as our pathetic politicians try to curry favour with us serfs by honouring our folk heroes. One must be sometimes tempted to value these honours slightly below winning a goldfish at a fairground rifle range (which is a trifle unfair to fairground rifle ranges).

'This is not for me. The honour is for the poor...'
Mother Theresa (on receiving the Order of Merit)

Ten Ways to Influence Those That Must Be Influenced (and get an Award)

1. Be born into the aristocracy, and don't marry below yourself.

2. Do good works, and make sure everyone knows about them (Sir Jimmy Saville).

3. Be responsible for the lives of thousands of young men (both ours and theirs) through having a high rank in our armed services. If involved in a war so much the better. The more you kill the better (Lord Montgomery?).

4. Make shedloads of money for yourself (through the hard toil of others) and give little bits away to charity, making as much noise as possible while doing so. Better still, inherit the loot from your mum and dad.

5. Write dweeby musicals and sing ghastly songs guaranteed

not to upset children or pets. When interviewed, never say anything contentious (Sir Andrew Lloyd Webber or Sir 'Heath'-Cliff Richard?).

6. Be a random road crossing or dinner lady for seventy-five years (Mabel Bagsworthy OBE) – John Major's slimy new way of showing he's a man of the people.

7. Work your whole life in the civil service without going mad. (Sir Eric Nerd).

8. Be an over-opinionated ex-footballer with severely questionable hair (all of them, but in particular, Sir Bobby Charlton).

9. Spend your whole working life exploiting Third World countries with a name like Sir Tristram Terribly-Posh, on the pretence of improving their lot (see page 56).

10. Bed royalty. Unfortunately, you might have to marry them as well (unless they're already married).

Ten ways of Making Sure You Are Never Offered an Award or Title

1. Speak your mind about the Government, making sure it isn't flattering.

2. Criticise the class system, or the whole way that honours are dished out.

3. Have anything to do with Fergie.

4. Be gay (unless a 'right-on' Shakespearean actor like Sir Ian McKellan, a Lord or MP).

5. Mention Republicanism.

6. Have anything to do with *Spitting Image*.

7. Be black. Unless you've cracked how to suck up to your white masters.

8. Open a horse-meat or swan-canning factory, and print *Appointment to Her Majesty the Queen* on each tin.

9. Simply get on with your life without hurting anyone, using anyone, being honest or attracting attention to yourself.

10. Write a book like this!

Far be it from me to suggest that the way the Honours were dished out in the olden days, when you could simply buy your title off the shelf, was slightly *less* hypocritical. What do you think?

The Awards Pantomine

'Being well known for their well-knowness, celebrities intensify their celebrity images simply by being well known for relations among themselves. By a kind of symbiosis celebrities live off each other...' **Daniel J Boorstin**

It seems that practically every week, some smarmy presenter invades our telly screens hosting some ritzy, glitzy, titsy show in which those enchanting and enchanted people from the entertainment business (in the loosest sense of the word) remind us (and each other) how totally fab they are.

'TV is an invention that permits you to be entertained in your living room by people you wouldn't have in your house...' **David Frost**

'The Awards Ceremony', as a form of mass entertainment, is a relatively new beast, but one which is expanding and mutating like Chris Evans' ego. Unlike the spectacularly politically incorrect Miss World (the living proof that brains don't necessarily go with beauty) or The Eurovision Song Contest (the living proof that Europeans are naff at pop music), these presentations are seldom given as the result of any particular competition, for it's the prize-giving itself which is in the spotlight. Its a bit like deciding who should get the medals at the Olympic Games by assessing what sort of year the athletes have had, or how popular they are with the fans.

The setting is always the same. Some horrid, razzed-up hotel conference room smothered in gaudy sponsors' logos with overloaded tables occupied by a whole bunch of 'must-be-seen-on-telly-in-case-Joe-public-thinks-we're-dead' stars and their hangers-on, who've paid an arm and a leg for the privilege of... hanging in. These overloaded 'guests' have stuffed themselves with food and drink, safe in the knowledge that a minuscule proportion of their 'being-there' fee will go to those that haven't *enough* food or drink and wouldn't even know an awards ceremony if it hit them on the back of the head.

'A celebrity is a person who works hard all his life to become well known, and then wears dark glasses to avoid being recognised...'
Fred Allen

Who Gets What?
What about the awards themselves? For a start, there is absolutely nothing these people can't find to award themselves for. The Best Actor in a Movie, The Best Actress in a Play, The Best Script, The Best Cinematography, The Best Special Effects, The Best Actor with a Wooden Leg, The Best Fish in a Radio Play, The Best Boobs on an Actress, The Worst Taste in a Documentary, The Best Young Actress who Got a Part *Without* Sleeping With The Producer – you name it, they'll give themselves an award for it.

It's Me! It's Really Me!
The bit I like best is when they are about to announce winners. Just as last year's recipient is about to open the

statutory golden envelope, the TV screen divides and each nominee is closed in on so that we are treated to the intimate witnessing of their reactions to either winning or losing. The losers have to put up the best performances of their lives, by not only pretending that they didn't really care about the result, but are delighted for the person who did win. We'd all love to see someone kick the table over, grab his or her rent–a–bimbo, and piss off fairly smartish in a high huff. Let's face it, everyone *loves* bad losers.

But we dutifully watch the winners automatically hug their partners 'without whose support none of this would have been possible', whilst feigning that sickly 'Who me? – But I'm so unworthy' expression. And then it's the awkward zig-zag through the tables full of big and little stars (some of whom have ceased to twinkle), who all pat them matily as they pass (to convince the viewers that they're still in the first division) and up to the stage where it's lots of multiple cheek kissing between the presenter and the presentee.

❛*Show business is sincere insincerity...* ❜   *Benny Hill*

Some of our more 'right-on' personalities, do actually see these ceremonies for what they are, but can't resist that extra shot of publicity. Have you noticed that even the self-styled brat-pack of show business - the Billy Connollys, Bob Geldofs, Ben Eltons or Dawn Frenchs still turn up to have their egos massaged, even though they go out of their way to try to give the impression that they're above it all. Pure, unadulterated, showbiz crap.

I'd Like to Thank...

The other bit I like most is when they give their winning speeches - that bit where actors prove that they're totally useless without a script and rock stars underline that they can't string more than a line of words together without a line of marching powder in their line of vision. Film directors and

producers suggest that their work is merely training for deity in the next life, while up-and-coming actors bore us silly with a list of the names of everyone from the make-up girl to the tea lady who really should have got the award instead of them.

Already-up-and-come film megastars, who unfortunately 'can't be with us tonight' (because they're probably collecting some more prestigious award somewhere else) insist that it was just luck (they don't mean it, but they insist it), and how much the award (once reminded what it is) means to them. Or what about those over-praised giants of the music business who feel that this dizzy platform gives them the right to bore us crapless with their soppy, half-baked views on the state of the world and how much they care? (Dead easy when you spend most of your time high as a kite, lounging by your Fender-shaped L.A. plunge-pool.)

Then, for the winners, it's back-to-the-table-time, tear-stained and ego-satiated, with the coveted award that usually looks like something you'd reject as a consolation prize at a fairground, even if you already had too many badly made cuddly toys.

Pick of the Pack

The final give-away at these ceremonies is most often one where the organisers have absolutely bugger-all left to award anyone for, but need to end on a big name (preferably nearly dead) to round things off nicely. Glittering prizes like - The Academy Award for a Lifetime Achievement, The Fellowship of the Guild of Whatever it Is for the Greatest Contribution to Whatever it Was, The Award for Being the Oldest Showbiz

Personality Still Alive (always won in the past by 100 year old George Burns who had been rumoured to have been battery operated for ten years but whose batteries finally gave out this year) or The All-Time Award for the Greatest and Cleverest and Kindest, Most Intelligent Person who Ever Walked on Planet Earth (which has to be handed on the following year).

The Bitter End

Guaranteed to have us rushing for the OFF button, these programmes usually wind with one of a predicatable gaggle of silly old showbiz buffers, like Sir Richard Attenborough (Grand Emperor of All Luvvies), going on and on, in their modest, self-effacing manner about how lucky they are to be so utterly fabulous and successful, and how honoured they are to have such marvellous chums in the business, with a sincerity that would shame the sadly missed Robert Maxwell.

Celebrities are intellectual fast food...   Lance Morrow

Why?

Any relatively sane person has to ask the question. Why do we continue to heap praise on those who, let's face it, have not only been simply doing their job but, through our loyal support (and cash) have already been awarded with fame and wealth? What is it in the human psyche that enjoys watching mere mortals built up to God-like status (but is just as happy to watch them plunge into obscurity?).

Celebrity is the advantage of being known by people who you do not know...   Nicholas de Chamfort

The answer must be the power of celebrity and glamour. We as a species are obsessed by it. Otherwise we would surely be glued to our screens watching awards for The Best Insurance Salesman of the Year, The Best Supporting Role in a Fast-Food Restaurant or, on the more technical side, The Best Performance as an Exhaust Fitter, or The Best Performance as a Jam Doughnut Filler.

CRAP CORNER

You probably think I'm a miserable, cynical, kill-joying old man. After all what's wrong with the community telling its heroes how much it loves them? On the other hand you might see these ceremonies, like me, as a gut-wrenching source of pure hypocrisy and false bon-hommie. Like:

CRAP! The panels that decide who gets the awards are the very people who make sure they get them too.

CRAP! The whole business of 'celebrity' feeds off itself. Famous people must be seen to be with other famous people.

CRAP! Most of the participants don't give a stuff about the individual charity that the collected money goes to (after the enormous expenses are taken out) and most would be hard-put to tell you what it was.

CRAP! If the producers run out of things to award for they simply invent another category. In this year's BAFTA Awards they made up a new bit for the best interview in a chat show, so that they could give the prize to the guy who managed to get Princess Di to spill the Royal beans.

CRAP! By thanking everyone but their mother-in-law in their acceptance speech, it helps them believe that the audience will love them even more. The fact is that nobody is remotely interested.

CRAP! Stars often use award ceremonies to bore us silly with their ill-thought-through views on practically anything.

CRAP! It seems daft to make a fuss of people who already do one of the most glamorous jobs, and so boost their already inflated egos.

If you agree, don't agree, or think the whole business is not worthy of comment, let me hear what you think. Turn to the last page for details.

By this stage, you must either think I'm just a tragic old cynic who can't see the good in anything or that the country we live in is so sad and corrupt that there's hardly any point bothering with the future. This whole book could be seen as the ranting of someone who believes the world we inhabit is doomed and that youngsters must simply accept that eventually they might well grow up to be the very people that I've taken the piss out of.

Protest among the young has not really been seen for a couple of decades. Although I poked fun at all those kids (like me) who marched against the bomb in the early sixties or demonstrated about public injustice or student grants, it can't be ignored that now we are in a period where adults, or those with power, have practically free-reign to do anything they like to whoever they want, without so much as a 'go forth and multiply' from those that it affects most - the young and seemingly powerless.

But, does making a noise and fuss about things do any good? The answer to this (despite my monumental, never-to-be-equalled distrust of those in power) is a resounding YES. Policemen, newspaper proprietors, town councillors, schoolteachers - in fact anyone (even politicians) need us - that's YOU - to keep them in their jobs.

Despite being weedier-than-weedy as individuals, our real clout lies in bulk. If everyone stopped buying those crap newspapers they'd dry up and shrivel like lizards' tails. If, by the time you read this the Tories have been kicked out after all this time, and if Labour don't fulfil their promises – you can kick 'em out too. And if one teacher's behaviour is unacceptable to the mass of the students he teaches, then together they can rob him of his job.

Uncool?

It isn't uncool to discuss what our politicians are doing to the country, or how the shit press are turning us into a nation of semi-literate morons, or how monolithic companies are controlling the quality, variety and price of everyday goods, or how sport is becoming simply another commercial bun fight, or how black people are still not getting a look in on the undeniable wealth that still exists in this country (and these are just my gripes!). It IS uncool, however, to let others act on your behalf – and stay silent.

So What?

Young people have, in the last ten years or so, been increasingly portrayed as apathetic, amoral and rather single-celled in the brain department. I bet that makes you feel great! Particularly as we adults have done such a great job of things!

So, why not drop someone a line to let them know what you really think? You could start with me...

If you have something to say about any of the stuff I've covered in this book (even if you think, like the title, it's a load of crap), write to me at the address below, with your thoughts. Let me know how old you are – you can't possibly be as geriatric as me! The best letters, be they angry, rude, funny, badly spelt or just plain daft, will appear in the back of subsequent printings of this book. If there are enough, I might even grovel to my nice publisher to bind them all together and make a complete book. Perhaps we could call it **C.R.A.P. Replies**. That'll serve you right.

John Farman, c/o Red Fox,
Random House Children's Books, 20 Vauxhall Bridge Road,
London, SW1V 2SA

Acknowledgements

Lords of Poverty/Graham Hancock/Mandarin; All the Trouble in the World/P J O'Rourke/Picador; Street Drugs/Andrew Tyler/Hodder and Stoughton; Post War Britain/Alan Sked and Chris Cook/Penguin Books; The Rise and Fall of the House of Windsor/A N Wilson/Mandarin; The Teenage Survival Guide/Anouchka Grose/Red Fox; The Essential Anatomy of Britain/Anthony Sampson/Coronet Books; Brewers Politics/Nicholas Comfort/Cassell; Social Trends 25 (1995 Edition)/HMSO; Chronicle of the Twentieth Century/J L International Publications; Young Peoples Understanding of Society/Andrew Furnham and Barrie Stacey/Routledge; The Last Green Book on Earth/Judy Allen & Martin Brown/Red Fox; The Whole Truth: The Myth of Alternative Health/ Rosalind Coward/Faber and Faber; The New Internationalist – July 1991/New Internationalist Publications; The Very Bloody History of Britain/John Farman/Bodley Head.